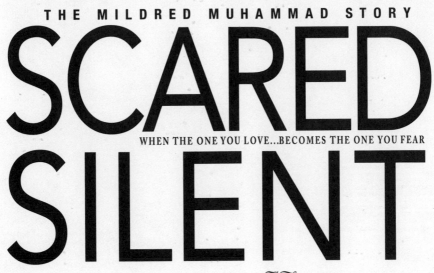

THE MILDRED MUHAMMAD STORY

# SCARED

WHEN THE ONE YOU LOVE...BECOMES THE ONE YOU FEAR

# SILENT

*A Memoir*

THE MILDRED MUHAMMAD STORY

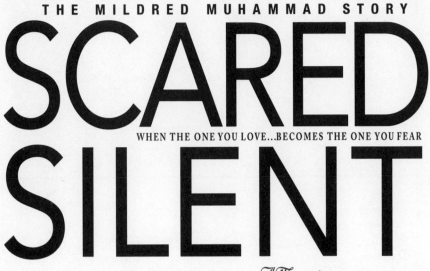

# SCARED
WHEN THE ONE YOU LOVE...BECOMES THE ONE YOU FEAR
# SILENT

*A Memoir*

# MILDRED
# MUHAMMAD

STREBOR BOOKS

NEW YORK  LONDON  TORONTO  SYDNEY

Strebor Books
P.O. Box 6505
Largo, MD 20792

This book is a work of nonfiction. Some of the names have been changed to
protect the privacy of certain individuals.

© 2009 by Mildred D. Muhammad

ISBN 978-1-59309-241-2

Cover design: www.mariondesigns.com
Cover photograph: © Keith Saunders/Marion Designs

Manufactured in the United States of America

THIS BOOK IS DEDICATED TO MY CHILDREN,
JOHN, SALENA, AND TAALIBAH
SO THAT YOU WILL ALWAYS KNOW THE TRUTH.

*"You don't have to have physical scars
to be a victim or survivor
of domestic violence."*

To the victims and survivors of domestic violence...
There is one suggestion that I would give to you. That is to stop *re-acting* and start *acting*. You know your abuser better than anyone. Rely on what you know and use it to your benefit. Follow your spirit, it will not lead you astray. Pray and ask God for guidance. Ask Him to put people and resources in place to help you. He will do it!!!
You should complete the safety plan in this book, which will help you to decide when to leave. Only YOU will know when that time is. Don't be afraid. Seek help from your local coalition. They have information regarding other organizations that can assist you.

**The 24-hour National Hotline for Domestic Violence is
1-800-799-SAFE**

Always remember it is NOT your fault and it is *never* too late to stand up for yourself! However, be wise, strategic, and careful...
If you want to contact me...Mildred@afterthetrauma.org. I will respond as soon as I receive your email. Our conversations will be confidential.

—MILDRED D. MUHAMMAD

# ACKNOWLEDGMENTS

First and foremost, I thank Almighty God, Allah, for bringing me and my children safely through. Thank You, Lord, for putting people (angels) and resources in place to help us along the way. It is by Your grace and mercy that we are here today.

To my children, John, Salena and Taalibah, to whom I've dedicated this book. Thank you for your love, your encouragement, your kindness...it was, has been, and continues to be my motivating strength to persevere. And to the new additions to my family—my husband, Reuben, and his children, Asaad, Omar, Jabril, Isa and Yusef...thank you for having the strength to be in my life. You've allowed me to trust and believe in love again.

To my mother...although you are no longer with me, I've felt your presence and love through it all.

To my sister, Adele (Maisha), and her husband, Chester Moses (who recently passed), thank you for allowing us to live with you and for your support.

To the Nation of Islam...thank you for your support. I am grateful for the teachings of the Honorable Elijah Muhammad, as taught by Minister Louis Farrakhan, which has sustained me throughout my life. I believe that I am of sound mind, body and spirit because of the teachings.

There are so many people who have helped me along the way, and for whom I am extremely grateful. Those who were in my life during the very difficult times of my marriage, its subsequent divorce, and the abduction of my children. I could not begin to pen all of the names, but know that I sincerely appreciated your help—whether you extended an understanding ear, provided me with sound advice, money, a sympathetic hug, or a compassionate prayer. Your kindness was more than heartfelt...it changed my life.

My longtime friends...Stanley and Pamela Barnes and Isa Nichols, you believed me when others didn't, in spite of what John said or did. Thank you for supporting me. Olivia Muhammad, you have been more than a friend to me, you've been my sister along the way and even to this day. Thank you for understanding, supporting, and praying with me. Above all, when circumstances became really tight, you didn't turn your back on me. Thank you!

To the Phoebe House and Staff...when I was at my lowest point, I had a place to lay my head, to gain my strength, to have friendships and to understand my struggle. I was nurtured, loved and given lifelong lessons that I continue to use to this day. I will always remember my experience there and take you in my heart. It was at the Phoebe House where I found my mission, my purpose in life...to start my organization, After The Trauma, which assists survivors of domestic violence.

To Monique Maye, my friend and attorney of Barnes & Maye Marketing. You've devoted countless hours representing me and my children. You've ensured we were treated fairly. Thank you for all that you've done.

To the staff of the YWCA, Deputy Roger Ward, Detective Whatcom, and all of the unknown names of those in law enforcement who assisted me and my children...Thank you! You helped me and my children to be together again.

To Monvelia Blair, thank you for the tools given to me during our counseling sessions in Tacoma. I still use them to this day.

To the victims' families and survivors of this terrible crime, my family and I pray for your continued healing.

To Audra Barrett, my literary agent. I am so grateful to you for taking my story into your spirit and helping me to find a publisher. You have become my friend. Thank you for believing in me and supporting me throughout this process.

To my writing partners, you've captured the essence of my voice and exposed the details of my life that needed to be told. Thank you for sharing your gift of the written word to bring my story to light.

To my publisher and editor, Zane, and my publishing director, Charmaine, thank you for believing in my story. I am truly humbled and grateful for this opportunity you are blessing me with.

To Norma Harley, of the Sherriff's Office in Maryland, you gave me my first opportunity to share my story. Thank you for your continued support for me and my organization, After The Trauma.

To the Economic Development and Training Institute and staff, thank you for allowing me to operate my organization, After The Trauma, in your facility. And for your ongoing support in assisting me with victims and survivors of domestic violence. Thank you for your continued support personally as well as professionally.

And to those who asked me to share my whole story, thank you for your encouragement. Writing my story has empowered me and helped me to realize my own strength. It has also allowed me to recognize how far I've come through that experience. I hope and pray that I have been an encouragement to you.

# PROLOGUE

I could not believe this was happening. The man I married, the man that fathered my children, could not be capable of such a thing. I sat in a hotel room riveted to the television set as images of John flashed across the screen. It was surreal. I walked up to the TV, put my hand on the screen—and whispered, "What happened to you?"

I was a zombie, not the real Mildred, the one who dreamed of simply being a good wife, a good mother and a good servant to God. I had just left a police station where an officer had looked me in the eyes and proclaimed, "Ms. Muhammad, we're going to name your ex-husband as the sniper."

For two years I had looked over my shoulder for two people: John, my ex-husband who had promised to kill me, and "the D.C. Sniper," who had terrorized the Washington, D.C. metropolitan area where I lived by randomly killing people. Now I was forced to reconcile that there was only one man—that John, the man who used to cuddle with me at night and fuss over his children during the day, was also the terrorizing gunman.

I remembered what John once told me: "You know I could take a small city and terrorize it and they would think it would be a group of people. But it would only be me."

Still, this was John posturing, wasn't it? Talking was far different from actually killing. Yet when police asked me if I thought John was capable of doing something like this, I surprised myself by not hesitating for one moment to reply, "Yes."

I knew he *could* kill. He was a military man and had fought in a war. I also knew that he had promised to kill me because he believed I had taken his children away from him. And I knew John to be a man of his word when it came to a threat or a promise of revenge. Still, over the harrowing months during which one person after another was gunned down by the man labeled as "The D.C. Sniper," not once did I think of John. Not once. It was unfathomable. The sniper had to be a madman. The sniper had to be inhuman. The sniper had to be like someone I had never known.

Now I was recalling every frightening comment John had ever made to me. He once said, "When a man hits a woman, it means that he has lost all respect for her. It would be easy for him to kill her after that."

But I did not foresee, not even in my wildest nightmare, that John would ever kill people who had nothing to do with me or our troubled marriage.

I stepped back from the television and realized my son was crying and my daughters were weeping into their pillows. I turned to console them, though I had no idea what to say. I held them close. They were scared. I was, too. In the past several hours, we had all learned that John was the sniper suspect and that police were searching for him. Then we had to hurry to pack and police sped us away from our house and to the hotel room where we were being held under police protection.

It is amazing how exhausting trauma can be, even when it is not accompanied by physical blows. The news had pummeled us. My son had nearly passed out when he heard the news. My girls were spent from the weight of one question: How could their father commit such a reprehensible act?

Once the children went to sleep, I tipped into the bathroom to let go of my own emotions. I had been "the good mother" for my children. I had comforted them until they closed their eyes. I had been the strong shoulder, the consoler. They only had one parent left and they deserved a good one. I turned on the water in the bathtub and sink faucet so they could not hear me. I sat on the cold floor of the bathroom, buried my face into a pillow and sobbed. I cried for hours, hoping that by daybreak when the children woke, I would be ready for the great unknowing that awaited us.

It was October 23, 2002. It would become a day of demarcation for me and my children. Before this date, my son and daughters were like other children, barely aware of the challenges that adults faced. But after their father was publicly named as the sniper, I watched the light in their eyes grow dimmer. They knew that the worst things were possible. That one day you could be romping in the yard with your parents and on another day you could sit in front of a television set, your heart nearly beating out of your chest, as you watched armed police officers search for your father.

When the person you love becomes the one you fear, you are scared to the core of your being. Everything you thought was real has become an illusion. It is disconcerting. You feel as if you are falling into a deep hole and there is nothing to hold onto because everything you thought was there is gone. You slip deeper. And deeper.

John was going to kill me, and now I knew that he had conspired to kill other people just to create a smokescreen. Soon I would learn all the details of how he planned to kill strangers and then shoot me down and have police blame it all on "the D.C. Sniper."

But he got caught. Thank God, he got caught.

When the person you love tries to kill you, the pain is unspeakable. How do you explain such an act to anyone? To yourself? What can you possibly say?

I had been a girl with simple dreams. One of my greatest prayers was to be a good wife. Now I thought of the many ways in which John had dismissed me and diminished my existence. I heard his familiar retort, "I don't mind because you don't matter."

I was thankful he had not killed me, and I grieved over those whose lives he had taken. I cried for their families, too. But the silencer on John's gun had silenced me in another way. Shame cut off my tongue. Fear paralyzed my throat. Surely people hated me, I thought. I was the reason innocent people were killed. A bullet did not take my life, but it would be years before I found my voice. Meanwhile, every gentle word I thought of I used to help my children heal. This is what a good mother does.

It took months, even years for my own healing. But now, seven years later—finally—I am no longer scared silent.

# CHAPTER ONE:
## FIRST MEETINGS, FIRST LIES
### SEPTEMBER 1983—BATON ROUGE

Women who have been involved with abusive men often say that their partners started out being exceptionally attentive and romantic. That was certainly true of John when I first met him. It was on a steamy Labor Day in Louisiana, and I had the day off from my job as a data processor at the State Department of Labor. What I remember most about that lazy Monday morning, except that it was hot, was that I had nothing special to do and nobody to do it with. I was a naïve twenty-three-year-old, living a sheltered life at home with my mother. My life revolved around church and work. I was ready to have my own life, as well as a real relationship. I wanted to meet somebody to love; I wanted to meet somebody who would care about me. That morning, my mother was bustling around the kitchen when I went inside to tell her that I was going to the corner store a couple of blocks away. As always, she reminded me, "Just be careful."

I had walked less than half a block when Valena, one of my best friends from high school, passed by in her car and offered me a ride. I certainly could have walked the two blocks, but I was thankful for the company. Valena and I were still close friends. In high school, I was a cheerleader, and she was on the pep squad. We went lots of places together—dances, parties, clubs. It was always fun being with her. Now that we were all grown up, the same thing was true: as soon as we saw each other, it was, "Hey, gurl, wassup?" Valena had another friend in the car, and we began laughing and talking the minute I climbed in. We were three girlfriends who were enjoying a day off in Baton Rouge, listening to songs on our favorite R&B radio station and generally having a good time.

On the way home, Valena said she needed to stop at another store up the street. She pulled into a parking space, and I stayed in the car while she finished her shopping. As I was sitting there, two men came out. One of them, a tall, good-looking brother, wearing sharp blue jeans and a sweatshirt, glanced in my direction. Our eyes locked. I felt vaguely embarrassed and I turned my head so he wouldn't come over. But, he did. Valena, who was right behind him, began talking to him. *Whoa*, I thought, *she knows him!*

"Who's your friend?" He used his head to gesture in my direction.

"This is Mildred," she told him.

He stuck his head in the driver's window. "Hi, Mildred," he said. "I'm John. What are you doing tonight?"

I had absolutely nothing to do, but I didn't want him to know that. My girlfriends and I often talked about how difficult it was to find a good man. Even so, I didn't want John to know that I was all that available.

That's why I tried to sound sincere when I said, "I have to check my schedule."

He asked for my number, gave me a beautiful smile, and said he would call later. After he left, Valena had some things to tell me about John. She said that, like us, he had attended Scotlandville High School where he had run track and played tennis. I was a year ahead of him and didn't recall ever meeting him. Valena dropped me off, and I went inside to think about his smile, which was probably John's best attribute. When I first met him, he had the kind of smile that everybody noticed; I wasn't the only one who said that his smile could light up a room.

John called early in the evening as he had promised, and we made a date for eight-thirty. He was at my front door exactly on time. I would quickly learn that he was on time for all of our dates. It was another plus in his favor. When he came in and met my mother, I also couldn't help noticing how respectful he was. Even more points in his favor. We drove down to a park by the river, a romantic spot filled with other couples doing what we were doing—walking, talking, laughing, sitting on the benches, and giving each other long, significant looks. Right away, John told me that he had two sons, but that he wasn't married.

At one point, he looked me straight in the eyes and said, "I'm looking for someone to share my life."

We were having our first serious conversation, and he asked if I was seeing someone special.

"No," I told him, "I'm just chilling until the right man comes along."

"Well, you've found him." John continued to capture me with his gaze.

"Is that right?" I asked.

"Yeah, that's right." He sounded confident of himself as we both smiled at each other. It felt good to be out with a man who was so quick to express his feelings. John seemed so special. *Hey*, I thought to myself, *finally a "man."*

When I asked him what had happened with his ex-girlfriends, he simply said, "Things didn't work out." He told me that with all the women he had known, after a while, they had done things that made him feel trapped. As soon as he got that feeling, he realized it was time to move on. According to him, he didn't have anything against marriage; he just didn't like to feel trapped. I was already intrigued by his thought processes so I asked him what made him feel that way. He told me that if a woman started nagging him or making him feel incompetent, he felt like less than a man. He wanted to be with someone who appreciated him and treated him as though he made a difference. I wanted to please him so I made a mental note never to nag him and to show him that he was appreciated and admired. When we said good night, he kissed me on my forehead and told me how much he liked being with me.

The next day he called to check up on me. It was sweet of him, and I told him that right away. He said that I was easy to talk to, and that he hadn't talked to anybody like he talked to me in a very long time.

"If there is anything I can do for you," he said, "let me know." Then he told me that he wanted to be there for me and that he wanted to make my life easier.

I was shocked that he was so straight with his words. I remember telling him, "You haven't known me long enough to say those things to me."

He replied, "There is something about you that lets me know that it's safe for me to talk this way. I know myself well enough to realize that if I can't do something, then I won't say it. If it comes out of my mouth, then I'm obligated to make it happen."

That sounded good to me. "Oh, then you're a man of your word, right?" "That's right," he answered, "I'm a man of my word."

And that's how our relationship started. From my inexperienced point of view, John was wonderful. He used all the right words and said everything I wanted to hear, but I was at a disadvantage: my ideas of how a man should behave in a relationship were all romanticized and based on television, movies, and hearsay. My father left my mother when I was four, and I had no relationship with him whatsoever. I don't even remember meeting anybody from his side of the family. In the last few years, I've thought a lot about what it means for a girl to grow up as I did. I've wondered whether the absence of a father image made me more vulnerable to somebody like John.

When I was growing up, my mother was the stable center of our universe. She supported the family by cleaning houses and working in restaurants. Any memories I have of my father are buried too deep to recall. There was only one family picture in the house with my dad in it. He was holding me and standing with two of my sisters next to him. But something must have happened when the photograph was being taken because his face didn't come out; it's just like a shiny blank. Everything I know about my father comes from what other people told me. Everybody said that he was tall, handsome, dark-skinned, and the life of the party; they also told me that he was a real ladies' man. My mother liked to tell me that I was his favorite baby girl, but I don't know if that was really true. Mama could have been telling me that to make me feel good about myself.

I was one of five children; my mother had my three older sisters and then it was nine more years before I was born. I also have a brother who is two years younger. My sisters were pretty much all teenagers or out of the house by the time I was old enough to retain many memories. When I was about nine, my father died. Even though we didn't know him, my brother and I went to the funeral with my mom and sisters. My father's body was in a closed casket with a United States flag draped over it. I looked for a photograph so I could see what my father looked like, but there wasn't one. My brother and I were sitting together; the only question was which one of us was going to cry first. We were told that Dad died in an accident in the Navy, but later, when I was about twenty, I was at another funeral with my mother, and I overheard some of my father's old friends talking. That's how I found out the truth. My father had died in a fire, and I guess you could say that he was also a victim of domestic violence. It seemed he and my mother were separated at the time and he was having problems with his current girlfriend who must have thought, if I can't have him, then neither will anybody else. While my father was asleep, his girlfriend padlocked the doors and windows on the outside of the small house in which they were living and set it on fire. My father's friends said that you could hear my dad screaming for miles while the house was burning. They said they came with axes to try to get him out, but they couldn't get to him because the heat from the fire was so intense. I feel terrible thinking about it even now. Just a few months ago, my sister found a photograph of my father, taken when he was nineteen. It was the first time I saw a picture of him. I began crying and couldn't stop for about three hours.

It was tough on my mother, living alone with young children to raise. She wanted better things for us, and she would have done anything to help her children. She struggled hard to pay the bills, but we managed. We were always in school; there was always home-cooked food on the table; and there was always love. My mother, who was one of fourteen children, came from a large, religious, Southern Baptist family. Her brother was a pastor and my uncle's church was a big part of our lives. We attended Sunday school as well as every service; my mother, brother, and I all sang in the choir. My mother always gave me two pieces of advice: "Live as near right as you can." And "Live as close to God as you can."

Some people complain about their mothers, saying they never got enough love. With me and my mother, it was the opposite. If anything, she loved me too much. She never wanted me to move away from her, get married, or have children. After finishing high school, I had attended Southern University for two and a half years, studying to get a degree in computer science, but I couldn't afford to continue. I had to drop out, get some quick technical training, which I did in data entry, and find a job so I could help my mother with the finances of the house.

I had wanted to go into the military, but my mom talked me out of it because she didn't want me that far away and she worried that I could get hurt. She said that people used to tell her to have children, but that nobody had ever told her how to let go. As far as she was concerned, the hardest part of mothering was letting her children grow up.

Soon after I met John, he told me some things about his childhood, and it sounded like he had never had anybody at all that he could depend on. John came from New Orleans, one of six children—three boys and three girls—but his father left all of them, when John was still very young, to start a new family and never looked back. John was always bitter that his father had abandoned the family, but the greatest tragedy of his early childhood was the loss of his mother, who died from breast cancer. He told me that he was five when his mother died, but I've heard reports from other family members saying that he was as young as two. The one thing everyone agrees about is that he and his mother were extremely attached and that she was holding him when she died. I don't think he ever got over his mother's death and he carried that sadness with him wherever he went. The image of him as a little boy in the arms of his dying mother also stayed in my mind. In our marriage, it was always hard for me to stay angry at him—no matter what he did—knowing what he had gone through.

After his mother's death, he and his brothers and sisters went to live with relatives in Baton Rouge. He didn't like to talk about what happened to him while he was growing up, except to say that they were mentally and physically abused by various adults in the family. He told me that he and his siblings tried to take care of each other as best they could. When I was reading about John's trial in the paper, it was reported that one of the people who hit him regularly was an uncle who was once accused of beating another child to death. John was a proud man who didn't like to appear vulnerable or have anybody feel sorry for him so the issue of his childhood abuse was not a topic he wanted to discuss.

People often ask me how he behaved when I met him and whether he seemed controlling, moody, or insecure, and I have to answer that he seemed much calmer and more stable than most people, but I had no real understanding then of his well-developed acting skills. Even so, he had a strong presence. Everything I heard the men in my family say a man should be, I saw in John. He had a steady job, and he was a member of the National Guard. He was a strong man with a strong handshake, and he appeared to walk tall. He was also extremely romantic, loving, and gentle with me. During his trial, I read newspaper reports of testimony from a woman he was dating in the last years of our marriage; she also described him in glowing terms as being gentle, considerate, and strong. Of course, during the early years of our relationship, I thought his loving words were all for me, but he was always exceptionally good with women. If he wanted something from a woman, he knew exactly what to say and how to say it.

Those times that he let his guard down, he did appear lonely and like he needed somebody to love him. I remember him telling me that, in his life, it was as though anyone who had ever cared about him wanted something from him. I was touched by his sadness, especially about the death of his mother. I was sure I could make a difference in his life. I wanted to show him how love looks and feels when it is genuine. I wanted him to know that I cared about him for who he was and not because of what he could give me. I promised myself that I wasn't going to disappoint or abandon him.

From John's history, one might have expected him to act gloomy and depressed, but back in 1983, nothing could be further from the truth. The John that I fell in love with was primarily a lighthearted man who liked to have fun. He would do things like pick me up from work and start driving in an unexpected direction. I would ask, "Where are we going?" He would point to the back, and I would see the fishing poles. We would head on down under the old Mississippi River Bridge where we would throw our lines in near the support beams. After we caught the fish, we took it to my house, cleaned it, fried it, and ate it. It was pretty good. Nights, we would go dancing or to the movies or just hang out. On the weekends, we would go to the park, museum, or zoo. Sometimes one or both of his sons would be with him; anybody could see how devoted he was to his boys and how much they loved him.

At first even my mother liked and appreciated John and would make him special things to eat. My mother, who really knew her way around a kitchen, could whip up all kinds of food and make it better than just about anybody else. I think she tried to make John feel at home because he was so respectful of her. If he wanted peach cobbler, she made peach cobbler; if he wanted pound cake, she made pound cake. In return he did little repairs around our house. He was always extremely skillful with his hands and could fix just about anything. We had some pipes under the house that were leaking, and he promised my mother that he would come over and fix them. He showed up right on time, crawled under the house, and started working. I crawled right after him and became his assistant. I loved that I could count on him to do whatever he promised to do. When I told him how much I appreciated that quality, he told me that he would always be that way, saying, "I never want you to lose that sparkle in your eyes when you look at me."

About two months into our relationship, I decided that I was going to go over to visit Valena, who I really hadn't seen since Labor Day. It was a warm day and I wanted to go for a walk.

"So, how's John doing?" she asked almost as soon as I walked through the door.

"He's doing well," I told her. "And our relationship is GREAT!"

Valena looked at me and breathed in and out, before she told me what she had found out. "Well, you know he's married, right?"

I remember saying things like, "What?" and "Ah man!!" and "What am I going to do now?!!!"

Valena asked me how I really felt about him, and I told her, "I love him, but he never said anything about any wife. He just told me that he had two sons."

"Yes," Valena agreed, "he has two sons by two different women, and he married the last one."

I felt as though somebody had kicked me in the stomach. How could this be happening? How could this be true? I was totally confused. John and I were together all the time, and I had seen no signs of a wife; he didn't seem like he had anything to hide; he had even given me his phone number. Although, of course, I never used it and waited for him to call me. But he never seemed to have any obligation to any other woman. He didn't seem to be worried about being seen with me. What was going on?

Before I left Valena that day, she said to me, "Well, Mildred, you've got a decision to make."

All I could think about was that decision and what I was going to say to John. I went to church regularly and all those "Thou Shalt Nots" and other messages about adultery began to flash in my brain.

When John called that night and greeted me with his usual, "Hi, Sweetheart," all I could think was, *John has a wife*, but I was so upset I could barely speak, let alone ask him about his lies. He asked if he could come over, but I was too hurt to see him. I told him that I had to help my mother with something. He asked me if I needed anything and I said no.

"Okay, honey," he said, "I'll talk to you tomorrow." Then he paused and used those three little words that every woman in love wants to hear: "I love you."

It was the first time he had said that to me. I said, "I love you, too."

Then I hung up the phone and burst into tears. I realized what I had to do, but I didn't know if I could do it.

That night I tossed and turned and couldn't sleep. At work the following day, I was a mess. Instead of doing what I was supposed to be doing, I thought about all the things I wanted to say to John about why our relationship had to end, and I wrote them all down on a piece of paper so I wouldn't forget what I wanted to say. I put the paper in my purse and was trying to get back to work when the phone rang. It was John.

"Hi, Tinker Bell," he said. Tinker Bell was a nickname he used for me because he said I was so little and cute. I called him "Sweetie" because he was so sweet to me.

"Hey, Sweetie."

"Just checking to make sure you have a smile on your face," he said.

I started looking for the paper on which I'd written down what I wanted to say to him, but I couldn't find it fast enough, so I put the conversation off once again, all the while knowing that I was getting in deeper and deeper. He told me again that he loved me and he wanted me to remember that while I was working. Then he asked, "Do you love me?"

"Yes." I couldn't deny it.

He said, "That's all I needed to hear."

In the meantime, I was thinking, *man, what am I going to do now?*

When I got home, my mom looked at me funny, as though she knew something was wrong, but I didn't want to tell her because I didn't want John to look bad. He called soon after I got home and told me that he wouldn't accept any excuses and that he was coming over. We went to the park because he said he had something he wanted to say to me and didn't want any distractions. I think I expected him to tell me about his wife and family, but I wanted to get out what I had to say first. Almost as soon as we sat down on a bench, I started talking and told him that I found out that he was married and that I was trying to find a way to end our relationship.

He said, "Please don't do that. You are the best thing that has happened to me in a long time and I can't go back to living without you."

I cried and told him that I was sure that what we were doing went against everything I believed. I also didn't want to be in this situation because I wouldn't want anybody to do this to me if I were married.

He was persistent. He pleaded with me, "Mildred, please don't throw me away. We can work this out." He told me that he wasn't happy in his marriage and neither was his wife. He said that they were simply going through the motions and it was only a matter of time before it would be over. He asked, "Can you please wait for me and not get involved with anyone else? I promise, I will not let you down."

"How much time?" As I asked that question, I knew the direction in which I was headed. I didn't want to lose him.

In retrospect, I can't help but notice how little anger I had toward him for lying to me.

My girlfriends and I were sort of indoctrinated to believe that men could do what they wanted and that a cheating man was not the same thing as a cheating woman. As long as the man was bringing the money home and taking care of the bills, everything else should be excused and forgiven. The woman was expected to keep quiet, cook, clean, take care of the children, and not cause any problems. So when I heard about John's marriage, I almost felt sorry for him because his wife wasn't giving him what he needed. I also felt tremendous guilt because I was helping him deceive another woman. But I didn't really blame him or get angry at him. They say that love is blind and that explains my state. I still thought of him as my knight-in-shining-armor, and the glare coming off of that armor blinded me.

It didn't take much for him to convince me that, even if I didn't want to be in a romantic relationship with him, we could still be platonic "friends." That same night, almost as soon as we came to that agreement, he had a favor to ask in the name of friendship. My mind was focused on his being married, but he had a different agenda that he was promoting.

He said, "I have something else I want you to know."

"What?" I asked. From the pained look on his face, I worried that he was going to say something really horrible. I was bracing myself. Could he be dying? What kind of confession was he going to make?

"I can't read." He looked uncomfortable as he told me. He then related an incredible story about having been in an accident and having lost his memory. According to him, he had recovered from his accident, but his memory of how to read was completely gone. His confession made me feel almost relieved because it was nowhere near as horrible as what I had anticipated. I also immediately realized that he was offering me a role in his life—one that would allow us to stay connected, even if we were no longer romantically involved.

I asked him some questions about the reading like, "Are you serious?" and "Does anyone know?"

He said he hadn't told anybody but me, explaining, "Everyone expects me to know things, and if they found out I can't read, they wouldn't understand, or they would laugh at me." He seemed sad and hurt; it was obvious that he was embarrassed.

John had graduated from high school so I asked him how he had accomplished that without being able to read. He told me that he had developed a photographic memory. If he needed to learn something, he would find some excuse to ask a friend to read it aloud to him. He said he told people that things sounded better when they were read out loud. He would memorize what he had heard and floated through school by memorizing everything.

I questioned him, "You've done all this just to survive?"

"Yes," he answered, "But it's getting old, and I need help."

He asked me if I could facilitate him learning to read. That's how our relationship changed from girlfriend/boyfriend to teacher/student. I soon discovered that he wasn't joking when he said he couldn't read, so we started with basics like "See Spot Run." I even took a phonics class at night so I would be better equipped to teach him.

We spent a lot of time meeting at the local library, as well as the library at Southern University campus. We worked hours at a time, and I would give him lots of spelling tests. It was tough going at first and required patience from both of us, but eventually we got past basic reading texts and moved on to newspapers, magazines, and books. Before long, he was really reading, and it opened his eyes to new possibilities for his life. Helping him with the reading and seeing the results was very exciting to me.

When we met, John was a sergeant in the National Guard and spent at least one weekend a month doing his service and training. He wanted to be in the regular military, but I think his literacy issues were holding him back. He worried that people would not respect him if they discovered his secret. As his reading and writing improved, he began to talk about leaving Baton Rouge. He thought that the best way for him to get ahead in life would be through the armed services. In order to get accepted, he had to take a battery of tests. He asked me to help him study for his military tests, and I did it happily. Yes, there was still a romantic undercurrent between us, but we both concentrated on his learning. If he called me at work, it was as likely to be a question about his attempts to figure out phonics and sound out a new word as anything else.

During these many months that we studied together, John continued to make a point of assuring me that he needed me in his life and nothing was going to stop him from letting me know that. We sometimes discussed his marital status, which I viewed as a serious problem. He continued to ask me to wait. I was trying to get some distance between us and would often back away emotionally; he hated it when I did that. In the meantime, he would also try to do things for me. Once when I was short of money, he offered to help me out. I asked if he was taking from his family to give to me, and he said no, he had plenty.

The give and take between us made me feel as though we were becoming good friends. John also began to confide in me in other ways. During the time we were romantically involved, he assured me that there were no other women, but he also told me that there *had* been other women and explained how he would arrange their names and phone numbers in codes he made up so his wife wouldn't figure it out. I remember thinking, "I don't want to be part of a harem." I recognized his behavior as being sneaky, but I didn't think it was a basic weakness in his character. Instead I made excuses for him; I thought he would be different if he were in a good relationship. I assumed he was trying to fill a void because he needed love and wasn't getting it. I didn't see his behavior with women as indicative of larger issues.

Once he passed his tests and was accepted into the Army, I cut off communication with him. I still felt extremely guilty that our relationship could be hurting his wife. It had been close to two years since we had met, and there he was, still married. Some people come into our lives for a lifetime; others are only there for a reason and a season. As far as I was concerned, my reason and my season were up. I suggested that he devote more time to getting things straight with his wife so that she could go with him wherever he would be stationed. He suggested that I go with him, and I said that I didn't think that would work; especially since he was still married. I told him to keep studying. I told him that I loved him; and I backed off, way off.

The day that he was leaving for basic training, I wanted so badly to phone him and say goodbye. But we had decided to let the relationship go, and I didn't want to make it worse. I spent November 5, 1985, his departure day, in my room crying. I woke up thinking about John and I went to bed thinking about John. I wondered what he was doing and how he was doing, and I wondered whether he missed me as much as I missed him.

Less than a month later, on December 1st, I received a letter from him, along with a one-way ticket to Fort Lewis, Washington. The letter said that he couldn't continue in his marriage any longer and he wanted me by his side. He said he was willing to do whatever he had to do for us to be together. One of the best things about the letter was that every word was spelled correctly.

# CHAPTER TWO:
## THE MILITARY EXPERIENCE

John always said the same thing to me: "We are going to be together for ninety-nine years. I can't promise you a hundred years because we never know what will happen. But even if we get divorced, we will still live together because I love you so much."

John may have specified ninety-nine years, but I was positive we were going to be together *forever*. Didn't he say that we would be together, even if we got divorced? If somebody said that to me now, the word "divorce" in a sentence about love would make me nervous. Then, I was a completely starry-eyed woman in love, who believed all of John's many romantic words; even when they didn't make total sense. Love was the motivating emotion in my heart as I quit my job, packed my bags, and prepared for my first plane trip. I was taking a huge and scary step, and I felt more than a little bit guilty about leaving my mother alone in Baton Rouge, but at twenty-six, I was determined to lead my own life. As the pilot circled the Seattle Tacoma Airport, known as SeaTac, I was full of questions about what the future would hold. Where would we live? Would I like it there? Would I find a job? Would I find a job I liked? What was my life going to be like? I was sure about only two things: I wanted to spend the rest of my life with this man who was so free with his words of love, and I wanted to make him happy.

John was waiting at the airport in a borrowed car so we could drive to Fort Lewis on a scenic road, framed by tall pine trees. As someone born and raised in the South, nothing had prepared me for the intense green vegetation or the cool temperatures. John had already found us off-base housing, a furnished one-bedroom apartment with a balcony, located right outside of the Fort Lewis gate. Soon after we arrived, we took a walk so I could become more familiar with the surroundings. Everywhere I looked, soldiers were out and about, alone or in groups. Mount Rainier, which was about sixty-five miles away, seemed so close that I felt as if I could reach out and touch the snow and ice at the top. Keeping in step with John, I felt secure and happy in this new world.

When John first talked to me about entering the military, I viewed his decision to become part of a peacetime Army as a practical and wise career move. The U.S. seemed far away from any kind of military action, and becoming a soldier felt safer and more secure than many other occupations. Then, in March 1986, less than six months after I arrived, the U.S. attacked Libya; everything changed in a heartbeat. The base was placed on alert and the soldiers were not allowed to come home. It was a scary time. I was watching the television news report of the attack. During the weather report, the map indicated a bad storm in our locale. A few viewers were so frightened by the booms of thunder that they called the station to ask whether the noise could be some form of bombing retaliation from Libya. I couldn't get over that some people were so nervous that they didn't know thunder when they heard it, but it also made me realize that I had been naïve about what it meant when someone joins the armed services. I started to be aware of the potential for danger in John's life.

While I was there to see certain things unfold in his military work, there were also other times when I was dependent on what he told me. In retrospect, I realize that his words were not always reliable. Nonetheless, since the D.C. shootings, I've read a variety of reports in the press talking about John's military career. Some of these reports downplayed his military service, giving him little credit for his time served. I've read stories, for example, saying that his primary duty was as the driver of a water truck. I've also seen other stories on the internet that gave him a more grandiose status, implying that he was some kind of covert operative, employed and paid by a top secret agency or terrorist organization. Neither of these versions of reality is true, that I know of.

John's MOS (Military Occupational Specialty) was combat engineer. This is a difficult and physically demanding specialty. John was only twenty-five years old when he became an expert in demolitions. He was highly trained in arming and disarming explosives. Combat engineers typically go into a terrain first in order to do reconnaissance work and disarm potential booby traps, mines, and other firing devices. This is dangerous work, and it is the work for which John signed up. As far as the Army was concerned, he was totally committed. This was where he wanted to be and what he wanted to be doing. Even when he was off-duty and home with me, his primary focus was on studying for his specialty or improving his physical strength and endurance so he could be better equipped to do his job. John started out as a PFC, private first class, but he told me that he would soon make sergeant, which was the highest rank he held in the National Guard. True to his word, he quickly became a Corporal (E4) and then Sergeant E5. This is the rank he held for most of his years in the military, and it is the rank he held when he was honorably discharged.

If I close my eyes and try to remember what he and I talked about during those early years of our being together, the answer is always the same: John talked about the military and what he could do to get ahead. He and his friends talked about their training and their weapons; they talked about what would happen if we went to war and then they talked about how to secure the peace. Just about everybody I met in the military community was the same in terms of being gung-ho; it was pretty much all military talk, all the time. John was full of plans about how he could advance as quickly as possible, but before he could make sergeant, he had to take a PLDC (Primary Leadership Development Course). There was a great deal of material that he had to read and study, and his reading and writing was still not where he wanted it to be. I would often help him with his reports. We followed a little routine: he would call me up at home or work and dictate what he wanted. I would type it up; he would make corrections or additions; I would type up the final copy. He would then take that to work.

John's graduation from PLDC was a big event in our lives. He was proud of what he had accomplished and so was I. He went to the barber to get his hair cut and lined perfectly, and that morning he kept changing his clothes to make sure that everything was as good as it could be. He was always particular about how he looked. I didn't think much about this because my mother had also taught me to pay attention to how I looked when I left the house. That was how people from the South are taught to be. This was a special day for John and his appearance mattered more to him this time than any other time. He had never graduated from a military school and knowing all the work he had to learn to accomplish this task (learning how to read) made it all the more important to both of us. I wanted to help him get ready, no matter what was going on.

When I met him, he was extraordinarily thin and looked as though he could be swept up by a strong wind. After he joined the military, he began to put more emphasis on conditioning his body. Eventually, the muscles in his arms and upper body were so pronounced that he looked like he had wings and couldn't put his arms all the way down. He approached exercise with the same enthusiasm he did everything else. First thing in the morning and last thing at night, John always did the same thing: one hundred pushups and one hundred sit-ups. He wanted to be the best. I actually knew something about body building because, at one point, I was training for competition status. When he learned this about me, he was surprised, but after we went to the gym together and I talked to him about the machines and how to use them, he realized that I knew what I was talking about. That's when he began to pay attention to my advice. We were both health conscious, and I made sure that we ate well—chicken, fish, vegetables, and grains. Neither of us smoked or drank. Personally, I couldn't get past the taste of alcohol, which I didn't like at all. If John ever drank, he never did it around me. Nor did he do any drugs. He had been a distance runner and tennis player in high school, and he would run every morning before leaving for work. At first he would run with other soldier friends, but when they saw how hard he worked at staying in shape, most of them decided it was too difficult to keep up.

"Don't do that," I told him. When some of the other soldiers saw how intensely John trained, they would become discouraged, but he couldn't modify his behavior. He took his soldiering and his training awfully seriously and there was little, if any, room for error. John had a great deal of zest for life, and when he was interested in something, he put his whole heart and soul into it. It was difficult for anyone to match his enthusiasm or dedication. He told me that his goal in the military was to become a member of the Color Guard. He admired the precision of how they stood and walked, and he tried to emulate their stance.

For the most part, John appeared to be well-liked and respected. He was the life of the party; a friendly guy who told jokes and made people laugh. He had three close friends—Doc, Burt, and James—who were always around. After he made sergeant, he often went out of his way to help soldiers, even those in other units. One night we got a call from a soldier who was reluctant to call his own sergeant. He told John that he was too drunk to drive back to Fort Lewis from California to make roll call the next morning. John began getting dressed and put me on the phone to get the directions and then left immediately to go pick up the "wasted" soldier. He drove all the way there and was able to get back in time the next morning for roll call. John liked the role of mentoring younger soldiers and was extremely interested in improving his leadership skills. He began to read various books on the subject and told me that it was his mission to become the best sergeant for his soldiers. There were, however, often superiors who were annoyed by his attitude. John said it was because he was too outspoken about the way things were run. He told me that when higher-ups came for visits or inspections, they would sometimes ask the soldiers questions. John said that he would be put way in the back or sent out on some detail so he couldn't speak up.

He always made sure that his TA-50 military gear was in tip-top shape. On weekends, I would often go with him to military stores to find items that might improve performance in the field. He would buy equipment that could make his stay in the field more comfortable so that he didn't have to rely on military issue. When soldiers are in combat situations, their gear can give them the edge that improves comfort and survival. John wanted to have that edge. We would buy food that tasted better than the standard issue Meals Ready to Eat or MREs, as they were called. When they were in the field, like many of the other girlfriends and wives, I would send packages filled with this food and other supplies.

John often said that he wished we had a yard so that he could spend more time training on his own. One time when he and his squad were in the field, I heard about a small house, within the apartment complex in which we lived, that was available for rent. It had its own yard. I decided to surprise him and made all the arrangements; some of our neighbors helped me move into this new space. When John returned, I picked him up at his unit and pretended to drive to our old apartment. Then I made a U-turn into the parking lot in front of the house. He said, "You didn't just move the furniture around this time, right?" He really liked having the private outdoor space. He put up his tent, and he would sometimes sleep out there as part of his training.

John's squad would regularly go into the field for thirty days at a time. He was a good student, and he took his training seriously. He was learning how to handle weapons and blow stuff up; he was learning about reconnaissance and how to leave an area without being noticed. He was planning for battle, wherever that battle might be. I remember his talking about how, in the military, you always need a plan. If Plan A doesn't work, you need a fallback Plan B; if that doesn't work, you need to be sure that you have Plan C at the ready and sometimes Plan D as well. After his military training, I noticed that no matter what John did, he always made sure that he had a plan and a backup. He realized that he could apply his military lessons to life, and he began to think everything through in a cold, militaristic fashion. That's one of the reasons why I eventually grew to be so afraid of him. His interest in weapons and explosives was not casual, and I eventually saw that he could make decisions with absolutely no thought to his emotions or anyone else's.

Soon after I arrived at Fort Lewis, I found a job doing data entry with a company in Steilacoom, a small town on Puget Sound. Steilacoom is only about ten miles from the military post, but because we didn't have a car, I had to take two buses to get there. It was a long trek, so I applied for a data entry job on post, which I got. Having the extra salary really made a difference in what we could do as a couple. As soon as John made Corporal, he decided we needed a car. He wanted a Corvette, but it was too expensive. I suggested getting a used Nissan 300ZX, but when we got to the car lot, we discovered that the payments on a used one were $395 a month. I didn't think we should pay that kind of money for a used car. We had no intention of buying a car that day, but a few hours later, John and I were driving through the Fort Lewis gate in a 1987 white Nissan 300ZX Coupe with a burgundy interior. The soldiers at the gate, who were looking at the car and not the soldier, didn't know if they should salute. We found out later that many questions were asked about how an E4 could afford such a car; some people even wondered whether he was selling drugs. They didn't realize that John and I were able to work together to get a doable payment plan. We had a five-year contract, and I think we were only late once.

During our early years in Fort Lewis, John and I were usually able to work together as a team. We made friends and socialized with other couples. John and the other guys would play poker or do guy things while the women spent time together. We appeared to be an ordinary young couple. We even went to church together at Grace Chapel. I was an usher, and John was a member of the men's chorus. He had a nice voice, but I used to tease him that he was lacking in the rhythm department. He couldn't sing, clap, and move at the same time.

However, not everything in our relationship was going smoothly. When his squad was in the field, he couldn't call or contact me in any way. These separations put stress on our relationship, and we began to have small, petty arguments. Many of these arguments were the typical domestic disagreements common for two people who are learning to live together. John, for example, was a neat-as-a-pin, spit-and-polish soldier. When he left the house in the morning, he looked perfect, but the house he left behind frequently looked like it had been hit by a tornado. I would say things like, "Why is it you can keep things straight for work but make such a mess in the house?" He would say things like, "I don't mind when you tell me what to do, as long as you don't whine about it!"

Sometimes our small arguments escalated to the point where we would barely speak to each other; when this happened, we were super polite, which could be even more irritating for both of us. Using "please," "thank you," and "excuse me" in almost every sentence, we argued politely about everything from which television program to watch to whether or not I got my house key out quickly enough. John could get so annoyed about the smallest things that he would stop speaking to me for days. I would attempt to smooth things over by enticing him with little peace offerings like making his favorite desserts. If he was really upset, he would turn away or ignore me. I always felt, however, that we were two people in love who were trying to make a relationship work and that these disagreements would get resolved. During this time, his behavior was never threatening or frightening in any way. Eventually we both realized that our disagreements were somehow directly related to our separations. Once we realized what was going on, we did seem to be able to talk about it, and we stopped having these kinds of arguments.

There were, however, deeper things about our relationship that disturbed me. John was the center of my universe, and I loved him unconditionally without understanding what that meant. He knew more about life than I did, and even then, he was skilled at manipulating others. I began to feel that he was taking advantage of my naivety as well as my love. There were several issues that really bothered me. It sounds silly and petty, for example, to say that he never bought me presents, but he didn't, and it hurt me. It wasn't about the gifts. It was about his attitude. I wanted to do things that made him happy. Why didn't he feel the same way about me? I was always shopping for him, looking for things I thought he might like. Early in the relationship, I bought him a gold watch. Soon after I arrived at Fort Lewis, he told me that he had never had a train set as a boy and that he had always wanted one. Well, it didn't take me long to find an excuse to give him his own train set, and he got down on the floor like a child and played with it. I bought him most of his clothes, and he liked that I did that. I was careful to choose things that made him look good because I wanted to help him increase his self-esteem. I wanted him to feel that he was smart and good looking. I even surprised him with flowers at work. He bragged about it to his friends. When he returned from the field, I would be waiting with a home-cooked meal and homemade cake, and candles and balloons. He ate up all the attention I gave him. I made a big deal about his birthday. He said that everybody celebrated his birthday because it was New Year's Eve.

John took it for granted that I would do most of the work of cooking, cleaning, and shopping. He expected the house to be clean, but he would leave the house at clean-up time. He said that as long as he was the major breadwinner, bringing home his paycheck and taking care of the bills, he didn't have to do anything else. He said that if I wanted presents, for example, I could buy them for myself. I would convince him to take me out to dinner for my birthday, and then he would be so moody and miserable, complaining throughout the entire meal, that I wished that I had not asked in the first place. Through it all, I remembered what he had told me about not wanting to be with a woman who nagged him so I tried especially hard not to complain. I realized that he had also sacrificed to be with me; he had left his wife in Louisiana. And, most of all, I realized that his life hadn't been easy. He wouldn't talk about his childhood often, but when he did, he would tell me how much he had wanted to have somebody who loved him. He would say things like, "I miss my mother; I wonder what it's like to have one." When he said things like this, it always made me want to prove my love.

I cut John a lot of slack; I was taking care of him in a way that he had never taken care of me. He took partial care of me. Take an average Saturday, for example. We woke up; John went into the kitchen and made a real breakfast—eggs and grits, toast and coffee—which he brought back to bed. We usually spent the day doing things together like going to the movies or the mall. So far, so good, right? The problem was that on at least half of these weekend evenings John didn't stay home with me. Instead, he would go out with friends. Many nights he didn't return until one or two a.m., or even later. He never stayed out all night, but he always had a separate life that I knew nothing about. When he came home really late, he would have some kind of lame excuse. At first, when he went out, I would be waiting by the window or the phone. I would be dreadfully nervous and hurt by what was going on. When he finally returned home, he was full of affectionate words. "How's my sweetie?" he would say. He used words that I wanted to hear, but his actions didn't match up. Nonetheless, his words made me question my expectations, and I wondered if I was being unreasonable.

I was so inexperienced about what goes on between men and women, and I had nobody to talk to about my relationship with John. I certainly didn't know any of the women at Fort Lewis well enough to confide in them. Besides, I had always been taught that you keep your problems to yourself and don't tell people your business. Other women would sometimes complain about their husbands and boyfriends, but I didn't think that was right. I didn't want to expose John. I also wasn't ready to hear anything negative about him or our relationship. In my head, the bottom line was that he and I had more good days than bad ones. I decided that he was just immature and that if I gave him enough freedom, eventually he would grow up and become more of a family man.

We weren't alone in having problems. Military life was difficult for many of the couples we knew on post. One evening there was a knock on our door. It was my friend, June, and her three small children. She had a black eye and she was crying. June was Filipino, and was also an extremely private person. If she came to us, she was really desperate for help. She told us that she and her husband had gotten into some huge argument, and even though she was holding her youngest and the other children were crying and screaming for him to stop, her husband began beating her. She was afraid to go home. I made dinner for everybody and John put bedding on the floor for them. The youngest girl, who really liked John, crawled into his arms and fell asleep as he sat on the sofa. June and her children didn't go home until the following morning after breakfast.

Standing on the porch, after they left, John and I started to talk about June and her husband. I remember him saying that when a man hits a woman, it is a sad thing. He then said something that I didn't expect to hear and that I found awfully strange, even at the time.

He said, "When a man hits a woman, it means that he has lost all respect for her. It would be easy for him to kill her after that."

"What do you mean?" I asked. "June's husband still loves her, right?"

"Maybe so," he replied. "But once a man has gotten over hitting a woman again and again, then it wouldn't be hard to see her dead." I think I was so surprised by what he said that my jaw must have dropped, but he continued speaking, "If I ever do that to you," he said, "take me out." I just looked at him and we went back into the house. June never talked with me about this incident with her husband again. I tried once to bring it up and find out if everything was okay. She told me that she was getting help from her family and community, and that things were better, but she didn't want to talk about it.

I had been at Fort Lewis a little more than a year when we discovered that I was pregnant. John and I were both excited but, about a month later, I began having cramping. I was losing the baby, and a friend took me to the doctor's office. I was able to reach John, who came to be with me. Both of us were crying, but John said it was okay; we would have more. I needed to get a D&C, which made me so nervous that I called my sister, Gloria, who was a nurse in Texas. Gloria was so kind and supportive, assuring me that this was the correct medical decision. Because John and I weren't married, I didn't have access to the medical hospital on the base so the situation ended up being medically traumatic as well as sad. John and I agreed that we both wanted children. He got serious about finishing the paperwork for his divorce, and we began to make plans to get married.

If a couple wanted to get married in any of the Fort Lewis on-base chapels, there was a requirement that they go through counseling. Once a week for a month, John and I met with several other couples and a counselor to discuss our issues and hear feedback. One of the things that John and I talked about was how we handled anger. When he and I were angry with each other, he would pull away emotionally; I would get quiet and not talk. We walked away from our counseling sessions thinking that we had minor issues compared to some of the other couples. I should also add that John wasn't really into the counseling experience and was simply doing what he had to do.

We were married on a Friday evening, March 10, 1988, at 7 p.m. at Grace Chapel. John was twenty-six; I was twenty-seven. He wore dress blues and looked sharp, just like he wanted to look. His hair was cut in a "flat top" or a "high and tight," as the military called it. I had a beautiful gown that I rented. Neither of us had family present and John's first sergeant gave me away. As soon as we got married, I phoned my mother so she could feel included. She cried and we both talked about how we wished that she could have been there.

My friend, Janice, was my maid of honor and she had helped me with food and decorations for the reception, which we held at the house she shared with her husband. John's friends put the drinks in the washing machine with ice. There was music, dancing, and laughing going on all evening. We had a lovely decorated wedding cake. Before the wedding, I had gone to a Michaels crafts store to buy a bride and groom tier for the top of the cake, but they didn't have any made especially for black people. I ended up purchasing the bride and groom separately and painted them black.

On October 2, 2002, when the D.C. sniper attacks began and I read that the windows were shot out of a Michaels craft store in Maryland where I lived, I remembered the bride and groom on my wedding cake. The sniper shot a woman in the parking lot of another Michaels crafts store, this time in Fredericksburg, Virginia. I don't believe in coincidences. It didn't even occur to me that the shooter could be having some of the same memories.

# CHAPTER THREE:
## DISAPPOINTMENT AND JOY

After we were finally married, life appeared stable and we were getting along really well. John went out fewer nights; he was more attentive and appeared happier and more settled. In fact, I was feeling blessed. Several of my friends at Fort Lewis were having such serious relationship problems that, in contrast, John and I could easily be viewed as the picture of marital bliss. I've seen statistics showing that domestic violence is an even larger problem among military families than civilian ones. During one five-year period in the 1990s, the rate of domestic abuse in the military was almost five times higher than it was in civilian families. The reasons cited include the stress put on relationships by long separations and low salaries. Experts also typically talk about what it means to live in a culture where violence is viewed as a problem-solving solution.

When we were living at Fort Lewis, I certainly knew my share of troubled couples and was friendly with more than one woman who would suddenly appear with suspicious-looking bruises. My friend, Janice, who had hosted our wedding reception, was always trying to get help with her husband, Jerry, who would sometimes punch her or hit her. Janice was an exceptionally pretty and kind-hearted brunette who had married her small-town sweetheart and wanted to save her marriage. She was always trying to get others to talk sense into her husband. It seems ironic in retrospect that John was one of the men who tried to intercede.

During this period, he and I were discussing the future. We were trying to make good decisions about where we would be settling down. We wanted to have children and we wanted them to have a permanent and secure home. We had pretty much decided that we liked the Tacoma area. John also talked a lot about Travis and Lindbergh, the two sons he already had. He missed them, and we made plans to invite them to spend time with us.

Unfortunately, life with John was not consistently calm and there were certain issues that were a constant in our marriage, but for the time being, more often than not, when something went wrong, we operated as a team. John, for example, had an accident with the new car. They called me at work from the hospital; I hurried over there, my heart beating, but he was okay. He was pretty shaken up, but nothing more serious. The car, however, was a mess. He was hit from behind and after the investigation, we were told John was at fault. This little accident with the car highlighted one of the difficulties of living with John. He was always making plans and contingency plans for the future, but he wasn't a cautious or careful man; frequently he would do something that blew all of our plans to smithereens. He liked living on the edge.

On some basic level, I was usually worried about his well-being. Some of my biggest concerns revolved around his problems with reading and writing. He didn't want anyone else to know about his shortcomings, and I felt as though I should always be on call to help him out. Although his reading skills had certainly improved, it didn't come easily to him. If we were taking a long road trip, for example, and there were unfamiliar signs and directions, he couldn't process it fast enough. When we drove together, I felt as though I always had to be on alert. There were other things I worried about. John hurt his shoulder, for example, lifting weights. The doctor told him not to aggravate it. He didn't listen. The end result was that he needed surgery. Then, there were the numerous times that he overdid it with his exercise program. He would get involved with what he was doing and forget to drink enough liquids. He would then end up dehydrated and at the hospital getting IV fluids.

In some ways, he was like a hyperkinetic child who couldn't resist testing the limits. Living with him, I never knew what was going to happen next. Any plans I made with him were likely to be broken, and I could pretty much count on him to do things that surprised me. He came home one day with three live tarantulas and a large fish tank; we had to go to the pet store once a week to buy the crickets. As to be expected, the inevitable happened, and two of them got loose. I wouldn't go back into the house until John found and secured them. I was also beginning to notice that if

I bought something for myself that he didn't like, it would mysteriously end up missing. This happened with a radio I bought, but it also happened with dresses, shoes, and even coats.

When I couldn't find something, I would look everywhere. John would watch me searching.

"Maybe you gave it away," he would say.

"No, I'm sure I didn't," I would respond.

I couldn't find an explanation for these disappearances, but I didn't dwell on the lost items. It didn't occur to me to suspect him of interfering with my wardrobe; I was still too naïve to consider the implications of this level of controlling behavior. John would sometimes get things out of the house by taking them apart. I came home and discovered that he had dismantled a clock that I liked. He said he wanted to see how it worked. I asked him if he could put it back together.

He said, "No," and threw it away.

One night he came home and told me he wanted to try to get accepted for Air Assault School; he thought it would be a good career move. I supported his decision and helped him with the planning and application process. The training school he would be attending was in Alaska so he would once again be gone for an extended period. By now, of course, I had made friends at work and on the post, so I didn't find his absences so lonely. While he was at Air Assault School, he was allowed to call home, which he did regularly. He told me that, among other things, he was learning how to repel out of helicopters. Some of the work he was doing sounded dangerous to me, but he was incredibly excited. The training was intense, but he thought things were going well. He sounded almost positive that he would get his pin and be able to move forward. But that's not what happened. When he learned he was disqualified, he was shocked. He didn't understand why; he was certain that he had done everything right and was as good as, if not better than, anybody else.

He told me that he wasn't ever going to volunteer for anything again. He said he thought politics was a factor in what happened and blamed what he perceived to be a quota system that determined how many soldiers of different races would be allowed to go forward. His experience with Air

Assault School marked the beginning of a change in his attitude toward the military. He shared his disappointment and anger with his friends, as well as with me. Other soldiers that attended with him were surprised that he did not make it, even though none of them did either. For weeks, John's failure to get his wings dominated his attitude and mood. He was also still having issues with one of his supervisors and this relationship was also souring his feelings about the military. He was still sure he wanted to be in the Army, but his attitude was changing; he was no longer 100 percent gung ho about everything life in the armed services had to offer. I still wasn't fully aware of his capacity to lose all enthusiasm for an interest that had once dominated his life, so I thought his change in attitude was a sign that he was becoming more mature and realistic about life, since nothing in life is perfect.

In the spring of 1989, I began to feel queasy and discovered I was pregnant. When I visited the obstetrician for the first time, John was by my side, as he was on subsequent visits. I hoped to experience natural childbirth, and since John was going to be my coach, we took Lamaze classes together. If we were going to be a family, we needed more space so we moved once again, this time into a two-bedroom apartment. John helped me shop for large baby items like a crib, high chair, and stroller.

"You already have children," I told him. "I want to have some say in naming our child." If we had a boy, which I thought we were going to have, I didn't want to name him John; I wanted our son to have his own identity. We finally made a deal. If we had a son, John would get to name him—as long as he didn't name him John. If it was a girl, I would get to choose the name.

John's two sons, Lindbergh and Travis, lived in Baton Rouge with their mothers, only a few blocks from each other. When John asked their mothers if they could come for a long visit that summer, everyone agreed that it would be ideal for them to come together. Lindbergh was seven and Travis was nine. Both boys were exceptionally intelligent and curious and they were already doing well in school. They were glad to see each other and really happy to be with their dad, who they were always anxious to please. We planned lots of activities. We took them swimming and sightseeing. We went to local parks and we spent a day on Mt. Rainier. John played baseball with them and we signed them up to play baseball with other children their age; they both did really well. My pregnancy wasn't showing yet, which was a good thing; I wanted the boys to become more secure about spending time with us alone without feeling threatened by the prospect of a baby brother or sister. It was important for them to be happy visiting us so that they would regard any children that John and I had as true brothers and sisters. It was time for us to be a family, and I loved that feeling.

I was feeling so comfortable and content that I didn't even notice how much time John was spending at the gym. He was "at the gym" for hours every weekend. He also went to the gym in the late afternoon after work. During that summer, he was usually home to have dinner with me and his sons so I didn't think anything about his gym time, except to worry that he might be overdoing it. That all changed after Travis and Lindbergh returned home. Once again, we started having problems. For one thing, John was spending too many evenings "out with the guys." For another, he seemed distracted and he was paying much less attention to me when he was home. Then, there was another issue. In our household, I was the one who paid the bills, watched the budget, and kept track of the money. John came home one day and told me that he needed some money to pay back a friend who had loaned him money. I didn't understand why he was borrowing money. John said that he had spent money on the car, but that made no sense to me. Where was the money going?

My pregnancy was making me feel bloated and tired, and I worried that I looked too fat. I began picking myself apart, trying to figure out if there was something about me that was making him act different. Did I need to look prettier when he came home? Did I need to make better meals? What should I do differently? I was feeling so generally insecure that I confided in my mother, something I rarely did. I told her just a little bit, saying that John was acting funny and different. I will never forget my mother's reply. She said, *"Sometimes a man can make you feel as though you are the only woman in his life—and you're not!"* I had wanted my mother to say something else, something that made me feel better, and I was sorry that I had confided in her. Later I would recognize the words my mother gave me as advice. I just couldn't see it then.

I decided to talk to John. I asked him what was wrong, why he was spending so little time with me now that I was pregnant, and where the money was going. My questions made him so upset that his eyes filled with tears.

He said, "I love you. I always try to show you that I love you. Why are you asking me all these questions?" He actually cried. John made me feel that there was something wrong with me for questioning his behavior, and I felt really bad and sorry that I had done so.

One afternoon, a few weeks later, I was sitting in the car waiting for him. I was holding some lottery tickets in my hand, and I dropped one of them between the car seats. When I reached down to get it, I noticed that something else was there. It was a silver comb, and it definitely was not mine. I didn't say anything to John, but I could feel my stomach start to churn. I didn't want to be suspicious, but I was.

The next day when I came home from work, I noticed that John had already been at the apartment and had gone out again. On an impulse, I hit the redial button on the phone. A woman answered. Her name was Danielle, and yes, she knew John, but she didn't know he was my husband. She was as surprised to learn about me as I was to find out about her. John had told her that he had two sons, but that he wasn't married. This sounded familiar!! I was still so disbelieving that my John could be unfaithful that I asked her if she was sure that she was seeing John. I asked her to describe how he looked, which she did. She even described our car. She said they had met at the weight room at the gym and she had been involved with him for about six months. She said she would see him almost every day. She thought of him as a real boyfriend, somebody with whom she went out on real dates, including long rides in the car. What she was telling me made me feel as though somebody was hammering on my heart.

As we talked, she sounded so sincere and honest that I couldn't help feeling sympathetic to her. She was nineteen and she told me that this was her first real relationship. It was apparent that she was very, very upset by my phone call. Together, we decided to confront him. I was unbelievably angry and hurt; I was also determined. I asked her if she wanted to come over to confront him and she agreed. I got right into the car and drove over to pick her up. She was extremely pretty and very young-looking. She also seemed so genuinely distressed that it was difficult for me to blame her; it was not her fault. I was really upset; she was so young. It made me feel sorry for her, but it also made me more jealous and angrier at him. Why would he choose someone this young?

The moment Danielle walked through the door of our apartment and saw John's picture on the wall, she said, "That's him."

It wasn't long before we heard John out in the hall. I asked Danielle to go hide in the kitchen. When he walked through the door, I tried to sound as I always did. I asked him about his work day and his time at the gym. He said that his day was fine. He asked if I had cooked anything.

I quietly said, "Yes, it's very hot. Go into the kitchen and see if you like it."

As he walked into our kitchen and saw Danielle standing by the sink, his first words were, "What are you doing here?"

"Oh, so you do *know* her?" I asked.

"No," he replied. He looked nervous, embarrassed, and genuinely frightened by the situation. I could see him trying to figure out what he could do or say next.

My world fell apart. I could almost feel the pieces hitting the floor around me, but I stayed incredibly calm. I was a pregnant woman, and I needed some immediate answers.

At that moment, to add to the confusion, my husband's friend, James, showed up at the door to pick up lottery tickets we had bought for him. It took only seconds for James to size up the situation and decide he wanted no part of it.

"I'll leave," he said, but John asked him to stay.

We were talking in the living room and James became nervous, so he asked us if we could take our discussion into another room. We left James in the living room with the TV set and went into the second bedroom. Travis and Lindbergh had been using it for the summer and we were planning on turning it into a nursery for the baby. Right then, it looked pretty empty, with a spare bed and one chest.

Poor Danielle was crying hard. Looking at her, I realized that she was an innocent victim in this situation. When I first met John, I blamed his wife for not loving him enough. Now I was his wife, and I loved him enough.

There was something deeper going on here and there was no way around it. I had to look at him without the rose-colored glasses and admit that he was a serious womanizer. I told him to look at what he had done.

"You have to make a choice here," I said.

He put his head on his chin as though he had to stop and think about what to say. Finally, he said, "Why can't I have both of you?" He was dead serious.

With two women staring at him, he must have realized that he couldn't talk his way out of it and was trying to figure out a way to appease both of us. He was in survival mode and didn't know what to do. I think he was more concerned about hurting her than he was about hurting me. I doubt if he was worried about losing me; he realized how difficult it would be for me to go anywhere.

"Let me choose for you," I told him. "You can stay with her and I'll go to the courthouse tomorrow and get the paperwork for a divorce. You can marry her, and then I'll be on my own. NO problem!"

John looked at her and then he looked at me and said, "I'm going to stay."

I told Danielle that I was sorry for the pain that she was feeling and the problems that he had caused. She was so broken up that I told her that I wished I could take her pain on myself. We hugged and she continued to cry. I left John and Danielle in the guestroom so he could talk to her for a moment, and I went back to the living room where a very uncomfortable-looking James was fiddling with the TV remote.

James was from Jamaica, and he was one of John's best friends. People even said they looked alike. When they were in the field, James didn't like sleeping on the ground and the other soldiers would tease him. They would say things like, "James, you sure chose the wrong MOS."

From my perspective, James was a good and straightforward guy. I asked him if he knew Danielle or if he knew that John was seeing somebody. He assured me that this was the first time he had met her and he knew nothing about any affair.

But then he asked me a strange question: "I thought you and John had an understanding. Isn't that true?"

I could tell from the look on James' face that he was genuinely puzzled by what was taking place.

"An understanding? What are you talking about?"

"I thought you both agreed that you could see other people."

I stared at James; there was absolutely no way that John could have thought that. John and I spent a lot of time talking about stuff like fidelity. About six months after I arrived at Fort Lewis, we were sitting on the couch discussing relationships. John said that he never wanted to be in a position where he was worried about me being with another man. He said that if a woman cheated on him, then he would walk out of the door. There was no question about it. I said that I was going to be faithful, but that fidelity works two ways. I didn't want to be worried about what he was doing either. He told me that I didn't have to be worried; he wasn't going to be doing anything. He acknowledged that he had been unfaithful in the past, but now that he had found the woman he was looking for, he wasn't going to be doing that anymore.

I took him at his word and believed him. We did agree, however, that we could go out with our friends, and we even established guidelines. We agreed that, for both of us, there would be no touching or slow dancing or deep eye contact or exchanging of phone numbers with members of the opposite sex. Neither of us could touch another person. That was the only understanding we had.

I looked at James long and hard. "He told you that we had an *understanding?* He told you that?" I asked. "And you believed him?" My tone was calm and almost conversational.

For as long as I can remember, people have commented on my ability to be calm in a crisis. The more upset I get, the quieter I become, even now. This time was no different; James said that I was so calm and quiet, it was scaring him. To James' relief, a minute or two later, Danielle and John came out of the guestroom. The only person who looked at all happy was James, when John asked him if he could drive Danielle home. James was so glad to get out of there.

In a little more than twenty-four hours, my trust had gone out of the door. Up to this point, I honestly didn't think John would be unfaithful to me. I had never even seen him look at another woman when I was with him. He would consider it a sign of disrespect to do that. Even though he had already told me some major lies, I still didn't know how good of a liar he could be and how easily I could be fooled. At that moment, I felt sad and foolish and incredibly hurt. What was I going to do?

Almost the second after James and Danielle closed the door and left the apartment, I felt my baby kick for the very first time! Twenty-four hours earlier, I would have shared that sensation with John. Now, I didn't even want to look at him. But that flutter in my stomach, caused by my baby's small feet, brought another realization: it wasn't going to be so easy to walk out of the door; no matter what I said. I had to stay and somehow make this marriage work. I had to get my emotions under control, for the sake of the child I was carrying. Of course this was easier said than done.

After everybody left, I asked John about the tears he had shed and the lies he had told me only a few weeks earlier. He didn't really answer my questions, but he did say that he wanted to go sleep in the barracks that night. I told him he wasn't going anywhere, and he had better stay in the apartment. This was something that we both had to face, and neither of us could run away. I went into the bedroom, closed the door, and spent the night crying into the pillow. When I woke in the morning, I found John sleeping on the floor in front of the bedroom door. I stepped over him. I was too upset to go to work the next day. For the next few weeks, I couldn't stop thinking about what had happened, and I would burst into tears all the time. With John, I went into my usual coping mode: I became exceedingly quiet, polite, and distant. I continued to go into the bedroom every night, alone. John slept in the other room. I was still cooking and cleaning and doing everything I was doing before, but we were having only the briefest of conversations about necessary items. John seemed cautious and scared. He didn't know what I was going to do. He was coming home promptly at five. If he was going to be even five minutes late, he would call. His attitude and behavior told me that he didn't want me to leave.

I realized that things had to improve between us. My crying couldn't be good for the baby. My mother would say that if I didn't stop crying, my child would also end up being a crybaby in life. I didn't know how true that was, but I didn't want to take any chances. I didn't talk to anybody about what had happened. As I always do in life, when I'm in crisis, I turned to prayer. I was seeking answers and guidance from God.

Finally, I told John that we needed to talk, and we sat down on the couch.

"John," I said, "I am going to wipe the slate clean. Everything that happened in the past doesn't exist. I forgive you for all of this, and let's try to make this marriage work."

John said, "Okay." He seemed both relieved and happy.

He said, "I'm sorry. I never meant to hurt you." Now, I know what he meant by those words and that what he should have said was, "I never meant for you to find out."

I promised him that I would never bring this situation up again, but I also told him that if I ever found out that he was with anybody else, I would leave him. I told him that if that happened, he could keep all of our material possessions; that I would get custody of any children we had, and he would get visitation rights. I would expect only two things of him: that he would take care of the children and that he would leave me alone. He agreed.

I put my hand out, as if we were meeting for the first time. He reached out for it. I introduced myself to him and said, "Hi, I'm Mildred. What's your name?"

"John, nice to meet you," he said.

We were going to begin our lives again. I never brought any of this up again. I never snooped through his belongings or followed him around or did anything that indicated that I didn't trust him. I said that I was going to start fresh and that's what I did.

As we prepared for the birth of our child, in some ways it did seem like a brand-new relationship. We had decided that we didn't want to know the sex of our child beforehand. I was so sure that the baby would be a boy that I hadn't even prepared any girl names. However, I did keep asking John what name he had decided on if the baby was a boy.

He always answered, "You will be surprised." I barely had time to think about what this "surprise" could mean before life dealt us another long curve ball.

About the time we were celebrating New Year's Day 1990, we heard that

John might soon be receiving orders to head to Germany. Our baby wasn't going to get to spend much time in the nursery we had prepared in our Fort Lewis apartment.

Our baby boy was born in Madigan Army Hospital on January 17, 1990, at eleven-thirty p.m. He weighed six pounds, thirteen ounces and was nineteen inches long. He was so beautiful, but John didn't reveal his name until it was time to fill out the official forms. That's when he said, "John Allen Williams, Jr." I just looked at him. I was certainly surprised.

He said, "I remember what you said, but this will probably be my last son, and I want him to have my name."

What could I do except say, "okay."

All was not well immediately after our son's birth. Within hours, the doctors told us that the baby had an infection and needed to spend time in the intensive care unit. Among the procedures they wanted to perform was a spinal tap. My little baby boy was crying so hard that I couldn't bear it. John held him during the procedure and I went outside to watch. I couldn't hold him steady; I was crying too hard. I stood outside in the hallway, gazing out of the window. By then, I was also crying, as well as praying with all of my heart.

"Dear Lord," I asked, "I know he's on loan to me, but please don't take him back right now. Please allow me time with him. Amen."

Just then the baby's crying stopped. The doctors completed their test. Lil' John cried so hard, he cried himself to sleep. They put him in his bed. John came out and walked me to my bed. After he left, I walked over to the ICU and put my hands on my son's little body. I prayed that anything that was not supposed to be in his body would be removed. I went to sleep, praying that my baby would be well. The next morning the nurse came in to tell me that my son was hungry and looked much better. I was so happy that I started crying again.

John returned later that day, along with some of my friends from work. They were happy to see me and the baby.

"What's his name?" one friend asked.

"John," I said.

"You mean I waited all this time to find out that the baby's name is John?" she said.

We all laughed.

I had seen the television series *Roots* and remembered what Kunta Kinte had done when his child was born. A few days after my son's birth, it was a warm evening and I took Lil' John outside to where we could both see the evening sky. I talked to him about what it meant to be black in America. I told him that we were descendents of slaves in this country. He didn't understand what I was saying, but I wanted to plant a seed and water it as time went by. I recalled what Kunta Kinte had said and the action he had performed with his child and applied it to Lil' John.

I lifted my son up to the sky and said, "Behold, the only thing greater than yourself."

My son became the joy of my life. And I thanked God for him, my first child. I wanted to do everything right. I wanted everything perfect; the best of everything for him.

Two weeks later, we found out that John's unit would be leaving for Germany in April.

# CHAPTER FOUR:
## WARNING SIGNS

Almost by definition, the military experience means never staying in one place long enough to get really comfortable. John left for Germany in April 1990 and, in June, the baby and I joined him in the town of Bindlach, where he was stationed. We were traveling light and had packed only our personal items; our Nissan was parked at John's sister's house in Arizona, where it would be waiting for our return. John had already bought a small European car, which we drove home from the airport.

At age thirty, after five years at Fort Lewis, I was much more experienced at dealing with life on an Army post and immediately began looking for work. It didn't take me long to find a job as an in/out processing clerk in Grafenwöhr, a training area for soldiers about forty-five minutes away. I was still nursing the baby, but Grafenwöhr had a daycare facility where Lil' John could stay; I was even able to walk back and forth to nurse him.

We lived off post in a small, furnished, two-bedroom apartment, right across from a cemetery. I used to enjoy looking out of the window and watching the local people carrying flowers and going in and out to visit gravesites in the park-like setting. I'd never seen a cemetery that busy. Some days it seemed more like a mall. Most of John's Army buddies had been sent to different places so neither one of us had friends on post. Germany forced us to be a family. For the first time in our marriage, we were together just about every night and weekend, and, as usual, we had an assortment of relationship issues.

John always loved playing with our son, but he was never the kind of father who got up in the middle of the night or got involved with the details of diaper changing, feeding, or burping, and Lil' John was one of those babies who refused to sleep through the night. He also had more than his share of childhood illnesses and required a great deal of care. I was tired much of the time. Living in furnished apartments was also beginning to wear on me. When we were at Fort Lewis, soldiers would often return from Europe with furniture they had purchased in Germany. Some of it looked really nice to me so I began to ask John if we could buy some furniture. His answer was always a variation of "We'll see." Something I particularly wanted was a rocking chair so I could rock the baby to sleep. Finally, I told John that I would go out and buy one myself.

Whenever I said something like that, he had three typical answers. "Hold on." "Give me a minute." or "Let me see." Eventually I realized that all three meant the same thing and if he had anything to do with it, I wasn't going to get what I wanted. And I didn't get the rocking chair.

I didn't know what to make of John's reluctance to purchase household items. It extended to the simplest necessities. I would buy four plates and put them in the cabinet. I would return home and two of them had mysteriously disappeared or been broken.

I would ask John, "What happened?"

He would reply, "I don't know, but we don't need more than two anyway."

More than once I remember shaking my head and saying, "Man, you are crazy."

One time I bought a set of twenty-eight various kinds of kitchen knives. John would use them as screwdrivers or makeshift tools to cut things or repair the car and one by one, they vanished. I asked him repeatedly not to use the knives for this purpose. It didn't take long before we were left with two steak knives—one for him and one for me. I would buy a new set of glasses and a set of dishes every six months. Finally I couldn't help but notice the trend. I stopped buying anything with a design and, instead, would buy only the most basic dishes—something usable so we wouldn't have to resort to paper plates. Then, I wasn't sure what the reason was for John's behavior. Now, I have two possible explanations. Perhaps he resisted the idea of being a family man and the household purchases represented too much domesticity. Or perhaps breaking objects I liked was a subtle way of breaking my spirit. But in Germany in 1990, I wasn't thinking like that. John was still affectionate; he was still telling me how much he loved me and I was a working mother who had real problems that seemed much more pressing than lost cutlery or broken crockery. For one thing, my son was sick all of the time. He had a million and one allergies, and he was developing asthma. For another, John's military career was not progressing according to plan and, once again, he was receiving the wrong kind of attention at work.

Midsummer, an M16 turned up missing on post. John phoned me to tell me not to expect him home for dinner; nobody was going home until the missing rifle was found. He then called again to say that the weapon had been found, but that he was being blamed for its disappearance.

"Why? What happened?" I asked.

He said that while he was looking for the rifle, he thought to check out the air conditioning. He hit the paneling hard in an upward motion; when he did, the weapon popped up. John told me that his superiors suspected that he had put the rifle in the air conditioning unit with the idea of returning later to retrieve it. They asked him how he knew that he would find the M16 in that spot. John said that he told them repeatedly that, like everybody else, he was only trying to help find the missing weapon. He told me that the incident was being investigated. He seemed upset but, to the best of my knowledge, nothing ever came of this. He sounded completely convincing when he told me about this incident.

On August 2, Iraq invaded Kuwait. Soon after this, John's unit received word that they would be going to the Persian Gulf. They were going into the Middle East and the units were having meetings on post to prepare them for what to expect, and not just in terms of what their military activities would be. The military wanted the soldiers to be prepared for the climate as well as the culture; they wanted them to be aware of what they could and couldn't do as well as places they could and couldn't go. The wives also had meetings; we were told that there would be times when we would have no idea where the units were being deployed. They realized that some men would write daily while others might not write at all, so they encouraged the wives to help each other and share information. John, who expected the worst, told me that the lifespan for a combat engineer in war could be as short as eight seconds. Maybe he was exaggerating, but he sure looked serious. He gave me instructions about the insurance policy, made sure all his children were covered, and put his papers in order. Everyone I knew was nervous, and the potential military action was the main topic of conversation.

On a cold, sunny day in December, I was at the base with all of the other wives, girlfriends, and assorted family members to watch our loved ones depart. There must have been about sixty soldiers and their families. We said our goodbyes in a large indoor reception area. Lil' John was with me and could only walk a few steps without falling down. The hardest part was not crying while we were waiting for the unit to board the bus. As soon as we were outside on the snow-covered ground, and saw the buses drive away, we all began crying.

Even though many of the wives opted to go back to the States until their husbands returned, I decided to stay where I was. I was in a foreign country alone, with an eleven-month-old son, but I was determined to make it and not leave the area. I wanted to be right there for John's homecoming. We got word that the war would begin on January 17, which is my son's birthday. All anybody thought about was the war. When I walked through the door at work in the morning, I looked up and saw the television that had been set for CNN. At home, I was glued to the set. We were getting information about the war as it was happening. It was instant news and I couldn't take my eyes off of the set in case I might catch a glimpse of John.

All of the wives were terrified at the prospect of hearing a knock on their door and seeing officers there to tell them that their loved one had been killed. I looked out of the window constantly, hoping I would never see that military sedan. I'm sure there were others who were doing the same thing. One of the women I worked with lost her only son; he had been in a helicopter that went down during night maneuvers. We all cried with her and tried to surround her with support.

My work at the in/out processing center put me in daily touch with what was going on. We saw the soldiers who were arriving in Grafenwöhr and did the necessary paperwork to process them into the system, and we saw those who were leaving. When soldiers were going home, among other things, we arranged the airline tickets for them and their families so we were aware of the discharges, honorable and dishonorable; we also handled the paperwork for those who would not be returning. We heard about the soldiers who committed suicide as well as those who were killed. I especially recall one group of soldiers in a tank unit who came through our office, laughing and joking; a short time later we heard that some of them were killed by friendly fire. It became depressing and upsetting. All I wanted to do was stay in front of the TV and watch the news. The only reason that I did anything else was because of my son. I hung a photograph of John on the wall, and made a point of showing it to Lil' John every day.

"That's Daddy," I told him.

He said, "Dada," and pointed at the picture.

Since so many wives had returned to the States, the housing situation on post had changed dramatically; apartments were suddenly available. John had been so happy when I had surprised him by renting a new house at Fort Lewis, and I decided to do the same thing and contacted housing and requested a two-bedroom apartment. A month later I was offered a lovely three-bedroom apartment on post, and Lil' John and I moved in.

One day in March, I was at work when I got a big surprise. The phone rang, and I heard John's voice saying that he was back. He told me that he had hurt his shoulder and they were sending him home. He had been gone for three months. I was so excited and happy. He had been sent back to another part of Germany about two hours away, and he asked me to pick him up at the Army hospital there. I arranged for the day off and, early the next morning, Lil' John and I were zooming along the Autobahn. When we arrived, we saw that John was still wearing his hospital robe. I immediately went over to him. I'd missed him so much and thanked God that he was alive. His shoulder was in a sling. He said very little. He couldn't get over how much our son had grown or how well he was walking. At first, Lil' John didn't recognize his father.

After John got dressed, we loaded his things in the car, and headed home. He barely spoke. All he said was that he'd had a hard time in Saudi.

"How?" I asked.

"I'll tell you later," he replied.

I was accustomed to living with a John who was typically enthusiastic and expressive. Whether he was happy, angry, or sad, his emotions always seemed close to the surface, and he expressed what he was feeling. I was expecting him to be his old self—full of stories and plans, as well as jokes. Instead, the John who returned from the Gulf acted like somebody had run over him and flattened him out. From the very first hug we shared after he returned from Saudi, he was different. His attitude seemed so altered that I asked him if he was still planning to be in the military for twenty years.

He said, "Why do you ask me that?"

I replied, "Because you seem different, and I can't put my finger on it."

He said, "Don't worry about it. We have plenty of time to talk."

It was apparent that he didn't want to discuss anything further so I left it alone.

He liked the new apartment, as I thought he would. At first, when he tried to sit next to me on the couch, Lil' John came and sat between us. When John tried to hold my hand, our son said, "No!" Lil' John just stared at his father. It was an adjustment for all of us. Finally, Lil' John looked at the picture on the wall and then looked at John. "Dada," he said.

"That's right," I told him. Once he made the connection, our son made room on the couch for the three of us.

For the next week, I continued to go back and forth to work with my son. John, however, had an additional week before he had to return to work. When I came home in the evening, he would be sitting in the apartment, staring into space. I would find him shaking his head back and forth. Sometimes it looked as though he had barely moved all day.

"Are you okay?" I would ask.

"I'm fine," he would reply.

He returned to work after a week, and I kept hoping things would go back to normal, but they didn't. He would come home on time every night, but he barely spoke to me. He would have dinner and play with our son, but he pretty much ignored me and wasn't sharing what was bothering him. Lil' John seemed to be the only bright thing in my husband's world, and he would play with him for hours on end. In May 1991, I began to have morning sickness and discovered that I was once again pregnant.

John appeared happy about this, but he was still distant and withdrawn. It was June before he began to even discuss some of what he had experienced in Saudi.

The first thing he told me was that he wanted to get out of the military. He sounded completely disillusioned and discouraged by the military.

He said, "The United States is wrong, and I don't want to be a part of this madness anymore."

He told me about his anger at having to dismantle bombs that our country had given Sadaam Hussein.

"How do you know they were 'our' equipment?" I asked him.

"They had 'USA' stamped on them," he replied.

John told me that he had thought long and hard about what he wanted to do. He said, "I want out and I want out now."

"What are we going to do?" I asked him.

We had based all of our plans on a twenty-year military career. We had nowhere to go and no money saved. John was now thirty. He had joined active duty service in 1985, and had already re-enlisted once. I asked him about his ETS—estimated time of separation from military service. The date he gave me was April 1994, but he seemed to think that there might be a way he could get out ahead of time. I suggested that he wait until the 1994 date. In the meantime we could prepare to leave the military.

He said, "Okay," and told me that he thought that was fair. Then he became quiet again.

John's behavior was scary. One minute he appeared fine; the next, he was confused. I wanted to do something, but I didn't know what. I asked him if there was anything I could do to help him through whatever he was going through. He said there was nothing I could do. He went to work in the morning. Otherwise, all he wanted to do was sit in the apartment, and he never wanted to do anything with me.

The only thing that held John's interest was his relationship with his son. When he came home, he would change his clothes and immediately begin playing with Lil' John. He would play with him as though he was also a child. They would run through the house, wrestling or playing hide and seek. There was only one television channel available for the English-speaking audience so we would buy videotapes—mostly children's tapes—

that they could watch together. Lil' John had a battery-operated car that he could drive himself. John would take him out and they would be gone for hours. John seemed confused and angry much of the time, but when he was with his son, he became calmer and more like himself.

When my pregnancy started to show, he was sure that it was going to be a girl, as was I. He began talking to my stomach, but he wanted me to tell him the girl name that I had decided on. He wanted to start calling the baby by her real name, but I wanted to be certain before I said the name out loud. The following week I had an appointment with my obstetrician, whose office was near my work. I was going to get an ultrasound. John took the day off from work so he could be with me and spent the day volunteering at Lil' John's daycare center. As soon as the doctor began the ultrasound procedure, he told us that he could see the sex of the baby and he asked if we wanted to know. John and I looked at each other before saying, "Yes."

"It's a girl," the doctor said.

John had always told me that he wanted a little girl. Now, he was so happy! He shook the doctor's hand and, when we stepped out of the office, he picked me up. I was incredibly happy whenever he showed those moments of enthusiasm that I associated with the "old" John. This time, when he asked me what I wanted to name our daughter, I told him Salena. I had seen a television program about a black woman who had been a slave; she had gone through tremendous hardships and, yet, she had preserved her strength and sense of self. I told John that I wanted our daughter to have a name that represented strength and that suited him just fine.

Although he was thrilled about having a baby girl, he was becoming less than thrilled with me. He was starting to question and find fault with every little thing I said or did. He would get annoyed about how many times I picked Lil' John up to hug or kiss him.

"He's a boy," he would say. "He doesn't need all that."

He would complain about how I set the table; he would complain about what time we had dinner; he would complain that I let Lil' John sit on the floor in the kitchen, playing with pots and pans, while I prepared dinner. He was nitpicking about every little thing.

There were times when I would say something like, "Since I'm not doing this the way you want, why don't you do it yourself?"

He would usually reply immediately, saying, "Oh, no, you are doing it fine." But then he would start finding fault again. He began to use phrases like, "You can't do that." Or, "We don't need that now."

John seemed to be turning into a control freak and I asked him if he was trying to control what I did and how.

"Oh no," he would say. "I'm just suggesting another and better way of doing what you are doing."

But, if I didn't take his suggestion, he would become angry and stop speaking to me for days. If I tried to make up and approached him with a peace offering like his favorite dessert or a flower, he would turn away from me and walk out of the house. To keep the peace, I began doing what he wanted the way he wanted, even when it wasn't the best way. I found myself changing to accommodate him.

John was becoming more consistently withdrawn and harder for me to reach. I could almost feel him purposely pulling back. No matter what happened, we had always been close. Now he seemed to be fighting that closeness. He talked much less about our future, and he stopped making plans with me. The only plan he wanted to talk about was getting out of the military. He wanted to do something to try to get out earlier. His attitude toward me would have made me upset, no matter what, but the fact that I was pregnant made it all worse.

One day in the late summer, I talked John into going to the park. It was a beautiful day, and we went to the kind of European park that you some-times see in movies or in paintings. Everywhere I looked I saw contented couples and smiling children. One of the main features of the park was a lake with paddle boats that could be rented. I watched other parents taking their children out on the lake, and I saw how happy they all looked. It was like a scene out of a movie, and I wanted to be a part of it.

I said, "I'm going to get a boat for us and we can paddle with Lil' John." As always, I didn't want to place any extra demands on him so I didn't suggest that *he* get the boat.

John looked at me with utter contempt and his tone was no less mean-spirited when he spoke. "You can't do that," he said.

His eyes were cold, hard, and angry. He had never before spoken to me with this degree of cold anger; he had never before looked at me this way. These were a stranger's eyes, and they frightened me.

I stood there staring at him. Why was my husband so angry at me? Why couldn't we go out on the lake and be happy like the other couples? Why didn't he want to be a part of this world? Even more important to me at that moment, why didn't he want to do something so small that would please me so much? At that moment, I felt as though my heart had been broken. John's fury at me because I wanted to go out on a paddle boat with my family on a beautiful day in a beautiful European park was, for me, one of the turning points in our marriage.

Until that moment, yes, John and I had problems, but he never looked at me as though he carried hate or anger in his heart. When I saw that look, I started to cry, and I couldn't stop. I simply couldn't stop. John said he was sorry, but "sorry" couldn't touch what I was feeling. On the way home, the tears would not stop falling. Once we were in the apartment, I locked myself in the bathroom. And I cried and I cried. I also think all of the worries and concerns of the previous two years hit me at once. I had been so worried about John and his safe return, and I tried so hard to make him happy. Now, here we were, and my simplest request was enough to make him angry.

I was crying so hard it hurt my stomach. I realized that I needed to stop crying because of the baby growing inside me and the little boy who hated to see his mother upset, but every time I tried to stop, I would cry harder. I was thinking, *Why is he so mean-spirited to me? What did I ever do to deserve it?*

John came to the door and apologized again, but I couldn't stop crying.

Finally, I said, "I'll be okay. Just leave me alone."

I could hear the television in the next room so I assumed he and Lil' John were okay. I decided to take a long bath to calm myself. I must have fallen asleep; the next thing I knew my son was calling for me. When I emerged from the bathroom, Lil' John was waiting outside the door. He was crying.

I asked him to stop crying, and he said, "Only if you will."

He was pretty smart for his age. After we comforted each other, he said he had a surprise and asked me to close my eyes. When I did that, he took me by the hand, led me to the living room, and turned me around. "You can open your eyes now, Mommy," he said.

When I did, I saw that John had prepared dinner and set the table with flowers. He apologized and said he hadn't realized how much he had hurt me until I went into the bathroom and closed the door. He promised that he would try to be more careful of my feelings.

After dinner, I put my tired little son to bed. He said, "Mommy, I love you and I'm glad you are happy again." I felt bad about having upset him and realized that I had to be more careful about how I behaved in front of him.

When I went back into the living room and sat on the sofa, tears were still falling. John was cleaning the kitchen. He came and sat down next to me. He apologized again and said that he really didn't know what had come over him in the park.

"I hope we're okay," he said.

"We're okay," I told him, as I wiped my tears away. What I didn't tell him was that I would never forget that look in his eyes and I would never stop wondering where it came from.

In the middle of the night, Lil' John got up and came into our bed with us. He really didn't like being by himself in his room. And I was really happy to have him with us.

# CHAPTER FIVE:
## THIS IS NOT THE MAN I MARRIED

I was still pregnant and Lil' John wasn't yet two when he was hospitalized with pneumonia. A kind nurse brought another bed into the room, and I slept there beside him until he was able to come home. John wanted to stay in the room with us, but he had to go back to work. Whether it was the air, the water, or the food, there was something about the environment where we lived in Germany that had an adverse effect on my son. Between his skin allergies and his asthma, he was sick all of the time, and I was constantly worried. Like John, I was also ready to go back to the States.

In the meantime, my husband's mood was not bouncing back as I had expected it to do. His disposition with me was all over the place. One moment, he was intimate, loving, and emotionally dependent; the next he was hostile and furious. But his disposition with our son never changed. It seemed the only thing that brought him any pleasure was the time he spent playing with him. Finally, after months of not wanting to talk about it, he asked if I wanted to know what had happened to him in Saudi.

I said, "Only if you are ready to tell me."

We put a tape in the VCR for Lil' John to watch and John and I sat down at the dinner table.

Almost as soon as he started to speak, I could see him becoming more and more agitated. According to him, he started having problems in Saudi; the black soldiers were being discriminated against. He said black soldiers and white soldiers could be in trouble for the exact same thing, but the black soldiers would get demoted while the white soldiers would get promoted. He talked to some of the other sergeants about this, and they agreed with him, but "they were afraid to speak up." He decided to try to do something about this and requested an appointment with a counselor from EEO (Equal Employment Opportunity) to try to get justice for the soldiers.

He told me that his request was granted, and when he went to bed in the large tent he shared with other soldiers, he expected to see the counselor the next day. That night, however, while he was asleep in his sleeping bag, there was an explosion in the tent. He heard soldiers running out, and he heard other soldiers calling for him, saying, "Where is Sergeant Williams?" The tent was filled with smoke, but when he tried to get out of his sleeping bag, the zipper jammed; he couldn't open it, but somebody had run back into the tent and pulled him and his bag out. When he and the sleeping bag were outside, somebody cut the bag open. The soldiers were all safe. The event precipitated an investigation to try to find out exactly who or what had caused the explosion. When it was completed, they said that John tried to commit suicide and take the other soldiers with him.

According to John, they then put handcuffs on him and arrested him. He said they didn't follow proper procedure by sending him to another unit. Instead, in front of "his" soldiers, they took his money, his TA-50, and his gas mask. He was particularly upset because they took his gas mask.

"How can you take a soldier's gas mask when there is talk about nuclear gas being released into the atmosphere?"

I remember saying, "I don't know, baby." He was so upset, and I was so upset for him.

"They didn't give a damn about me, babe," he told me. "They finally sent me to another company, and they put me in what felt like a dungeon. They hogtied me and left me there with my head on the floor for hours." He stood up and continued talking. "They treated me like dirt. I didn't deserve that, Mildred." He was getting more and more upset. "I didn't deserve that. I wanted to be a soldier. I cared about my soldiers. You tell me, why would I try to hurt them?" He walked over to the window.

He continued, "They wanted me out of there because they didn't want anyone to know what they were doing." At this point he was crying. I went over to him to put my arms around him, but he pushed me away.

"Do you understand?" he said. "They tried to kill me, baby. I saw the blasting caps on that white boy's bed, and he is a private. They believed a private over a sergeant. How could they do that?"

At that time, I honestly believed that my husband had experienced the worst kind of racism. He was crying. He looked as though he was in terrible emotional pain. How could I not believe him? It's interesting, but until that time, he and I had rarely, if ever, discussed racism. We had both grown up in the black community in Baton Rouge. The students in the elementary, junior and high school we both attended had been all black. The college I attended, Southern University, was predominantly black. In the Army, we both made friends from all races. We had close friends who were black, white, Hispanic, and Asian. I had never heard John complain of racism before.

Racism is not a general topic of conversation among my friends. If you are black in this country, it's going to have touched you in some way. Where I grew up in Louisiana, there were very clear lines about places you could and couldn't go and things you could and couldn't do. Employment opportunities were also affected. I was sympathetic to what John was telling me. Once, in Baton Rouge, I spotted an ad in the paper for a job that seemed right up my alley. After dialing the number listed, I was informed that I should come right over since the job was still available. When I arrived at the office, however, and the person taking applications looked at me, he said, "I'm sorry; that job is no longer open."

"But I just talked to you on the phone," I responded.

The person stammered and started to say, "But you don't sound..." Then he stopped himself. I know he was about to say, "But you don't sound black." Instead, he kind of ducked his head and said that the job had just been filled.

As I was leaving the office, a white woman came in and I heard her say she was there about the same job listed in the paper that he told me was filled. I saw that she was being handed an application to fill out.

I told John about this and other experiences. When I was finished talking, he said, "Well, I've never experienced anything like that. Every place I went for a job, I got it."

"Are you telling me," I asked John, "that this is the first time you've experienced racism?" I found this almost difficult to believe, but I couldn't argue with his experience.

"Yes," he said, "and I don't like it."

"Welcome to the real world," I told him.

He said, "It's not like this in the United States."

"Maybe it's just less out front in the United States," I suggested.

John came over and apologized for pushing me away, and cried some more. When I looked at him, I could see that he was still both angry and upset.

After we put Lil' John to bed, I was having cramps. John suggested I go to bed. And he said he would be up for a while. Later, I woke up. John was not in bed, but I heard sounds coming from the living room. I tiptoed into the living room and saw him crying into a pillow. I didn't want him to know I was there so I tiptoed back to bed. About an hour later, I heard water running in the shower. A long time later, he came to bed. I could tell that he was trying not to wake me, but I let him know I wasn't asleep. He put his head on my shoulder and cried some more.

He said, "Why did they do that, babe?"

Even now, I can remember his tears and the depth of the pain he was feeling. It seemed as though his spirit had been crushed. Despite all the love I felt for him, I was helpless to do anything. It was apparent that he was so deeply hurt that only God could help him.

The next morning, which was a Saturday, we were awakened by Lil' John. I started to get up to make breakfast, but John told me that he would do it.

"Okay, big man," he said to Lil' John, "let's go into the kitchen." I heard them laughing and playing, and John's spirits seemed to have improved, but later that day, while he was looking out the window, he saw one of his lieutenants. "See him," John said to me. "He knew what happened to me, and he didn't do anything to help me." Once again, I could see his dark mood settling in.

I was still expecting that, any day now, John would become more like the man I married, but it wasn't happening. Instead his dark mood was evolving into a permanent fixture. His old 'get up and go' was missing. He seemed to have lost interest in not just in me, but in life itself. At that time, I knew nothing about depression or what it meant. I didn't come from a world that discussed psychological symptoms, and I didn't have a clue about John's moods. I couldn't say anything to one of his superiors, or even a chaplain, about his mental state. I still wasn't one hundred percent sure that he wasn't going to change his mind about the military, and I didn't want to do anything to jeopardize his career. If he was hurt further in the military, I sure didn't want him to blame me.

As I was watching John and thinking of what I could do to help him, it came to me that he could write a letter and have those soldiers who witnessed this experience sign it. When I spoke with him about it, he was excited. He began recalling the details so he could be accurate in his writing. As we were completing it, *60 Minutes* came on. I suggested to John that once the report was completed and signed, we should send it to Ed Bradley with a letter explaining what we wanted. He liked the idea.

We went about getting the signatures from the soldiers. We visited one soldier whose wife was present. She reviewed the letter and thought it was very well written and before her husband signed the letter, his wife asked, "Are any of the soldiers who signed this document white?"

"No," we said.

"Unless you have one white boy's name on this document, they will not listen to you," she warned.

We sat back in disappointment, listening as she explained the subtleness of racism there.

"They can get away with it over here and that's why it is in the open," she said. "They know no one will look into it or care about what we do."

I saw the light leave John's face.

"Well, we have to at least try and see where it takes us," I said.

They agreed and her husband signed the document.

We submitted the document and sent a copy to Ed Bradley. A few weeks later, John received a letter telling him he had an appointment to go to the commander's office. We both went. First, we met an E7 who spoke to us before we went in to see the commander. He asked us questions about why we were there.

"You need to be careful with what you are doing," he said. "They don't like *us* to make waves for them."

I thought he was trying to talk us out of what we were doing, but we still went into the commander's office. He had the report in front of him and began asking questions.

"When the investigators came to speak to you about this incident, why didn't you answer their questions?" he asked John.

John didn't answer. He just looked at the commander.

I was shocked but tried to hide it. He hadn't told me of the investigation.

"Sergeant Williams, what happened in Saudi, in your own words?" the commander asked.

John didn't say anything.

"So, since it appears you are not going to cooperate, this meeting is over," he said.

John stood up, saluted, and we left the office.

When we got to the car, I said, "What just happened in there?" I was calm in my speech so as not to incite an argument. "Why didn't you answer him? Why didn't you tell me of an investigation?"

He looked at me. "You ask too many questions," he said.

*Who is this man?* I thought. *Where is my husband? What is going on?*

After that day, the incident never came up again. I didn't question him about it. We placed the paperwork in our files and we didn't hear from Ed Bradley.

I continued to try everything to lift John's spirits. I suggested walks, movies, and outings. Some of the people in my office would come back on Monday mornings and tell me about trips they had taken to other parts of Germany or Europe, so I suggested to John that maybe we could do something like that. He wanted no part of it. I suggested doing things that we used to do in the States, like visiting museums. There was even an American military museum in Germany. The old pre-Saudi John would have loved going there. The post-Saudi John called it a "museum of death."

He said, "What's wrong with Americans, that they want to celebrate how they kill people?"

Sentences like this always made me think of him as being essentially non-violent. But time proved that this was another example of the ways in which his rhetoric and his actions didn't always match up.

Over the years, I have thought many times about what John told me about his experiences in Saudi. I have gone over and over the details he gave me. When he cried to me and told me that he was blamed for something he didn't do, I certainly believed him. Since then, of course, I have come to have some second thoughts. I believe absolutely that something happened to John in Saudi that threw him into a deep depression and completely altered the way he viewed the world, but I don't know what that something was and will probably never know.

During John's murder trial, I read reports in the paper that gave a completely different version of what happened in that tent in Saudi. Some of John's supervisors said that he routinely complained that he wasn't being treated fairly because he was black. John had a series of problems with his platoon sergeant, Kip Berentson, and I had heard about them going back to Fort Lewis. According to interviews in *Newsweek* and the *Washington Post*, Sgt. Berentson said that he believed that John threw a thermite grenade in a tent that held sixteen soldiers, including Berentson. Another one of his superiors, a captain named Rick Martin, was quoted in the *Chicago Sun-Times*, saying that the grenade pin was found near John's bunk. As the primary suspect, John was removed from the unit, but there was insufficient proof for a formal arrest. The captain also referred to the M16 that had gone missing in Germany. The captain indicated that John had confessed to hiding the rifle to get another soldier in trouble.

Did John throw that grenade or was he blamed unfairly? I will probably never know the truth about this incident. John wept as he questioned why he had been treated the way he was, but were those tears sincere? Was he crying for the reasons I thought he was? Or was it all part of some kind of act? By the time he and I separated, I had ample evidence that he was able to lie when it suited his purpose; I had seen firsthand that he could push those tears out as a manipulation when he wasn't being honest. He had the capacity to lie in a way that I couldn't understand then and that I can't understand now. And I know better than anybody that he could and would cover up his lies with more lies. But if nothing that John told me about these events was true, I still wonder why none of these serious incidents were found on his military records. If he was guilty, why wasn't he reprimanded? If his military superiors thought he was disturbed, why didn't they do anything? Why didn't they at least recommend that he see a psychiatrist for further evaluation? Finally, if he did all that he was accused of, why did he receive an honorable discharge? Why was he awarded medals for time served in the Gulf? These are big questions for me. As I've become more and more involved with the issue of domestic violence, I've become aware of the problems that angry soldiers are causing within military families. Who knows how many returning soldiers walk among us as time bombs waiting to explode? This is a community that needs help for both the soldier and his family.

Soon after John cried and told me about his experiences in Saudi, we had another situation to face. One day, when I went to work, I began cramping so badly that I had to go to the doctor. It was only November, and our daughter wasn't due until February. The doctor determined that I was starting to dilate, and he hospitalized me. They released me a couple of days later with the understanding that I was to be on complete bed rest for at least a week. This time, John was really there to be counted on. He took time off from work and stayed home. He did all the cleaning, shopping, and cooking, which was a real job. When you're living on an Army base in Germany, and you are hungry, you can't order up a pizza. If you want dinner, somebody has to shop and cook. John took care of us. I still remember him sitting on the edge of the bed reading Dr. Seuss' *Green Eggs and Ham* to both Lil' John and me. He seemed happier staying at home and not going to work.

On Saturdays, he and I often went to the base in Nuremberg, which was about an hour away. There was a larger PX there where we could stock up on groceries and household supplies, and there were a variety of other shops. One week, when we went to Nuremberg, I decided I wanted to get my hair done before the baby was born. John and our son went off to the PX and I headed for a hair salon. The stylist, a beautiful Jamaican woman with a lovely lilting accent, and I started talking while she worked on my hair. Sometime in the conversation, she asked about my religion. I told her that I had been born and raised as a Baptist.

She asked, "Have you ever heard of Louis Farrakhan?"

I told her, "No."

She told me something about who he was and said that he was an important black religious leader. She looked a little surprised when she said, "You're from the United States and you've never heard of Minister Farrakhan?" I told her that I was from Louisiana, and the only person I knew who fit that description of religious leader was Martin Luther King, Jr.

"You have to hear Minister Farrakhan," she said to me. She gave me two tapes and told me that I needed to return them after I watched them; she wanted to give the tapes back to her son. I promised to bring them back the following Saturday.

That night, after dinner, John and I sat down to watch the tapes the sister gave me. The first tape was a history of black people from the beginning of time. It talked about the scriptures, about our time in Africa, and it talked about slavery and the effect it had on us as a people. It talked about some of the ways that we had been mis-educated about our history and our spiritual heritage. It took some of the scriptures and explained what was happening in a real, chronological, and historical way. The second tape was of Minister Farrakhan speaking. I was accustomed to hearing the words of Reverend Martin Luther King, Jr., who taught that integration was the primary goal. Minister Farrakhan said something else. He said that the black community has to build strong families and strong communities. He essentially said that we shouldn't be worried about whether or not we were being accepted by the white community. He said we had to worry about whether or not we were accepting ourselves. He said racism is not something we created, but it's something we have to deal with. We have to know who we are and we have to assume responsibility for our own actions and how we treat each other.

While John was watching that tape, he kept saying, "That's right. That's right."

For me, these two tapes were life-changing. I was raised as a devout Baptist. I always prayed and read my Bible every day. I had been in the choir, an usher, and a Sunday school teacher. I was taught never to question anything in the Bible; even if it didn't make any sense.

"You don't question God," my mother would say.

"But, Mama," I would say to her, "I don't understand and understanding is important, right? In all of your getting, get understanding, right?"

"Mildred, just read your Bible," my mother would tell me.

When I finished watching those tapes, my belief systems were shattered. I was no longer going to be able to believe like I did before and, from that point on, I would not believe anything without researching it for myself. I felt as though I had been lied to my entire life. Now, who or what could I believe? It was like something exploded in my brain. I cried for two days straight. For two days, I also stopped praying. Soon, I began praying again, but I remember praying, "Oh Lord, I don't know who You are, but I've got to call on somebody to help me. Please, whoever You are, help me. I am truly a lost sheep in the wilderness."

It wasn't long before I realized that what was dear to me was my relationship with God, and my mother gave that to me when I was young. That belief and trust was solid, but now the foundation was on shaky ground. I had to strip down and start looking at my beliefs. I could no longer blindly accept what somebody told me. I was going to start questioning everything, and this attitude would eventually reach out into all parts of my life, including my relationship with John.

I don't know exactly how those tapes affected John. I only know what he said, which was, "Why didn't we know about this man? He is right in the States! Why did we have to come all the way to Germany to hear about Minister Farrakhan? When we get back, we have to find him!"

Many of the newspaper reports after the terrible D.C. shootings said that John had been a Muslim since the 1980s. These newspaper reports were wrong. John knew nothing about Islam and had no interest in pursuing the religion until after we heard Minister Farrakhan in Germany in early 1992.

The following weekend I returned the tapes to the sister in the hair salon and thanked her. She said, "So what did you think?"

I told her that we had watched the tapes. They had caused us to question everything about our lives and the direction we were going to take. Both tapes were informative and very penetrating. We had no idea the level of deception that had been imposed upon our people and life would never be the same again for us. We were taught wrong and we had to correct that by researching for ourselves what we were being told. I thanked her for the tapes and for loving us enough to inform us.

She said, "Sister, be blessed."

It was only a week or two later, on February 1, that we were in Nuremberg shopping for baby items. I was still working full-time, and I was feeling pretty tired. Salena was due on February 10. I told John that I needed to stop at the commissary to get something to drink; I was extremely thirsty. My labor pains started no sooner than I had selected something. I remember saying to the cashier that I really needed to purchase the drink quickly because I was in labor.

"Oh Lord, just keep the drink," she said.

I walked slowly to the car; my lower back was hurting badly.

As soon as I got back in the car where John was waiting, I told him I was in labor. We drove forty-five minutes, one way, to the hospital in Eschenbach. I told John I forgot to put the bag in the car and we needed to go to the apartment to get it before we went to the hospital. We had to pass the hospital to get to the apartment to get my bag. When we got to the apartment, I was feeling so weak that I couldn't walk up the stairs. John had to carry me. We called the hospital and described my pains to the nurse. The nurse asked a series of questions.

"Is this her first child? How far apart are the contractions?"

After answering the questions, John asked, "How soon does she have to be there?"

The nurse replied, "A minute ago."

We had planned to leave Lil' John with Mae, a co-worker who was also pregnant, but we didn't have time.

On our way to the hospital, Lil' John was getting upset because I was crying. The labor pains were hurting so badly.

Lil' John said, while crying, "Mommy, are you okay?"

I had to show him I was fine, so I took a deep breath, wiped my face, looked at him in the backseat, and said, "I'm fine, honey," smiling the whole time.

"Okay, Mommy," said Lil' John. He stopped crying and began smiling and singing.

John looked at me and said, "Girl, you are something."

When we got to the hospital, I got a wonderful surprise. While passing the rooms, I saw Mae. They allowed Lil' John to stay in the delivery room with us, but I was having a lot of pain and was worried that he might get upset if I started moaning or screaming. I asked John to take him down the hall to stay with Mae. He returned, stating she already had her son and would watch Lil' John. John was by my side and was trying to comfort me. He put his hand on my stomach during a contraction.

I remember saying, "I love you, baby, but if you don't move your hand, you will lose it." He smiled and held my hand. I was in so much pain and the labor was too advanced for them to give me any medication to ease the pain.

When Salena arrived in this world, she weighed seven pounds, eight ounces and was twenty-one inches long. She was exceptionally quiet when she was born. She had tears in her eyes and she was blowing bubbles. She was so beautiful. Her hair was straight and I remembered that Lil' John's hair was curly. I wanted her to be like the woman after whom she was named; I wanted her always to preserve her strength and sense of self. As with Lil' John, John went with the nurse to watch them bathe Salena.

He always said, "I want to make sure they give us the right baby."

Right after Salena was born and cleaned up, the nurse and John rolled her into the room that I would soon be sharing with Mae and her baby boy. John put his finger in Salena's hand; she grabbed it and wouldn't let it go.

When Lil' John met her there in the hospital, he said, "Hello, Sawena (he had trouble pronouncing the "l"), I'm your brother, John." He was so sweet.

I was in the hospital for three days and they allowed Mae and me to have our babies with us the whole time. It was wonderful, having Mae as a roommate, and we were able to help each other.

John and I took Salena home on a beautiful snowy day. The back seat had two car seats. "I'm going to take care of Sawena," Lil' John promised. John had been given time off to be with us. He was glad to be home, and I was glad to have him there. I remember being on the sofa with Salena while John prepared dinner and having Lil' John get his book and his chair to sit next to us.

"Mommy," he said, "can I read to you and Sawena?"

We all became so close during this period. I couldn't think of another place that I wanted to be. John was on full alert for Salena's cries. After I fed her, he would hold her until she fell asleep. A few days later, we took Salena outside and as I did with my son, we presented our daughter, Salena Denise, to the universe.

A week or so later, however, I was still in pain and I needed to go to the hospital to have a small surgical procedure done. John took the children to daycare and me to the hospital. He stayed with me until I went in for surgery. He said he would be there when I came out. However, when I came out of surgery, he wasn't there. While I was in the room alone, I began shaking uncontrollably and couldn't reach the button to contact the nurse's station. I couldn't think of any reason why John wouldn't be there to help me. I really felt alone and scared. I finally stopped shaking and fell asleep. When I woke up, John was sitting in the chair. I asked him where he had gone and why it took him so long to return. I also explained to him that I had been shaking uncontrollably and couldn't stop.

His eyes met mine with a dreadfully cold, empty stare and he said, "I don't like hospitals." It was bitter cold outside, but his attitude was even colder. "You're fine now," he said. "Why are you complaining?" He seemed angry, but he continued talking. "I'm going to get the children," he said, "and bring them back to see you." I told him that the children wouldn't be allowed in that part of the hospital.

"Okay," he said. "I'll just go home then." And he left, just like that. No kiss, no handshake, nothing. It was as if I didn't exist. After Salena's birth, I thought we were getting closer again, but that intimacy was gone with the snap of a finger, just like this.

The next day he appeared at the hospital to pick me up, acting as if he was always the loving father and the attentive husband and making sure that the nurses and as many people as possible saw him in this role.

"There's Mommy!" he said to the children as he came over and kissed me on the cheek.

I couldn't help but wonder who is this man? Why was he so hateful yesterday and so good natured now? What is going on? Later John told me that he was angry at me for being sick. I told him that it was beyond my control and there would be times when I would feel sick and would be sick. He said he wasn't going to get angry at me for that reason again, but he did. This was not the first time John got angry at me for not always functioning at full capacity, and it would not be the last. It reached the point that if I wasn't feeling well, I didn't tell him; I didn't want to face his anger. I kept it to myself and kept going.

Salena was a little over a month old when we received orders stating the post was closing and John was being moved to Fort Ord, California. We were happy to be on our way back to the States. We packed, had our things picked up by transportation, and stayed in a hotel for a few days until our flight was ready. During that time, the news was focused on the Rodney King trials. Police officers were being tried for beating Rodney King. I remembered the videotape evidence and the verdict: "Not guilty!" *How could this be?* I thought. John and I both watched the news of everything exploding in Los Angeles. We were amazed at the verdict and the reactions of everyone.

The day came for us to leave Germany. We got on a plane for an eighteen-hour flight back to the States. I was happy to be going home. It was a large plane; three aisles. Salena was in her baby seat next to me in the middle aisle and John was sitting in the next aisle beside mine, in an aisle seat, with Lil' John next to the window. As usual, they were two little boys playing together. As I watched John, I was thinking, the man who had gone to Germany had focus; he was optimistic, happy, and ready to take on the world in a positive way. The man who came back from a war zone, Desert Storm, was quiet, unsure, reserved, and angry all the time. Very, very angry, and extremely good at hiding it. *Who is going to help him?* I thought. I didn't know how or what to do on my own, or who I should turn to for help.

# CHAPTER SIX:
## HIGH STRESS

I remember my first trip to Safeway in California after we returned from Germany. After two years of shopping in a PX the size of a small convenience store, my jaw dropped at the sight of all that food and all those choices. It took me about an hour to walk down each aisle, in awe of the selections and the quantity of the food. After that, it took me another thirty minutes to purchase food. I was truly amazed.

Both John and I were relieved to find ourselves in the California sunshine and away from the darkness our time in Germany had come to represent. Fort Ord was unique among Army posts because of its beautiful setting on Monterey Bay. When I walked out of the two-bedroom trailer we rented on post, seagulls circled overhead, and I could see the Pacific Ocean. There were times we sat on the porch watching Salena and John play. John was smiling. When I looked at him, a glimpse of the man I married was present.

The two years we spent at Fort Ord were so filled with events, good and bad, that the time passed almost in a blur. Almost as soon as we arrived, I started looking for work and, consequently, for childcare. The daycare providers we interviewed were women who cared for children in their home on post. One of the first women had a very good setup for children and she appeared competent and kind. We were about to finalize some arrangements when John looked at her and said, *"If anything happens to my children, I'm coming after you."* I didn't see the look in his eyes when he said that, but apparently she did. She said that with that level of threat, she would rather not take care of our children.

Another time, we visited a woman, who again looked as though she would be suitable. John was carrying a voice-activated tape recorder, which he left behind in her house. When he went back to get it, and the woman discovered that she had been taped, she was livid.

"I don't think I want to have anything to do with you or your children," she said.

John told me he wanted me to work, but then he did things to sabotage my being able to do so. "I'm not trying to hold you back," he assured me, but his behavior indicated otherwise. One day after he left for work, I went out and interviewed daycare providers without his knowledge. I was lucky because I found a wonderful woman, Joyce, to care for our children. Her facility was off post in Seaside. It was a little distant but I liked her spirit and the way her home was set up to care for children. It would prove to be the best decision made for our children. Soon after, I received a letter that a job was available at the Naval Oceanography Center. I accepted the position and we were on our way to living again...or so I thought.

During our first few months at Fort Ord, John stabilized into a kind of neutral state. He wasn't loving and affectionate, but he wasn't mean and nasty either, which made him a whole lot better than he had been. I could live with neutral.

Our lives got better in sunny California. We both began to make friends again, and we did things together: we took walks; we went to the beach where the children played in the sand and learned to love the water. When we settled, we found out there was a Nation of Islam Study Group in Seaside. The meeting was on Sunday afternoon at 2 p.m. Like all Nation of Islam meetings, it began and ended with a prayer. In between there were scripture readings from the Holy Qur'an and the Bible, as well as teachings aimed at helping us to understand who we are and how we should treat each other. All of the teachings revolved around learning to live our lives in ways that are pleasing to God. While at a meeting, a Minister said that when God breathed life into man, He gave each of us some of His spirit. When we awaken that spirit—that part in each of us that is Divine—we awaken the *self-accusing spirit*. Awakening the *self-accusing spirit* within ourselves is the beginning of true understanding—the beginning of our spiritual evolution and growth. The *self-accusing spirit* is what helps us make choices that are ethical, moral, and righteous.

I know that when people hear that I am a member of the Nation of Islam, they get scared. They think that means that I must hate people of different faiths and races. That's not what we are taught. For me personally, Islam and the teachings have provided me with deeper insight into the scriptures of both the Holy Qur'an and Holy Bible. The teachings have helped me truly understand my role as a black woman, a mother, a sister, and a friend in this society. Islam did not become my new religion; it became my way of life. I have found that through the teachings, I am able to do as my mother instructed me when I was still a child—"Live as near right as you can and as near to God as you can." As a Muslim, I now add the words, "Insha'Allah" (If it be the will of God.)

Going to these meetings, I loved hearing more of the teachings, and they reverberated with me on the deepest level. They reached my spirit and I stopped looking to external forces for help and looked within. In the Nation of Islam, we are taught not to be blind followers; we are taught to study the Holy Qur'an and we are also taught to study the Holy Bible and all prophets. We make no distinction among prophets. We are taught to honor truth and to search for it in all things. I know the teachings also had a profound effect on John. Whenever we attended meetings, he became more conscious of himself and his surroundings and began to treat me better. John was so taken by the teachings, he asked what we had to do to become members. He was told that although I could become a member right away, he would have to wait until he was out of the military. Both of us, however, could continue to study and attend meetings.

As I was studying, I learned that if you have wronged someone, you should go back and ask for forgiveness. I had never stopped thinking about my part in the hurt that I had inflicted on John's first wife, Carol, which in part still bothers me today. *If only I could go back*, I thought. However, to do that would be denying my children. And that I could not do. I decided to write her a letter, apologizing for my part in the breakdown of her marriage to John. I never heard back from her, but I was glad that I had mailed the letter. When I told John that I had written Carol, he looked at me and shook his head.

He asked, "Why did you do that?"

I said, "I felt guilty for my part in the breakup of your marriage, and in studying the teachings, I'm supposed to go back and ask forgiveness from those I've wronged." I asked him had he apologized to her. He told me that he had already apologized to her.

In September, I discovered that I was pregnant again. We are taught in the Nation that a husband should be sensitive with his wife; especially when she is pregnant. John responded to these lessons and he tried to be more considerate, but he was still nowhere near as engaged with me and our relationship as he had been before he went to Desert Storm. I began to notice that his competitive streak was becoming more pronounced within our household. He frequently appeared to be competing with the children for my attention. At other times he competed with me in an attempt to be the favorite parent. In short, he became jealous if I paid more attention to the children than I did to him, and he also became jealous if he thought the children were more attached to me than they were to him.

In December 1992, my mother phoned and asked if she could move to California to live with us. I explained to her that we lived in a small, two-bedroom trailer and if she didn't mind that, I would discuss it with John and call her back. I had two small children; I was almost four months pregnant; and I had a full-time job. By now my mother had a variety of medical problems ranging from arthritis and cataracts to diabetes and heart problems. I wanted to do whatever I could to help my mother, and I also thought it would be good for the children to get to know their only living grandparent. I discussed my mother coming to live with us with John. He was receptive of the idea and after talking about it some more, he agreed. I called my mother right away and both of us were incredibly happy. She arrived in early February 1993. Our little trailer was small so she knew she was going to have to share a room with the children, but she said she didn't mind.

My mother's arrival coincided with another change in John. He decided that he was going to change the way he looked. He went to the barber, and when he returned, he was sporting a crew cut. I asked him why he cut his hair so low. He said he wanted to look different. Along the same time, he announced that he was going to stop wearing any colored clothing. Henceforth, if he wasn't wearing his Army uniform, he would only be wearing black. He also began distancing himself from me again. In our living room, we had a sofa and a loveseat. If I was sitting on one of them, he would sit on the other and avoid being next to me.

Soon after my mother moved in, John came home one afternoon with a new male friend named Steven, whom he had met at the Salvation Army when he was giving away some of his old colored clothing. Steven seemed to be intelligent and well-spoken.

"He has no place to live," John told me, "and he's going to be staying here."

It upset me at first; I was uncomfortable having a total stranger in the house with me and the children. John insisted that he wouldn't do anything to put his family in danger. I repeated that I didn't think it was a good idea.

John said, "That's too bad; he's staying."

He was determined, and I was reluctant to make a big fuss; my mother had recently moved in, and I didn't want John to start giving me grief over this. My thinking went along the following lines: he was willing to compromise and accommodate my mother, so I should do the same for his friend.

Steven wasn't around much during the day, but he slept on the couch, and he was there every night for dinner. Although he was always respectful to me and my mother, the conversation between the two of us was mostly limited to sentences like, "Have you seen John?" or "Please pass the string beans." He would show up at about the same time John did every night, and he would leave in the morning with John. When he was in the house, Steven tried to be helpful and fit in with the family, but his primary relationship was with John. They quickly became best friends, and I could hear them talking, always talking, about the things that interested them.

Right after Steven moved in, our lives became even more complicated. A serious charge was made against John, and, once again, his problems with the military became the primary focus of our lives. An E7 (sergeant 1st class) accused John of threatening to kill him and his family. I learned about it from John, who told me at the same time that he already had an attorney and the attorney was a woman. He gave me a few details and then he stopped talking to me about it. He treated me like a stranger and wouldn't discuss the case with me at all. I heard him talking to Steven as well as other people, but not to me. If I asked him any questions, he got annoyed and told me to stop "interrogating" him so I stopped asking. In his head, once again, I had morphed into the enemy. Then, out of the blue, he told me that the attorney said she needed to see both of us, as a couple.

When we got to the attorney's office, she had a question for me.

"Do you know how serious this is?" she asked.

She told me that if John was tried and found guilty, he would be taken directly to Leavenworth. She told me that they would have shackles in the courtroom and that I should be prepared for all possibilities.

The attorney asked John why he hadn't talked to me, and he told her that he didn't trust me. Then, the attorney looked at me and asked what I had done to make him feel that way.

I told her, "Nothing."

The attorney told John that he had better start talking to me. She also said that she wanted me to be in the courtroom so that the jury understood that John was a responsible family man. She asked if we had any other family in the area. I told her that my mom was living with us.

"If you can," she said, "have her in the courtroom also." The attorney also told John to line up as many friends as possible to go to court to act as character witnesses and to show support.

On the way home in the car, I asked John why he hadn't talked to me.

"I think you are part of the establishment."

"What does that mean?" I asked.

"I think you will try to talk me into pleading guilty."

"Are you guilty?" I questioned him.

"No," he answered.

"Then why would I tell you to do that? Besides, I need you here to help me raise the children. I don't need you in jail."

Then he said something awfully strange that I was never able to figure out. He turned to me and said, "People say I shouldn't trust you."

"Who are these people?"

He never answered that question.

The day of the trial, my mom and I headed off to court. I told her that John was accused of threatening an NCO, but I don't think she fully understood everything that was taking place. Even so, she was worried.

She asked me, "What's going to happen to us if he is arrested?"

"Don't worry, Mom, we'll manage," I told her. I hoped that I sounded more confident than I felt.

I was eight months' pregnant, and I was so huge that I was unsteady on my feet. At that time, Lil' John was three; my daughter Salena was a year old; and I was still working full-time. I think I was so tired from my life that I was simply numb. When I got to the courtroom, as the attorney had warned us, the shackles were there to be put on John should he be found guilty. I became terrified. I wasn't comforted by the fact that John's attorney had told us this was one of her first cases, and she was also incredibly nervous.

From the very beginning, the trial went well for him. The sergeant who had made the accusation wasn't very convincing in his testimony. He said that John had threatened him and his family, but that he didn't immediately tell his superiors about it. The sergeant talked about John's tone of voice and the threatening look in his eyes, but when asked why he didn't report the threat at the time that it allegedly happened, John's accuser had no good answer. Even in my anxious state, I could tell that the sergeant wasn't a compelling witness. In the meantime, John had arrived in court with close to twenty character witnesses, all of whom appeared ready to testify for him. They were all there to say that he was a good soldier, a good friend, a hard worker who did his job well, and was always there to help others. The judge only allowed four people to testify on John's behalf.

When the jury of officers came back with the "not guilty" verdict, the courtroom was filled with shouts of joy. So many people were happy that it was amazing to see. Earlier John had pointed out a high-ranking officer sitting in the back of the court.

"See that guy," John said. "He's waiting here so he can watch them take me away."

When the verdict came in, I turned to look at the officer. I could read the disappointment on his face. He quietly left the courtroom. Later that day, after we got back to our house, John came into the kitchen and apologized for mistrusting me.

He said, "I should have known that you had my back, but with other people whispering in my ear, I didn't know what to think." I had no idea who these other people were. He promised that it wouldn't happen again.

At the time of this trial, I was still convinced that John wouldn't hurt anyone, and I didn't believe the sergeant. Now, with the wisdom of hindsight, I remember the disbelieving looks John's friends and other people gave me when I tried to convince them that John was planning to kill me. After John's arrest, when the media was searching for information about his background, I kept expecting to read more background about his military history, including details about this trial, but I never saw it mentioned.

Almost immediately after the trial, I began having contractions. My baby wasn't due for more than a month so my obstetrician put me on bed rest. It was a good thing my mother was there; she and John had to take care of everything while I tried to concentrate on not having the baby.

When our first two children were born, John was attentive to my labor pains and needs. This time, when I woke John to tell him that I was in labor, he tried to convince me that I wasn't having any pain. "Go back to sleep," he mumbled. When I insisted I was in labor, he said he was tired and wasn't ready to get up. After much pushing and prodding from me, he finally woke up.

My mother yearned to see at least one of her grandchildren enter this world, and I had promised her that she would be able to come to the hospital with us, but the only car that was working was the Nissan 300ZX, a two-seater. I woke my mother, telling her that we were going to the hospital. My plan was that I would crawl over into the well in the back. When John saw my mother in the kitchen, he said that she couldn't come. My mother said that she understood, but I saw the sadness in her eyes as we drove off. When the car turned the corner, I began crying.

"I want my mom to come," I pleaded with John. "We can make room."

"We don't have time," he said.

"I'm already in pain. A few minutes won't make any difference. I promised her. Please, John, turn around and get my mom. Please, John, please."

At the next stop sign, he turned and looked at me. He made a U-turn and went back. My mom was sitting on the steps crying. We pulled up to the house and I opened the door. John rushed into the house to get me a pillow and some blankets, and he picked me up and placed me in the space in the rear. My mother got into the passenger seat. She held my hand the whole way.

"Hold on, Mildred. Just hold on," she said.

When we got to the hospital, I was about ready to give birth, but the nurse said the doctor needed fifteen minutes to get there, so I had to wait. I kept talking to my mother, saying, "I'm so tired, Mama. I'm so tired."

I think my mother thought I was going to die because she responded, "Please stop saying that, Mildred, please."

Our daughter, Taalibah Aanisah Muhammad was born on May 1, 1993 at 1:52 in the morning. She weighed seven pounds, three ounces and was twenty-one inches long. She was beautiful. As he did with all the children, John went with the nurses to watch them wash her. When he returned, our youngest baby girl was in his arms, and he didn't want to let her go. He wouldn't let me hold her; he wouldn't let my mother hold her. I finally convinced him that I had to nurse her. When he left the room, I gave Taalibah to my mom, who held the baby until she began crying. The hospital told me that Taalibah and I could stay for three whole days if I wanted to do so. Did I want to rest and bond with my newest daughter? Yes, I did. Did they have to ask?

John's interest in the military was not reignited while we were at Fort Ord. Although he went to work and did what he had to do, being a soldier was no longer a top priority, and he began to focus on other things. He was thinking about what he was going to do after he left the military; in fact, he was already starting to use our yard to repair cars for other soldiers for a price. In the weeks surrounding Taalibah's birth, John had a new preoccupation that seemed relatively harmless at first, but became scarier and scarier as time went on. It started when, all of a sudden, two ten-speed bikes arrived in the yard—one for John and one for Steven. I asked John where they came from. He said he found them and gave me a loud, "don't ask any more questions" look. He and Steven spray-painted both bikes a flat black. I thought to myself, *what is going on? What are they doing?*

Within a few weeks, the strangest things began happening. John and Steven began night rides. They would head out into the dark night on their black bicycles in their black clothing. John didn't always announce his comings and goings so, more often than not, I didn't even know that they were out riding around until they returned. The most frightening part of these night rides had to do with the black bags they both carried on their backs.

When I asked John what was inside the bags, he got angry and said, "You ask too many questions."

The bags they were carrying looked like rifle bags to me, but I wasn't sure.

*What were they doing at night on black bicycles*, I wondered. I was concerned, but I also thought my imagination was running away with me. I would ask, "Where were you?"

He would reply, "We were out riding."

Something was going on, but I didn't know what, and I didn't know what I could do about it. I knew John well enough by now to know that he was not engaging in random and spontaneous jaunts on a bike. By now I realized that most of the things he did were calculated and scheduled. I considered talking to somebody about what was going on, but who could I talk to? If I told somebody, "My husband and his friend go out riding their bicycles at night," nobody would pay much attention to me. One day, on the evening news, we heard a report of a man who had been shot in the neck during his commute home from work. I looked at John and he looked back.

He said, "Don't ask." Years later, when I was about to testify at John's trial, I told the prosecutors about these rides.

John's night rides ended as strangely as they began. One day Steven left and didn't come back. I didn't see him leave; he didn't say good-bye. The few things he kept in the house were gone. John said he didn't know where he went or what happened to him. I asked John if he was coming back.

He replied, "I don't think so."

Soon after that the bicycles disappeared as well.

Years later, right about the time John and I were separating, I overheard him telling a friend of his about Steven and what they were doing on those night rides. From what I gathered, John and Steven had gone out at night on their bicycles to a place where soldiers from John's unit were guarding some equipment, including something that John referred to as C-4. When I first heard this, I thought John was saying C40, which I thought was some kind of airplane, so it all didn't make sense to me. Later I realized that he was saying C-4, which I learned was a type of explosive used in the military. I heard him saying that he and Steven had a plan to get their hands on some of this explosive. When they reached the place where the C-4 was kept, John threw something to distract the guards. Then, it was supposed to be Steven's job to grab the C-4 and run. John said that when he threw a rock in the direction away from the C-4, the guards responded as he thought they would and followed the noise, and that Steven was actually able to put his hands on the C-4. But at that crucial moment, Steven panicked, jumped on his bike, and rode out of there.

When I heard John telling this story, I began to understand why I never again saw Steven. He must have realized that John was taking him places he didn't want to go, and he was smart enough to get out.

Once Steven was out of the picture, John began to put more of his focus back on the children, but our relationship continued on its downward path. We weren't really communicating. If I asked questions, for example, it was a big problem. When I first met John, it wasn't an issue if I asked him anything. I should also add that I was becoming more of a questioner in general. The Nation of Islam classes stressed understanding and truth in all situations. The women's classes were also teaching me to think before I spoke and to consider my words and what I was saying. All this was making me ask more pointed questions, which John hated. He also hated it when I made direct statements that could be misconstrued. A simple question like, "How was your day?" could trigger the following sort of conversation:

He might reply, "Why are you asking?"

I might answer, "Well, you look a little upset. Is anything wrong?"

He would probably then say, "What makes you think I'm upset?"

I would probably then answer, "Well, the look on your face."

"That's your interpretation," he would tell me before walking away.

Remember that John prided himself on being able to hide what he was feeling. His need to conceal his emotions had intensified over the years, particularly with me. I could sometimes actually see him changing the expression on his face so that I wouldn't be able to tell what he was thinking or feeling. It was getting harder and harder to talk to him. He had gotten to the point of holding an expression on his face, going to the mirror to examine it and change it. He didn't want anyone to identify the expressions on his face

We were also having some problems in how we handled the children. Although John continued to play with them, he was also a demanding father. This was particularly true in his relationship with our son. Basically he wanted Lil' John to be perfect in every way. John seemed much too quick to address anything that he perceived as a weakness or imperfection in our son. As Lil' John progressed past the toddler stage, his father began to focus on ways to *"make him stronger."* John could sometimes be hard on his son; he seemed to think this would make Lil' John better prepared for life. I thought Lil' John was pretty perfect. He still had some health issues such as asthma that needed attention, but John didn't want to accept it, and he would sometimes even try to prevent me from giving Lil' John his medication.

John seemed to get some kind of satisfaction from criticizing me in those areas in which I put the most effort. He knew how important it was for me to be a good mother. He knew how hard I worked at keeping the home clean and preparing food for my family. He knew, through practice, where I was sensitive, and he knew which words pushed my buttons. He was very strategic in upsetting me and was always pointing out how I could have done something better. John could have an exceedingly hard, contemptuous, and dismissive tone, and he made little snide comments that would cause me to react. Much of the problem was not in what he said, but in how little he said and how he said it. I was constantly reacting to his tone of voice, and I hated that.

Having my mother living with us didn't make our relationship any easier. When my mother lived across the country, I was able to hide things from her. Now, she could see for herself that we were not the picture-perfect couple. And at this point, we had been married only five years. My mother also thought that John was too harsh and controlling with the children. She would never talk to him about something like this; instead, she talked to me. It goes without saying that she also didn't like the way John spoke to me. However, my mother was first and foremost a religious woman, and she put the family first. She would never say anything like, "Why do you put up with it?"

While I was cooking dinner one night, John began complaining about something, and I started to cry. My mother must have heard me; she came into the kitchen. "Mildred, you stop that crying right now," she said. "You suck up those tears and you pray…You don't let him know that he's upsetting you, and you do whatever you have to do to keep this family together."

Both she and John were polite to each other. When they were upset about each other, they complained to me. Consequently, I felt caught in the middle, with John tugging on one arm and my mother on the other.

I returned to work after Taalibah's birth, but I was almost immediately informed that the post was downsizing and I was going to be let go. I was pretty upset about this, but John said, "You always wanted to stay home with the children. When your job is cut, you don't have to go back to work. I can take care of you and the children."

The idea of being totally dependent on him financially made me nervous, but he was extremely convincing.

"I promise you," he said, "I will not let you down. You will not regret this."

I agreed, but even as I smiled and said, "Yes," I didn't feel right. I felt as though I was giving up control of my life.

We soon learned that all of Fort Ord was being downsized in anticipation of the post's eventual closing. John received orders to go to Fort Lewis, the base where we started, and in a sense, we were going home.

By now, we were a two-car family, and in September 1993, we began the drive up the California coast. John and Lil' John were in one car; my mother, Salena, Taalibah, and I were in the other. We purchased walkie-talkies so we could communicate with each other. It was our last family trip, and John seemed almost light-hearted. For the first time in years, his good mood lasted more than a few hours. Our new home was on post, in family housing. It had a large yard and a playground right beyond our backyard. The children really liked it. John acted as though he was actually happy. He was laughing, playing, talking, and generally behaving the way he used to before Desert Storm. It was good to feel that spirit around again, and I didn't want it to end.

John was allowed a generous amount of time to get us situated and set up. When it was finally time for him to return to work, he gave me a hug and a kiss and was off. I was feeling so happy. It had been a long time coming, but I honestly thought the John I knew and loved was back, and everything was going to return to normal again. Or at least that's what I hoped. At the end of his first day at work, he came through the door, not smiling as he had been when he left. Instead he appeared angry and agitated. I asked him what happened.

"This is not going to be a good place for me," he said.

"Why not?" I asked.

"Everything was fine until this lieutenant in my unit told me that he was going to make my life a living hell."

John told me that the lieutenant was jealous since John went to Desert Storm and he didn't.

"That's crazy," I said. "How can he take that out on you?"

"I know," he told me. "But it doesn't matter. We have to plan to make a living outside of the military. I'm not going to become a slave to these people. I'm ready to get out."

"What are we going to do?" I asked. He only had a few months left to serve, but we still had not made a concrete plan as to what to do next.

"Let me think about it," he replied, "and I'll let you know."

# CHAPTER SEVEN:
## OPEN FOR BUSINESS

As John prepared to leave the military, we needed to find a way to make a living. He had a wonderful idea—why not start a mobile auto repair company? There was a real need for this kind of service. He was a good mechanic. We had a plan: he would fix the cars, and I would do the paperwork and be responsible for publicity and getting new business. I got a business license. Since John had a short time left in the Army, they moved him to a new position: dog catcher. This was actually good; it gave us the time to plan our business.

On January 1, 1994, we opened our business and called it Express Car/ Truck Mechanic. John was thirty-four, and I was thirty-five. We began advertising the business and received our first customer for an oil change. It felt so good, getting that first check. We were proud of ourselves and our ability to make this happen. As time went on, more customers called and John was able to service them. I created our personalized work orders and we decided he should wear black jeans and a black sweatshirt until we ordered uniforms. We used our 1987 300ZX as our work vehicle.

By April 1994, John was officially honorably discharged. We had enough clients, civilian as well as military customers, to sustain our business. This business could really pay off, or at least that's what I thought. The idea was simple enough: When customers had car trouble, all they had to do was call us. John would then head out and fix their vehicles on their own site. Customers liked that they wouldn't have to take the time to drive the vehicle to a mechanic and then wait around to get it fixed. If customers called while he was out doing a job, I would page him; he would then call me, and I would give him the new work order.

I was extremely optimistic about our business and our future. I was sure that this was our time to make things work. With John out of the Army, I also expected his mood to improve. He wasn't going to have any more superior officers to complain about; I was positive he would be a happier person. What I didn't anticipate was that almost as soon as he stopped complaining about the military, he would have something new to find fault with. As far as our business was concerned, he quickly began to have problems with it, and as usual, problems with me.

Our business meant a great deal to me. Neither John nor I came from a place where we had very much growing up. I saw this as our chance to give our children opportunities that we never had. As our company started to succeed, I began to realize that John and I were not on the same page. I wanted the business to grow and I wanted to grow with it. He wanted to limit what we were doing. He wanted to control the business, and he wanted to control me, but none of this was immediately apparent to me.

Soon after we opened, I began attending networking meetings for small business owners in the Tacoma area. After a few of these meetings, I was able to tell more people in the community about the services we could provide, and we soon started getting offers from companies, as well as individuals, to repair vehicles. I was proudest of the contract we had with the Department of Labor. There was a "Welfare to Work" program in Tacoma that had available funds set aside for repairing clients' vehicles so they could go to work, and we were awarded the contracts. It was easy to see that getting new business would be no problem. I was so excited. But John quickly became angry. Instead of being proud of me, he was resentful. Why should I be the one who went to meetings? Why did he have to be the one to fix vehicles? And when he went off to fix those vehicles, why did I have to know where he was going? Why did he have to respond to his pager?

When we started out, John was the only one repairing vehicles, but within six months or so, we needed to hire another mechanic. Since I was always trying to find ways to grow the business, I had this idea that we should always try to make our little company look larger than it really was. John and any other mechanic who worked for us would wear a uniform with our company name on it. They also wore gloves so their hands were always clean. John thought of doing this, and it really impressed people.

Despite the way he complained about the business to me, the majority of our customers loved John. He always showed different faces to different people, and when he was acting like his most generous outgoing self, he created a lot of goodwill. He also had a way of falling into situations. One day he called me to tell me that he had come upon an older couple by the side of the road. Their car had broken down. "We need to get these people home," John said. He asked me to meet him. He got their car up and running, but he wasn't sure if it could make it the whole way to their door. He drove the couple in their car. I followed in our truck. We drove and drove and drove for what seemed like more than an hour over winding roads and who knows where until we got them home. It turned out that the gentleman was a major executive at Ocean Spray. We got some new business, as well as a year's supply of cranberry products, which was fine with me; I love cranberry sauce.

One day, not that long after our business opened, I was walking through downtown Tacoma and I noticed a sign in a window offering tax and bookkeeping services. When I went in, I saw a pleasant-looking woman, about my age, sitting at a desk. I told her that I was looking for a bookkeeper since I was operating a business for the first time. I wasn't clear about setting up books, but I wanted to do it right. Her name was Isa Nichols. I asked her did she know that her name meant "Jesus" in the Qur'an.

"No," she said. "But that's a good thing."

We laughed. She had a good spirit. She was to become important in my life. I tend to be a private person, and it had been a while since I'd had a close friend with whom I could share things. Isa was exceptionally kind, as well as generous with her business advice. Our relationship started out on a professional basis. She became our bookkeeper and consultant about operating a business. She and I also had things in common which gave us more to talk about than how to do taxes. We both had children; she had an elderly father living with her; I had an elderly mother living with me. We soon found ourselves talking about our children and activities for seniors. Isa was also a spiritual woman, striving to live in accordance with her strong beliefs. I was drawn to this quality in her.

When she joined our operation, I took John over to her office so that he would know who she was. Isa and I didn't gossip, but she did tell me that she had noticed John around the neighborhood. She was surprised when she found out that he was my husband; she didn't think he was married. Lots of people didn't think John was married, and even more didn't think that he was married to me. We had decided it would look more professional if we didn't automatically tell customers or business contacts that we were a couple. Inadvertently, this behavior probably helped John's M.O. when he was trying to impress a new female client.

Isa had lots of sound advice, which I wanted John to hear from her, not me. An ongoing disagreement that he and I had revolved around the way he handled money. Theoretically, when customers paid John, he was supposed to bring the money back to our office so I could deposit it in the business account. John preferred to handle payments, particularly cash, as though it was for his personal use. He put it right into his pocket, and he didn't want anyone else to know what he did with it. Isa would patiently explain to John, time and time again, that it made good business sense to put everything through the bank account. For one thing, it allowed for better record-keeping. For another, showing regular deposits and a healthy balance in the bank would give us credibility and, for example, make it easier for us to approach the bank for a loan, should we ever need one. Isa would tell him that we needed to adopt a more professional approach. John would tell Isa that he wanted a "ma and pa" business, not some "big" thing. Isa would tell John, "When you have a business, and it's successful, it's probably going to grow. You have to be prepared to grow with it." John would nod and agree with Isa when she was there, but then he would turn around and do whatever he wanted the minute she left.

Isa asked him, "Well, how much cash do you need in your pocket every day for expenses, and parts, and walking-around money?"

"A hundred dollars a day," he replied.

"Good," Isa said, "So, let Mildred deposit everything into the account, and then she will give you a hundred dollars a day from that, and you can keep track of your expenses."

"Okay," John would agree in front of her, but when it was the two of us alone, he continued to do what he always did: He took the money he got from customers and spent it on himself or on parts we didn't need. Consequently, our cash flow was limited.

"I thought you agreed to follow a more businesslike approach," I would say to him.

"I said that in front of her," he told me, "but I'm not going to only carry around a hundred dollars. I'm going to have what I want. I'm going to do things the way I want. This is my business, and if I run it into the ground, then I'll run it into the ground." John continued to handle the money he got from customers the way he wanted. As soon as it was possible to do so, I was able to get a portable credit card machine, which the other mechanics used as well. Since so many people preferred using credit cards, John was often forced to do so as well.

He always had to feel that he was the one in control of everything. As loose as he was with his own accounting practices, he expected me to account to him for every penny. If I bought parts or spent money on the business, I had to get his approval and show him every little receipt. The same thing was true, even if I went to the grocery store. He would give me a set amount and then would complain if I went a penny over. I even took a calculator to the store with me so that he wouldn't reprimand me later.

When he and I were alone, his tone of voice when he spoke to me could get pretty unpleasant, but in front of others, he seemed to restrain himself. There were, of course, exceptions. One day Isa was in the office, and she heard the way John talked to me. I saw the look in her eyes when she noticed it. Later, she pulled me aside. "Does he always talk to you that way?" she asked.

"What way?" I replied.

"Rude and disrespectful," she answered.

I don't recall my response, but I'm sure I attempted to cover up the problems in our relationship.

It would be misleading if I said that John was always in a bad mood. Every now and then I would see a glimpse of the lighthearted man that I fell in love with. He was frequently in a good mood with his friends, and he had several really good friends. His best friend was probably Robert

Holmes. He and Robert, who was also a skilled mechanic with a repair business, were old friends from the military. After the D.C. killings, Holmes was the person who called the authorities to say that he believed that John was the sniper. Later, Holmes told me that when he contacted the FBI, his primary thought was that if he didn't call the authorities about John, he would see my name scrolling at the bottom of the news, stating that I was killed by the sniper. I will always feel grateful to Holmes for figuring out that the D.C. sniper could be his good friend, John, and for following through on his fears and doing what he had to do.

Another person with whom John and I both became friendly was Stanley, a local guy with car troubles, who entered our lives as a customer and became a good friend—almost like a brother—to both of us. After two or three car repairs, John invited Stanley over to the house for dinner. At one of these dinners, Stanley, who had a background in marketing, offered to help us market our new business. We were originally operating the business out of our house, but within the first year, we learned about a Tacoma incubator, designed to help fledgling business operations like ours. We were able to rent office space and a garage there for a reasonable rent, and we were able to get uniforms for the mechanics. Stanley was particularly fond of the children and took the time to get to know each of them individually. In my children's world, he will always be their Uncle Stan.

The majority of our customers adored John. People were always calling and telling me how great he was. He was young, only thirty-five, but customers felt safe with him, trusted him, and spoke of him as if he were older. If they heard he was coming to fix their cars, they thought nothing about leaving him keys and an open check for the repairs. Strangers didn't see the side of his personality that I saw. Stanley, who spent more time with us, however, became aware of the degree to which John was hurtful to me. When John started yelling at me about something he thought I was doing wrong, I didn't fight back. Instead I would sit at the table with my head down. Stanley came to my defense. "Stop yelling at her," he said. Stanley is the only person I ever remember standing up to John.

With John, I was always trying to get to a place where things would calm down and we could start acting like a real family, but it never happened.

If everything was starting to normalize, then he would somehow create a new problem. He often had accidents that were really not accidents, or he would get tickets for speeding or parking in the wrong spots. John loved being the center of attention, and if nothing was going on, he seemed to create drama. He was sometimes like a child who gets into trouble so he will be noticed.

It was probably during those first years in our business that I began to see how easy it was for him to begin lying again. If I caught him in a lie, then he would tell a bigger lie. He thought he could explain his way out of anything, and he often did. It was also beginning to be apparent that a fair number of his lies revolved around women. Many of our customers were single mothers. John loved playing the role of knight-in-shining-armor for women who didn't have fathers for their children. At some point, he was even giving money to other women, but it took me quite a while to figure this out.

One day, John brought a car he was fixing back to the house because he needed to get something. When I saw him, I noticed something missing.

"Where is your wedding ring?" I asked.

"Sometimes I don't wear it," he replied. "If I'm in an engine, I take it off and put it in the ashtray till I'm finished working. Depending on the job, the ring gets in the way and I don't want to mess it up."

"So you're not trying to make it appear as though you're not married?"

"Of course not," he assured me.

But things were happening that I couldn't help noticing. He would come home for a couple of hours and then leave after dinner, saying he had an appointment. Since I kept track of appointments, I would question him.

He would say, "Oh yeah, this customer came up to me, and I forgot to tell you."

"Wait," I would reply. "How are you going to fix a car in the dark?"

"We'll turn on the porch light," he'd say. "Gotta go. See you later."

There were too many times when I couldn't reach John on his pager. At first my primary concern was that we might lose business; I wouldn't be able to dispatch him to the next job. He would tell me that he couldn't call me back because he was under a car or that he didn't have quarters for a pay phone. Most people were still not carrying cell phones. Good little problem solver that I am, I went to the bank and got rolls of quarters. That didn't work either; he would claim that he couldn't find a pay phone that worked. I explained to Stanley the problems we were having with communication. He suggested we get Nextel phones. Since he was a representative at that time, he got them for us. I was pleased; I thought that I would be able to reach John when I needed him, but it didn't always work out that way. One day, I called John to let him know I was going to the store to pick up a part. A woman answered his phone. We did one of those, "Who is this?" "Well, who is this?" routines. Finally I hung up and called back. This time, John answered. He denied that a woman had been on his phone, and said the mix-up must have been crossed wires, which was, of course, impossible. I asked Stanley about that. He said the circuits are only programmed to that particular phone and there isn't anything called crossed wires.

Probably the biggest indicator that John was seeing at least one woman revolved around his strange behavior once a week on Tuesday. This was the day that he regularly disappeared. I never knew where he was and I couldn't locate him. When I questioned him, he said he was going to the gym. That's the way it was, and there was nothing I could do about it. He had a cover-up story for every situation. When he came home with red marks on his neck and I asked how he got them, he said they came from a "hot tail pipe." When he had scratches on his back, he told me he was "on the ground under a car."

There was even one time when a woman called the office complaining that John refused to fix her car unless she provided sexual favors. Stanley got involved in smoothing over this mess. John was absolutely adamant that the woman didn't know what she was talking about and was just jealous and trying to make trouble.

Looking back, I see that I could have done more about finding out where he was during his frequent unexplained absences, but by this time I was overwhelmed. I was the person who was responsible for bringing in new customers and running the business. I had three small children at home. I had to care for them, even while I was working. I was the one doing the cooking, cleaning, and shopping. While my mother really loved the children and helped, she was no longer young and was limited in what she could realistically do. There were also times when she placed a fair number of her own demands on me. She had frequent medical appointments and needed me to help her organize them. John and my mother also never really got along. He would say that he was happy that the children had their grandmother, and she would tell me that I had to do everything I could to hold my family together, but there was a lot of tension between them. I continued to be stuck in the middle negotiating, interpreting, and trying to keep the peace.

However, I was still making excuses for John. My priority was keeping my family together. It's probably fair to say that my priority was also having a business to pass on to our children. I wanted to keep our plans intact by having this business as a legacy for them. And I thought John felt the same way. However, he was still taking the time to construct elaborate lies. He was extremely persuasive, and his stories were sometimes almost plausible. When I would get most upset, I would always consider the promises he and I made to each other about not letting our children grow up like we did, without both parents. More than anything else I wanted an intact family. I had a dream about what a family should be and that's what I wanted. That's what I was holding on to.

I don't think I was ever much happier than when I was in the kitchen of our house in Tacoma watching John, Salena, and Taalibah playing out in the backyard. In the winter, we would all go down the hill in back on sleds and tires and just about anything that would slide. In the summer, we had a pool for the children. When I was in that backyard with my children, I felt as though I was in heaven. It was the kind of setting I wanted them to have, and I didn't want them to have to give it up.

When we were settling down in Tacoma, we both got involved at the local Mosque. I liked that he was becoming friendly with the men. These were good people with good values. With the men and women at the Mosque, John played a role and always acted like he was Mr. Responsible Family Man. I wanted so much for him to be that person that I did everything I could to help him appear that way. For example, I never complained about him to anyone, not even my mother. I always covered for him. Like women in abusive situations the world over, I didn't want people to know too much. I also didn't want people forming negative opinions of him.

At the Mosque, I was a member of the women's group. That's where I met my good friend Olivia. Like Isa, Olivia had a deep spirituality. I was incredibly pleased to have made two good friends in Tacoma. I admired and respected how they related to God and how they were able to relate to my spirit. Maybe because we were in classes together, Olivia particularly always seemed to sense what was going on with me, even though I didn't tell her. She says that when she first met me, I even walked with my head down, and that I was like a Stepford wife. She couldn't understand what was going on; to the outside world, it looked like I had everything a woman could want: a hard-working husband, beautiful children, a professional life, as well as lots of material pluses like a nice house and a car. But Olivia saw my deep unhappiness, and she tried to help me. When we talked, our conversations were filled with scriptural references. She frequently suggested passages that I could read to help me look at my circumstances spiritually and would often suggest reading for me to get a better understanding.

When Olivia first met John, she liked him. She would teasingly call him Similac, the name of a popular infant formula. That's because she thought he looked so young, and he was younger than me. Later, when Olivia learned more about John's military background, I remember her saying, only half-jokingly, "Mildred, you do know that you are sleeping with a trained killer, right?"

"Yeah," I responded, "but he's never going to do anything to me."

"Okay," she replied, "but I'm just bringing it to your attention."

Olivia was my authority in the women's class I attended at the Mosque. Even so, she never gave me any direct advice about my marriage or John; instead she encouraged me to think of myself as a woman of God. She helped me become more aware of what that meant. She helped me raise certain questions about myself and my life. Here's an important question that I began to ask myself: As a child of God, shouldn't I be living a life filled with love and respect? As children of God, shouldn't we all be living lives filled with love and respect?

By the end of summer 1995, the biggest buzz in our community was about the Million Man March that Minister Louis Farrakhan was organizing to take place in Washington, D.C. on October 16. Everybody was talking about it. This was going to be about black men recommitting themselves to taking responsibility for their families and taking care of the women and children; it was about stopping crime and making commitments to community as well as personal growth. John quickly decided that he wanted to attend. I was thrilled. He was going to hear a strong message encouraging him to be a respectful and loving husband. There was a lot of fuss and preparation that went on getting John out the door and on his way to Washington. One of my sisters lived in the Washington, D.C. area so I called her and asked if John could stay with her and her husband. She said yes, and when John was at the Million Man March, he was there with them.

After John was arrested, there were many reports that he attended the Million Man March as a member of Minister Farrakhan's security detail. This is totally untrue and is probably one of John's stories that he told people. At that time, John was not a member of the Nation of Islam; he was one of many, many black men who wanted to be part of that historical moment. After the march, I talked to one brother who said that when he got on the plane to Washington, he looked around. For the first time in his life, he was on a plane filled with black men. He said, with a smile, that it was a sight to see. He said it was an indescribable experience and was struck by the feeling of love between these men. It inspired him to do better for his wife and his children. I think most of the men came back saying the same kinds of things.

At the march, Minister Farrakhan asked the men to take a pledge. This is an excerpt from that pledge:

*I pledge that from this day forward I will never raise my hand with a knife or a gun to beat, cut, or shoot any member of my family or any human being except in self-defense. I pledge from this day forward I will never abuse my wife by striking her, disrespecting her, for she is the mother of my children and the producer of my future. I pledge that from this day forward I will never engage in the abuse of children, little boys or little girls for sexual gratification. For I will let them grow in peace to be strong men and women for the future of our people.*

I was thrilled when I heard that John had taken the pledge. Wow, I thought. This is so important! I was even more pleased when he came home and started acting differently. I'm not talking about a small change. I'm talking about a *drastic* change. It wasn't gradual. It was noticeable right away. He had made up his mind to be different. Once he made up his mind, he could do anything. That was how he did things. Suddenly he was less demanding; he stopped yelling at me and was speaking to me in a nicer tone of voice without harsh or critical words. He was coming home for dinner and spending more time with the children. Bills were getting paid on time, and he seemed completely aware of his responsibilities. He had made a decision that he was trying to honor. Whatever had happened during the Million Man March appeared good for his spirit, and he was on a high. I was cautiously hopeful, but some things didn't change. John was still holding on to the money he made and not turning it over to the business.

When he returned from the Million Man March, we were both regularly attending Nation of Islam meetings, but I was the one who was most enthusiastic about joining. John was involved with activities at the Mosque and friendly with the other men, who, for the most part, really liked him. But, as far as joining was concerned, he was holding back. I had no such reservations and became a member in January 1996. A year later, I had become secretary of the study group, and the teachings were speaking to me on a profound personal level. Unfortunately by the time I became a member, John's behavior had started to revert back to where it was before the Million Man March.

Nowhere was this more apparent than in the business. The more I did to try to grow it, the harder he worked to sabotage my efforts. When I brought any of this to his attention, he would say things like, "It's all mind over matter, Mildred. I don't mind because you don't matter."

# CHAPTER EIGHT:
## I CAN'T DO ANYTHING RIGHT

One day, John and I were having a discussion about the pros and cons of relocating the business. "Let's make a list," I suggested. I took a sheet of paper, a pencil, and a ruler, and I made a line down the center of the paper. On one side I put "Pros"; on the other I wrote "Cons."

"The line is crooked," John said.

"It's good," I replied. "There's nothing wrong with it."

"No," John insisted. "You have to do it over."

He refused to speak to me until I drew the line to his satisfaction.

This was a fairly typical exchange. He loved playing mind games with me, and I didn't know how to play back. I always had to dot all my i's and cross all my t's to his satisfaction. So far, my eight years of marriage to him had made me so accustomed to his kind of emotional abuse that I didn't really question his behavior. Instead, I tried to tailor how I spoke to him, knowing that if I didn't ask the right questions or use the right words, the conversation could take a strange direction. Then, he would catch me in some kind of circular logic that made no sense. Once, I asked him why he was so angry, and he said something like, "Why would you say I'm angry? Is it because of the look on my face that you have associated with being angry? It would be best for you to ask me if I'm angry instead of assuming, because you know what to assume means, right? It means you make an 'ass' out of 'u' and 'me.'"

We had these kinds of exchanges regularly.

He was always looking for something to complain about, no matter what I did or how I did it. He complained about how I handled customers; he complained about how I answered the phone; he complained that I was a bad mother; he complained that I was a bad wife; he complained that I was a bad housekeeper; he complained that I was a bad Muslim. He never stopped telling me what I was doing wrong, and he didn't particularly worry about whether or not even he believed what he was saying. When John first went into the military, he would practice expressions in front of a mirror so that nobody would know what he was thinking. I never knew whether he actually believed half of what he said.

The thing about him is that he didn't think that he needed to follow normal rules of behavior. If he was looking for ways to rationalize or explain away something he was doing, he would find somebody else to blame. By the time our business was a couple of years old, there was a lot that John needed to rationalize, and I was his favorite person to blame. Express Car/ Truck Mechanic, which had started with so much promise, was in trouble. John had cut way back in terms of the amount of work he wanted to do, so customers were complaining and bill collectors were calling. I had no idea what he had done with the money he had put in his pocket. It had gone in a variety of directions. For example, after our son started karate lessons, John made an investment in a karate school. He partnered with Felix Stozier and the school was moving along pretty well. There were parents bringing their children to be trained and Lil' John was attending also. There were times Salena went with them; she liked doing everything her big brother did. However, eventually John lost interest and the school was closed.

I think he was helping at least one other woman with some of her bills. (And, yes, I remembered how he had offered to help me when we first met.) He had a way of spending whatever he got his hands on, and he made sure he was the one who held the money. I had been waiting for a $3,000 tax refund so that we could pay some bills. I was in Chicago at the time. I called and asked him had the check come in; I needed funds while I was there. He said the check didn't come. John took the check when it arrived, signed it, and cashed it. When I returned from Chicago, I called the IRS; they said it had been sent. I requested proof from them. To my shock, I received proof that the check had arrived and had been cashed. I showed John the proof I had received. However, he still continued to deny knowing how this could have happened, even while he was also telling me that he didn't have to explain anything to me. Once again, I heard the "I don't mind because you don't matter" explanation.

During this period, it was becoming more and more apparent that John was involved with another woman and that she was influencing how he treated me. He was rarely home, but the minute he walked through the door, he would take charge. If I was in the kitchen, making lasagna, he would come in and start adding ingredients that I never used. I could see that he was getting cooking tips from somebody else and trying to incorporate them into what I was doing. The house could be immaculate, but he would start commenting on how I could do things differently or better. He didn't want the children to spend too much time in front of the television so, if they were watching a program when he came in, he would turn it off, saying that I was letting them watch too much TV, implying that my parenting skills were somehow lacking. When he was in the house, the stress level hit new highs.

On those rare occasions when we went to a restaurant or a movie, he continued his complaints. The waitress wasn't efficient, the food was too expensive, people were talking too loud, and the seats were uncomfortable. It didn't stop. At home, he suddenly started listening to different music. He was playing all these love songs, and they sure weren't for me. I could feel it. He would sit there listening to Toni Braxton with a dreamy look on his face.

As far as the children were concerned, he expected them to run to the door to greet him with a hug when he came home. They did that with me, and he was annoyed if they didn't do it with him. He liked playing with all the children, but it wasn't always stress-free. A favorite household game, for example, was Monopoly. Everyone enjoyed it. John, however, didn't agree with all the rules and would insist on changing those he didn't like. It was confusing and got to the point where our son didn't want to play with him anymore. The same thing was true with something as simple as a game of tag, which the children liked playing. If John was home, they would sometimes go out of their way to play it in another area so he wouldn't see them and interfere with what they were doing.

John always went out of his way to relate to all children, but, in truth, he paid more attention to other people's children than he did to his own. He had strong ideas about discipline and how he expected *his* children to behave. However, he did not want to be known as the strict parent so, he would tell me to carry out his wishes about discipline, simply because he said so. Frequently, I wasn't prepared to do this, which would get him furious. As far as discipline was concerned, he couldn't stand it if the children weren't fulfilling something that he wanted, and he was always harder on his son than he was on his daughters. He simply hated that Lil' John had asthma and wanted him always to act big and strong without any vulnerability. When it came to dealing with our son's asthma, my friend Olivia said that she always thought of me as being like a single mom, who had to do it alone. Lil' John's asthma could sometimes become dreadfully severe; emergency trips to the hospital were not unusual. Once, when he was running around in his pj's, I noticed he was wheezing. I quickly got the peak flow meter that measures oxygen and told him to blow into it. It didn't even register. When I called the doctor, he told me to meet him at the hospital, where even after a treatment, Lil' John still couldn't get the meter to budge. He ended up having to stay for four days.

John seemed to almost blame me for our son's asthma and acted as though it was something I was making up. He didn't acknowledge the value of preventive medication and would say things that encouraged our son, who wanted to please his father, not to take his asthma medication. I ended up having to hide it in applesauce. John's underlying message seemed to imply that real men don't have asthma. At one point, he suddenly started complaining that I didn't know how to take care of Lil' John's asthma. He had all kinds of pronouncements about asthma and what it meant and what should be done for it. Once again, he tried to get me to stop giving Lil' John his medication. I asked him, "Are you dating a nurse?" At John's trial for the D.C. killings, a nurse from Washington State testified that she had been in a relationship with John during this time. She described him as being kind and attentive.

John and I also began to argue about what it meant to be a good Muslim. I think one of the reasons why he was first attracted to the Nation of Islam was that he thought it was going to help him control me. Instead it had the opposite effect. The teachings, counseling sessions, and the women's group, of which I was a part, were making me more and more aware of what it means to be a spiritual woman—a child of God. Instead of looking to John as my ultimate authority figure, I turned to God, but John would tell me that in Islam, a wife should follow her husband in everything he does. "You are supposed to submit to me," he said. "You are supposed to follow me."

I responded, "Wrong. I am supposed to follow you when you are following the teachings and have a comprehensive knowledge of what God wants you to do, and I'm not seeing that." I also began to feel that he was more interested in Islam as a way to control others than as a way of spiritual growth.

As my marriage and the business began to unravel, more and more I was finding solace in my inner spiritual life. I was busy reading the Holy Qur'an, reading the Bible, and studying the teachings. John was paying lip service to what he was learning, but he wasn't following the teachings. It goes without saying that he continued to stay out night after night.

I looked out the window at about one or two in the morning, and I saw a car pull up in front of the house. He was in the driver's seat. He got out and a woman came out of the passenger side to change seats. I saw them hugging each other. When he came inside, he began telling me what detained him for so long. He had seen an army buddy he had not seen in a long time. They began talking and the time got away from him. However, when I told him what I had seen, he looked at me and walked away.

I told him, "There is no Godly reason for a man to be out, leaving his family insecure after nine o'clock p.m., unless he is working. That's what Minister Farrakhan says. So what is your reason? You leave us unsecure at night. I am doing your job, locking the house and making sure we are safe. That should be your job."

The more I learned about the teachings of the Nation of Islam, the more I tried to follow them, and the more I became aware that John wasn't following any spiritual path. When he was coming home in the middle of the night, it was clear that he wasn't being divinely guided. It was clear that the spirit he was bringing into the house wasn't good and that he wasn't teaching my son and daughters an example of the way they should behave. So I started to withdraw and detach from him emotionally.

In the summer of '97, John's middle son, Lindbergh, came for a visit, which was a great event for my children, who really loved and looked up to him. Lindbergh had developed into a tall, good-looking thirteen-year-old boy. He was really smart and nice, but he did have some problems with his father. I think Lindbergh couldn't understand why John had been absent from his life for so long, and he was angry about it. John was hard on all his sons, and sometimes he would say things that were really hurtful. Lindbergh would wait until John left the house and then he would either go off to be by himself or go outside and punch the house. Once, I went outside, and I could see that he was hurting his hands from all the punching he'd been doing. Other times he would look as though he had been crying.

Since Lindbergh was John and Carol's son, I felt as though I couldn't do that much to protect him or get involved in their decision-making regarding him. But I wanted to help him find a way to channel all that energy, so I signed him up for a karate class in the martial arts school that Lil' John attended. When Lindbergh was visiting, John made a point of being home more often in the evening, but he still wasn't around that much. I didn't want Lindbergh to feel that he had made the trip all the way from Louisiana and was being neglected so I tried to plan little trips and take the children places. We went to Mount Rainier and we did other special things. Lindbergh and I became extremely close. It was fun having him there with the children. Sometimes Lindbergh would go with John to help him fix cars.

When we got close to the time for him to go back home, John suddenly made an announcement: Lindbergh wasn't going home. Then, John started to tell all these stories about how Lindbergh had been abused and how he wasn't going to send him back to more of that treatment.

I clearly remember saying to John, "I thought you said you would never try to take Lindbergh from his mother."

"Well, he says he's been abused and neglected," he responded. "What am I supposed to do about that?"

I said, "You're supposed to talk to Carol and see what's going on." I did not add that Lindbergh certainly didn't look abused or neglected to me.

John didn't call Carol, but he did get an attorney, who told him that he had a case for custody and drew up some papers asserting that Lindbergh was in a dangerous position if he went back home and charging Carol with different kinds of abuse. Carol would call and John would not talk to her. That made me angry. I asked Lindbergh about the things his dad was saying but he wouldn't say anything. At this point, John wasn't sharing everything with me, and I didn't have all the information.

He did ask me to go to court with them so we would present a family unit, which I did do. The judge read the papers and said that he had no jurisdiction in Tacoma, Washington and Lindbergh had to go back ASAP. John got really angry at the attorney. "I thought you said we would win!" he yelled. "You just took my money!"

The attorney apologized before repeating what the judge said: We had to send Lindbergh back. This was on a Monday; we got Lindbergh a plane ticket for Thursday. Wednesday night, when I came home from a Mosque meeting, I found John packing his clothes in a large duffel.

"What is going on?" I asked him.

He stopped what he was doing for a minute and said, "I'm running away with Lindbergh."

"No, you are not," I told him. "You can't do this. There is a court order."

"Yes, I can. We're running away."

"And what are the children and I supposed to do while you are on the road?" I asked him.

"Do you think I'm going to send him back, knowing all this stuff he said?"

"Well, I don't know all the stuff he said," I told him, "because nobody told me, and I never read the reports. You can't go anywhere with this boy. Besides, I don't know why you are doing this right now."

I guess I must have stopped John in his tracks when I said no, but I was worried about what he would do. I got Lindbergh and put him in the children's bedroom. I locked the door and windows from the inside and slept sitting up against the door in the room with the four of them.

The next morning, when Lindbergh was ready, I said, "It's time to leave for the airport."

"I'm not going," John said.

I got in the driver's seat; Lindbergh got in the passenger seat; finally John got in the back. It was extremely quiet in the car so I turned on the radio.

We made it to the gate just in time. Lindbergh gave his dad a hug, gave me a hug, and said "I love you, Dad. Love you, Mildred." We both told him we loved him, and he left. This was before they had all this airport security, so we were able to go to the gate and watch the plane go down the runway. As soon as it took off, John did an abrupt right face and walked away from me. He didn't look to see if I was behind him or next to him. When we reached the car, I got back in the driver's seat; John got in the back seat. As soon as we arrived home, he got in his truck and drove off.

This was another turning point in our relationship, and I believe he really started hating me since I wouldn't help him keep Lindbergh. I didn't want Carol worried about her son and I didn't want her to be hurt in this way. I was not going to be a party to John's plans in that direction.

At Lee Boyd Malvo's trial, Lindbergh testified about what happened that summer, saying that his father manipulated him into believing that he had been abused by his mother. Lindbergh said that John put these ideas in his head so firmly that they were "embedded" and that it took his mother months to "decode" him from the belief that he had been abused. During the sniper trial, Lindbergh and his family testified on Lee's behalf, John's young accomplice in the sniper shootings, to support the theory that John had brainwashed Lee.

After Lindbergh left, I know that John felt that he owed me little loyalty and that he could no longer trust me. His tone and his attitude toward me became even colder and harsher. But despite all of the problems, I continued to stay in the marriage. I know now that I should have been strong enough not to put up with this treatment. I should have loved myself enough to have not stayed in this situation, but at the time, I felt as though I couldn't have done anything else.

It had been nine years since we'd taken our vows. One day blended into the other with little relief. Not only were things between us getting worse and worse, the business into which I had put so many hopes and dreams was still falling apart. There were few positive moments, but one of them involved a visit from John's oldest son, Travis. Like Lindbergh, he also questioned why his father had paid so little attention to him. During this time, John was picked up by the police for unpaid tickets and ended up spending the weekend in jail; we didn't have the bail money. He didn't want anyone to know he was in jail for the weekend. So, to those who asked, I said he was out of town. I told the children some kind of complicated story so they wouldn't know what had happened to their father.

We had so little money by now that I took a weekend job at the *News Tribune*. I worked on the shift stuffing advertisements in the paper. While I was working, I expected John to be home with our children. However, when I called to check on the children, I found he was not there. When I would come home, he would pretend that he had been there all along. I knew better. I was trying to do everything, and it was getting harder and harder, particularly since John was getting meaner and meaner. When I attempted to discuss my unhappiness, he was disinterested and avoided conversation. Once I remember him saying, "You have to understand that there are times when I don't mind discussing this kind of thing. But keep in mind that it doesn't matter what you think. Your happiness and the way you feel is not dependent on me. So if you have a problem, you have to correct it; I am not responsible for your happiness."

Finally, I turned to members of my Mosque and talked to one of the brothers in the study group. I said that John was relating to me in a harsh, unkind matter. I told him that he was rarely home. I told him that he had neglected the business to the point that there was little left to save. I asked for his help. The brother did go to John, but it didn't take John long to convince him that I was making things up. The brother came back and told me that he had tried talking to him, and John had told him that I was trying to get attention by telling untruths.

Later, John would say to me, "Let me tell you something. Nobody is going to listen to you. I got this all wrapped up. You'll see."

By trying to get somebody to talk to John, I opened up the floodgates. From that day forward, he started complaining about me to anyone who would listen. He said so many things that were plain hurtful: the business was having problems because I was neglecting it and refusing to answer the phones or respond to the customers; I was a bad housekeeper; I was a neglectful parent; I was a nagging wife. To hear John tell it, I made his life a living hell with unreasonable demands, unfounded jealousy, and selfish ways.

I was in terrible shape, suffering from fatigue as well as severe depression. I would go into the bedroom every night and pray and cry. My friend,

Olivia, looked at me with concern in her eyes. She called me day and night to make sure that I was all right. She called me at least five times a day at prayer times. "I don't know what's going on with you," she would say, "because you're not talking to me. But let's pray together."

Nothing helped, and I was so depressed I didn't know what to do with myself. I phoned my doctor and the minute he got on the phone, I began crying.

When I got into his office, I started crying again.

"Mildred," he asked, "what's the matter?"

I said, "I'm doing the best I can, but I'm not doing anything right. John thinks everything I do is wrong. I'm not a good wife. I'm not a good mother. I'm not a good daughter. If everything I do is wrong, then why am I here? There is no point in my being here if everything I'm doing is wrong. All I do is cry. I just can't stop crying."

The doctor told me that I was extremely tense and suggested giving me five milligrams of Valium to help me calm down so I could get some sleep. I remember my response to him. Thinking about it now, considering that I was contemplating suicide, I can't believe the condition I was in.

"Valium?" I said. "I don't want to get addicted to that stuff."

He assured me that a few milligrams of Valium weren't going to turn me into an addict. I went home and went into the bedroom and closed the windows. I wondered if I could get the doctor to give me enough Valium to kill myself. I thought about other ways of doing myself in and worried about making a mistake and failing at suicide since, according to John, I had failed at everything else.

Soon after that, I had to deliver a package to one of the elders in my study group. When I got to her house, I noticed that she had a tape called "God's Healing Power" by Minister Farrakhan. I asked her, "Can I borrow that tape?" When I got in the car, I put it into the tape deck and started listening. It was a lecture about suicide. What are the odds of something like that happening? I started crying so hard I had to pull over. That tape really spoke to what I was feeling. I listened to it over and over. I'm so thankful for that tape. The more I listened, the stronger I became, the more I realized that suicide wasn't the way out.

# CHAPTER NINE:
## "YOU NEED TO GET AWAY FROM THIS GUY"

I was sitting at the desk in the shop doing paperwork for the business when John came in, pulled up a chair, and sat down very erect. I thought he was going to tell me what happened on the last appointment, but he spoke just four words: "I want a divorce."

I started crying. Strange as it may seem, until this moment, I somehow thought we were going to be able to work things out, and I was still trying to be the good wife. Now I was surprised, confused, and hurt. I managed to ask, "Why did you bring up divorce? Once it's out in the atmosphere, it's going to happen."

He explained that he didn't want to be tied down and he assured me that he was sure about what he was saying. "I'm not happy and I just don't want to be married anymore," he said.

John knew, as I did, that you don't play around with the word "divorce" unless you mean it. But once he said the word and it was "out there," it was inevitable.

After he left the office and I stopped crying, I didn't know what to do next. I felt as though my world was coming to an end. When I married John, I followed my belief that women submit themselves to their husbands. When I said "I do," I meant I would give over to John all power over me. I yielded any authority I had to him. I trusted him unconditionally. Before him I had not trusted anyone in that manner; other than my mother. This was years before I knew that, on faith alone, I should only submit to God. Any other human being would have to first earn my trust.

When I tried to call John, he wasn't answering his phone. I needed to talk things out with someone. I called our minister at the time and I told him that John had walked in and asked for a divorce.

He said, "Sister Mildred, calm down and everything will be all right."

I hung up the phone and stopped crying. I began thinking that maybe divorce might be the best thing for both of us. John would no longer have to hide what he was doing. He might be happier. He could still see the children. We might all be better off.

I locked up the office and drove to the park, which was my favorite place to go since it was on the water. I pondered all the pros and cons of getting a divorce. The negative was that John wouldn't be there. The positive was we would still be working the company together, so I would have finances. He was already acting like he was free, so this scenario wouldn't be so bad.

I thought and I cried. I prayed and asked God to give me the strength to go through the divorce—and to continue to provide for me and the children. After that I was confident in my decision and started on my way home.

I had been at the park for about two hours. When I got home, the children greeted me at the door. They were hungry, so I started making a huge pan of lasagna. I had to go out of town on business. My mom and John were going to care for the children, but I didn't want them to have to cook while I was away.

I was in the kitchen when John came home. I heard the children running over to him. For a while, they were all playing in the living room. I was standing at the counter, preparing the lasagna to put in the oven, when John walked into the kitchen.

"Have you thought about what I said?" he asked.

"Yes, I did," I said, without pausing or looking at him.

"What do you think?"

"I think that's a good idea," I said.

John started breathing hard, fidgeting around, and acting very nervous. "Divorce?" he asked, as if he was checking to make sure I understood.

"Yes, that's what you asked me in the office," I said, still not looking in his direction.

He paused. "That's not what I want," he said.

I stopped what I was doing and looked at him. "Why did you say that?"

"It was to just scare you and let you know what was on my mind," John said.

"If you put divorce out there, it's inevitable," I insisted.

"I don't want a divorce," he repeated. "I don't want us to be separated. We have children to raise."

I had done my thinking and praying and I felt stronger than I had earlier in the day. "I don't want to be with anybody who doesn't want to be with me," I said.

"That's not it," John said. "I just wanted to scare you."

We went into bedroom to talk. John called his sister for her to talk to me. He sat on the bed, rocking back and forth, and saying, "I don't want a divorce."

His sister told me not to pay any attention to John. Then she asked me to give him the phone—and I did.

I heard John say, "I didn't mean to say that. I didn't mean that. I don't want a divorce."

As soon as John saw that I wasn't afraid of the idea of divorce, he decided we should stay together. But the word "divorce" stayed in the back of my mind as a possibility and I began to do research on it. I discovered that one of us had to move out and I learned the amount of time we had to be separated. I found a legal aid place that could do my paperwork. I got a legal book from the library and read it at the office. I didn't dare take the book home. It was in my mind that our marriage would probably end since John had spoken the word out loud.

I looked at the Qu'ran for guidance also and found that it said a husband and wife had to be separated for four months before you can start divorce proceedings. In the book *The Religion of Islam*, it said that there can't be any sexual contact between the two people during that period—120 days— or if there is, you have to start all over, counting the separation time.

I didn't want to start over. Although I didn't openly pursue a divorce, my mind was set on it.

After John returned home the night he talked to his sister, he recommitted himself to working on our marriage again. We opened up the shop together at 9 a.m., closed at 5 p.m. and then came home with the children. Everything went well for about a month, then John started staying out late again. He always said it was on an appointment, but it wasn't. Who fixes a car at nine at night? His deceit gnawed at my self-esteem. But John was a master at deceit, allowing me to know just enough to make me feel worse about myself, to second-guess my value as a wife, a mother, a person.

On another night John was supposed to assist in an event for the Mosque. They could usually count on him, but this night he didn't show up. Someone from the Mosque called me. The person was concerned and frantic; it wasn't John's character to not keep a commitment. I told them I didn't know where he was—and I didn't. I became concerned, too. As it got later, I started calling hospitals and friends looking for John. I even called the morgue.

I was awake all night. John had never spent the entire night out of the house. It was near daybreak when I called the pastor that he was helping to renovate a space for a church. I asked him if he had seen John.

"Mrs. Muhammad, I'm not going to hell for anybody," the pastor said. "I'll tell you what he did. He picked me up at the airport and drove me past your house, so I would know where you lived. Then he brought me back to my house."

The pastor thought it was a strange thing for John to do since he had to pass his house to get to our house, then turn around and take the pastor back home. Plus, since it was dark at the time, the pastor couldn't really see and said he still wouldn't know how to get to our house in the daytime. He also said, once he got inside his house, he looked out the window and saw John make a U-turn and park.

While the pastor and I were talking, John came in.

"Where have you been?" I asked, holding the phone by my side, where John could not see it.

"I've been where I been." He shrugged. "I don't get a greeting?"

"As-Salaam Alaikum," I said.

He did not return the greeting. "I was with the pastor," John replied.

I gave him the phone and said, "He's on the phone." John was shocked to hear that.

The only thing John said to the pastor was, "Uh, yeah, I understand."

He turned and walked out the house as he continued to talk to the pastor on the phone. I walked behind him. "Where are you going? Where are you going?" I asked, as he ignored me and continued talking to the pastor.

He opened the car door. He said, "I'll talk to you later," hung up the phone, handed it to me, and got into the car and drove away.

I stood there and looked at him leave. I am not one to yell and be belligerent. I calmly walked back into the house. I am reserved with my emotions. I have to wait and see the truth I am facing. Usually, when I find out the truth, I simply accept it and do whatever I need to do to move on.

John came back later that evening. We sat down and talked. He said, "I just don't want to feel like I'm trapped when I'm married."

"I don't want to be with anybody who doesn't want to be with me," I said. "I want a divorce."

In spite of everything, John acted as if he didn't understand. "Why?" he asked.

"You are behaving like you're free; you may as well be free," I said. "Now you don't have to report to me, or tell me when you're coming home."

John moved out a month later. He told me that he had gotten a hotel room. Even though he was gone, one of our friends, George, who was in the military with John, needed a place to stay when he came up from Florida, so John told him he could stay with us. But he didn't tell George we were separated.

When George arrived, John was at the house, dressed in his work clothes. At night, John stayed at the house late until our friend fell asleep. He'd return early enough in the morning to make George think he had slept right there at the house.

But one afternoon, George came to me and said, "What's really going on? I may be crazy, but I'm not stupid. I know something is going on."

"John and I are separated," I told him. "He's living somewhere else."

George thought about the bond our families shared. Our children were close to one another; his wife and I were friends and we had all gone places together as couples and as families.

"You can't do this," he pleaded. "You have to give him another chance.

Have you done all you can do? Can you try again? You have these children to raise."

I hate to admit it, but I wasn't confident enough to continue saying no to our friend, who kept asking me the same questions and raising the same issues about the children over and over. After the friend left, John and I decided to go get help from another friend of ours who was a counselor.

Early on, she asked me, "What are the things John does that you don't like?"

I listed several things immediately. "I don't know where he is living. The only way I can contact him is with a pager. And if he doesn't answer that, I have no way to get in touch."

She looked surprised. She turned to John. "What's up with that? Why can't she have a number to call you directly?"

"She can have my pager," he said, refusing to compromise.

Then, since we were trying to reconcile, she asked John, "When do you think you can come back?"

"I want to make sure it is a decision that can help both of us," he answered.

He returned home on a Friday two weeks later. He apologized to me and then he took the children into the living room and apologized to them for the pain he had caused them.

"I will do everything I can to make sure you have what me and your mom didn't have," he promised the children, explaining, "Your mom and I didn't grow up with a mother and a father."

He assured them he would always be there. The children hugged him and went to bed. They were happy and I was, too.

We had an incredible, fun-filled family weekend.

Then Monday came and we returned to the counselor.

"I don't think I'm ready to come home," John announced during the session. "I just had to make sure that we were making the best decision."

I suspected that John's motive was much more selfish than the one he was offering. I was furious that he had put the children through all this chaos while he made up his mind, and I wasn't going to allow them to go through this kind of up and down again. It had been apparent for some time that he was seeing at least one other woman. I recalled that, when my brother Charlie visited, John actually took him with him to "collect money" from women whose cars he had fixed. But John always entered the houses alone and kept Charlie waiting in the car for as much as an hour and a half. My brother said to John, "If my sister finds out what you are doing, she is going to leave you." John's response was, "And if she does, all hell is going to break loose."

I was finished. I'd had enough. I was done. I didn't want to be married to John for one more minute. What I wanted was for him to pack up his madness and go.

I tried to speak in a confident tone that would convince him. "You just wanted to see if you could pull me toward you," I said. "But as of today, you have to go."

We went home and John packed. It was September 9, 1999. We would never live together again as husband and wife. Years later, I would find out from my children that the woman who was our marriage counselor and friend had actually helped John to take care of the children after he had kidnapped them, although she indicated to me she had not seen him after I called her. My daughters told me their father would take them over to this woman's house for her to comb their hair. I was furious with her. But after a while, my anger subsided and I thought about how John could manipulate anybody into thinking what he wanted them to think. He fooled a lot of the people he went to for help. He was good at brainwashing.

John was convinced he could talk anyone into anything. He was sure that whenever he wanted me with him, all he had to do was ask. But when he saw that I had stopped waiting for him and made up my mind that I wouldn't put up with any more of what he was doing, his attitude toward me changed. Suddenly, he wanted to try again. But I held firm. It was over, and I wasn't going to be his wife.

He came to the door and gave our son flowers to bring me. Then John Jr. would ask, "Mommy, please let Daddy come back. He's trying." It hurt me so to tell him no, but it hurt me worse that John would use his own son to participate in his madness.

I didn't like it when he would use the children or put them in the middle of our problems. It was obvious what he was trying to do since he had never bought me flowers before. Throughout our marriage, I wanted a husband who would buy me gifts he knew I wanted or needed. He never did this until this separation. He knew I needed a coat badly. He gladly bought me a coat. He started taking care of my car for me, without being asked. Normally, he was too busy fixing other cars and I took mine to outside mechanics.

But when none of these material things or gifts won me over, John started seriously harassing me. He did some obvious things like bugging my phone and making tapes of my conversations, looking for "evidence" of infidelities that didn't exist. But he also did things I couldn't imagine someone doing to another person, like changing my phone number without my permission. Since his name was on the phone bill, all he had to do was call the phone company and request a new number—and that's what he did more than once. He didn't share these new numbers with me, so my friends couldn't call me and if I was out, I couldn't call home either. One of his friends called to check on me. She said John gave her the number.

"Give me the number," I pleaded.

"No," she said. "John will be mad at me."

I couldn't believe it. "You mean to tell me, you are not going to give me the number?" I asked. "You know Lil' John has asthma and I may have to call 9-1-1. Wow."

Right after that, John called. "You thought you got away, didn't you? As many times as you change the number, I will change it, too," he said. "I know people everywhere. You are not going to get away from me."

He changed the number without my knowing it five times, until I called the telephone company and a representative said he would put a code on the phone so no one could change it from the number he was giving me. He said, as he was talking, he could see that someone was calling in to try to change the number yet again.

John rationed the amount of money he gave us for food. I spent about $200 a month for food while he was living with us, even though he insisted I give him the receipts to prove I was spending the money on food. After he left, my mom, who was diabetic, still lived with me and I had three small children. John started giving me $50 for food, and I had to make it last for a month.

I called the social services department for food stamps but since we were still married, John's income had to be counted in the equation, which meant I did not qualify for aid. The bottom line for my family was that this meant somebody couldn't eat. I gave the children and my mother the food, and I started looking at not eating as simply fasting. I made it a spiritual practice, so it wouldn't bother me. I was losing weight, but I didn't tell my children or mom what was going on. However, Lil' John, who was nine at the time, asked me why I wasn't eating.

"I'm fasting," I offered.

"Mom, you've been fasting for two weeks," he said.

"I know, honey. I'm trying to receive words from God to help me with what I'm going through."

He said, "You can have my food."

"You, Grandma, and your sisters have to eat, honey. I will be fine. I want you to eat your food so you can be strong."

When I insisted I had enough, he asked, "Is it Daddy? Does he give us enough money for food?" To appease him, I took a spoonful of his food.

"You should feel better now," he said.

"I do. Thank you, John."

John still had a key to the house. One night, while I was in the bed half-asleep, I heard someone open the door. My hearing had become so heightened to any noises. I heard the key going into the door and assumed it was John. Still, it scared me; it was so late. Shortly after that, he was in the bedroom standing at the foot of my bed. He was so calculating. He planned everything, and I didn't know what his plan was for me. Then my spirit told me to be still. And so I was still. He walked around me for two or three minutes. I did not flinch or move a muscle until he was gone. I had always listened to my spirit and that night I listened intently. My spirit would guide me throughout my ordeal with John and I believe it is why I am alive today.

I figured John must have entered the house through the garage. The second time he came it was also at night. I was sitting in the living room in the dark. It was about 10 or 11 o'clock. I stayed up late; I needed some quiet time to think about what was going on in my life. I didn't have on the television or radio. I was just sitting in the dark trying to figure out what to do next.

I heard the key go into the front screen door and then into the big door. I got up and was trying to look out the front window to see who it was. The front porch light was out, which was strange; I had turned it on. Suddenly, the door swung open. I ducked behind the sofa. But on my way down, I glimpsed the intruder.

There was a hall light on that also shone on the front door. John couldn't see it from the outside, but that light allowed me to see his face. It had all happened so quickly, but now, realizing it was him, I jumped up from behind the sofa.

"What are you doing?" I asked. He jumped and was surprised to see me.

"I was coming to check on you all." He spoke calmly, as if it wasn't unusual for someone to sneak into their almost-ex-wife's house late at night.

I looked him right in the eyes. "You could have called," I said.

He didn't say another word. He closed the door and left.


John's visits left me more frightened than I had ever been of him. He didn't look at me the same way he used to. He stared at me with a cold, distant look. I had seen the hardness in his eyes when he stood over my bed and I saw it again on that second visit, when he threw open that front door.

That morning after his second visit, I checked the porch light and found it had been unscrewed. I fixed it. I made it a practice each night to double check everything—the doors, the windows, the locks.

The third time, I saw him coming. The bathroom light was on for the children and I was in the bed. I peeped as he was coming in the door, then I closed my eyes. I thought of his military training as a combat engineer; his vision was better than mine because his eyes had already become accustomed to the dark. If I had opened my eyes to see, he would have seen the whites of my eyes while I was squinting and trying to focus. So again, my spirit said, "Be still."

My door was partially open and he slid through that opening without touching the door. Right then my daughter Taalibah woke up and ran to him, yelling, "Daddy!"

John picked her up and I opened my eyes as if I was just waking up. He leaned down, gave her to me, and walked out of the house.

The next day I called the locksmith, who told me it would be two days before he could come. On the day I made my call, John came by and said there was something wrong with the dead-bolt lock and that he needed to get it off the door and replace it. He demonstrated that the key would not fit.

"It will be fine," I said.

"Give me your key," he insisted.

He took the lock out of the door, leaving a big hole. When he pulled it out I saw a straight pin fall to the ground. I know John didn't want me to see it, because I realized that the pin was the reason the door did not work. Nevertheless, he left with the lock. After he left, I also noticed that for some reason the screen door wouldn't lock anymore either.

That night we didn't have a lock on the door at all and I was terrified. I got a kitchen table chair and propped it against the door handle. I stayed awake all night, sitting in the chair, clutching a knife so I could defend my mother and children. I did the same thing the next night. The next day, the locksmith came and I relaxed some, knowing that John no longer had a key to my doors.

John's abuse took many forms. He didn't pay the rent, so we were being threatened with eviction. He didn't give me enough food money. I was worried about how I was going to provide for all of us.

One day there was a knock at the door. I looked out to see who it was and saw my friend, Olivia. I didn't want to let her in the house; she would look around and I was ashamed of what she would find. When I finally opened the door, I stepped outside to greet her.

"As-Salaam Alaikum," I said.

"Wa-Alaikum Salaam," she said. "Wassup? I can't go in the house."

We both laughed.

"Yes," I said, moving to the side to let her in.

She looked around, just as I thought she would.

"I thought the house wasn't clean or something," Olivia said.

I led her out to the deck.

"Okay, tell me what's going on," she said.

"No, no one would believe me."

"Try me," Olivia said.

I told her everything that had happened between me and John.

"Okay, I've heard enough," she said.

She walked into the kitchen and looked in the cabinets. Then she looked in the refrigerator. There wasn't much food in either place. She looked at me and I put my head down.

"Get your scarf; we're going to the store," she said.

"Olivia, you don't have to do that," I said.

"Did I stutter?" she asked.

I laughed and said, "Okay, okay."

"Bring the children so we can give your mom a break," she said. Then she went in my mom's room, spoke to her and took her order for what she wanted to eat.

First, Olivia took us to the grocery store. "Okay, Chica, get what you need and what you want."

"Olivia, that will be a lot," I warned.

"Wait a minute, did I stutter?" she asked again.

I laughed. I then filled two baskets with food. After the store, Olivia took me and the children to a restaurant. When we finished eating, she ordered my mom's food. The children were happy and laughing. We talked about the teachings and she told me to study 2nd Peter regarding a virtuous woman.

"I want you to work on yourself and let Allah deal with John," she said.

At home, we put away the food and Taalibah took my mom her food.

"Thank you for being my mom's friend," Lil' John said.

"You are welcomed," Olivia said.

"I love you, Sis Olivia," Lil' John said.

"I love you, too," she said. "We have to take care of your mom, right?"

"That's right," agreed Lil' John.

Salena gave Olivia a hug. I walked her to the door.

"Okay, Chica, I know you're not going to call me, but I'll be checking on you," she said.

You don't leave a friend like that, which is why Olivia is still my best friend today.

When John came over to give me $50 for food, he looked in the refrigerator and the cabinets and saw all that food. He was furious. "Where did you get all of this food?" he asked.

"From Allah," I said.

John came by the house one day waving a recording tape in my face; he referred to it as evidence.

"I'm going to destroy you with this tape! I'm going to get you off that pedestal you think you're on!" he hollered. "You're nothing, and I'm going to make sure everyone knows it, b@#%h!"

I don't know what was on the tape—or if there was anything on it. I do know that once John recorded a tape of my friend Olivia and I talking about our lives, which got him extremely angry. I also found out from the phone company that my phone wires were set up so that someone could wiretap my conversations.

John was convinced I was having an affair with the guy in the internet chat room. But I wasn't. I had cut off communication with everyone else, so I began chatting with people on-line, trying to get advice on what to do next. I had friends on a site called Black Voices, which had an African American chat room for people of different ages. I talked to people on the site, asking them for advice.

The next time he came to the house he said he wanted to see Lil' John, because our son was sick. I refused to let him in. I was frightened. He knocked and I opened the door a little. He shoved the door. I pushed back, but he was stronger. He pushed me and the door so hard that I fell backward onto the floor. I jumped up, took a swing at him, and missed. My first thought was that I had to be out of my mind to do that. I looked at the expression on his face and I was sure I knew exactly what was going through his brain.

*He's going to kill me*, I thought. I ran to the back of the house and into my bedroom to call the police. My mother passed me in the hall. I heard John say, "She's having an affair, Mom."

By the time the police arrived, John had left. I explained what was happening. They asked if John's name was on the lease. I said yes and they informed me there was nothing they could do. They left papers for me to fill out to get a restraining order.

A few days later after the situation had calmed down, John came over again. He was nicely dressed and wearing a shirt and tie. He said he wanted to talk to me so we went into the garage. As he spoke, I saw the cold fury in his eyes.

"You and Olivia are not going to raise my children," he said. "You have become my enemy and as my enemy, I will kill you."

I was petrified but I tried not to show my fear. "I've been sleeping with the enemy all this time, so what else can you do to me now?" I said.

John walked hastily toward me. I ran to my brother, Charlie, who was visiting. When John saw Charlie, he left.

"John looks mad," Charlie said.

"John said he's going to kill me," I said, breathless. "He means it. I saw it in his eyes."

Charlie shrugged. "John isn't going to kill you. He said that to scare you."

"Well, it worked." I was trembling inside. John meant what he said. He would not have said it unless he meant it. From John's point of view, when he said, "I will kill you," it was him giving me his word. He always said that his word was his bond.

I also knew John never did anything without a plan. There was no question in my mind: John was figuring out a way to kill me without getting caught.

I went to the police department and filled out a four-page form asking for a restraining order. I was crying so much I could barely see the papers. I could not believe my life had come to this moment. I kept thinking, "How did we get here?"

I went to a phone and called a friend. I told her what I was doing. I said, "I don't think I should do this."

She told me I should. "You have to protect yourself," she said.

The day of the court hearing, I was scared. I went to the courthouse alone. My legs shook as I walked. I thought I might faint from weakness. At all times, I stood where I could watch all the doors. I planned my escape route, just in case I saw John. I had stopped crying. I was frightened, but I felt as if I was on a mission.

John didn't show up. The judge read the forms I had filled out and said, "You need to get away from this guy."

"Yes, sir, I'm trying," I said.

With that, the judge granted me a lifetime protection order. I still carry it with me to this day.

# CHAPTER TEN:
## MISSING

After receiving the restraining order, John and I agreed that the children would visit him every other weekend. We didn't write up a formal agreement. We just talked about it and settled on that arrangement. We were waiting to go to court for a parenting plan. A friend of his, someone I knew, would come to pick up the children and take them to see John.

The date of the first weekend visit was Friday, March 10, 2000, our twelfth wedding anniversary. Tommy, one of John's good friends and an old service buddy, picked the children up at the house about 6 p.m. He returned them Sunday evening so they could prepare for school on Monday.

The next visit was Friday, March 24. The same friend came to pick them up. Before leaving, he turned and asked me for Lil' John's nebulizer and medications for asthma.

"Why?" I asked.

John was doing well and had not had an asthma attack in a long time, so I didn't give Tommy the medication or the nebulizer. If I had felt that my son needed either, I would have sent them. After they left, I immediately began missing the children. Still, I hoped they'd have a good time with their dad.

On Monday, my mom's birthday, Tommy dropped off the children just in time for school. I had to scramble to help them get ready so they could be on time. They seemed their usual happy selves. But later in the day, Lil' John called to say he was having an asthma attack.

Months later—and even today—I ponder that call, wondering if John used Lil' John to carry out what he had planned. However, on that day, my brother who was visiting at the time, rushed to school to get my son.

Sometimes Lil' John wheezed to get attention. I had to listen to his breathing to determine if he needed a treatment or not.

When my brother and Lil' John arrived home, I could tell that my son was struggling a little to breathe. I gave him a treatment. Shortly after that, I called John to explain what had happened and asked him to pick up the girls.

Later that evening, John called to say he wanted to take the children to Odyssey I, which was an indoor family fun and game center. He said Tommy would come by and pick up Lil' John.

"That's fine, John. Just have them back by five-thirty," I said. "We're taking Mom to Old Country Buffet for her birthday."

He agreed.

Just before Tommy arrived, I explained to Lil' John what was happening. He gave me the oddest look.

"What's wrong, honey?" I asked.

"Nothing," he said, continuing to stare at me.

"You sure?"

"Yes, ma'am."

I walked out of the bedroom and went into the kitchen. I turned around and found Lil' John standing behind me, just staring. "Honey, you know you can tell me what's bothering you, right?"

He looked like he wanted to cry. "Yes, ma'am," he said, reaching up to give me a hug.

I knelt down and hugged him.

"I love you, Mommy," he said.

"I love you, too, honey," I said.

But something about the way he said it, concerned me. I watched him and thought he didn't know how to tell me what was going on inside of him. Before I could say anything else, there was a knock on the door. It was Tommy.

I walked Lil' John to the door. As Lil' John was walking out, he looked back once more, stopped, and waved.

"Bye, Mommy."

"See you later," I said.

The doorbell rang at five-thirty that evening and I assumed it was the children. Instead, Tommy was standing there alone. He handed me two dollars and a message written on notebook paper. It said: "Happy Birthday, Grandma. I love you, Taalibah."

I couldn't fathom why my child was sending a note. "What is this? Where are my children?"

"With John," he said.

"What time is he bringing them home?"

"He said you should call him."

Then Tommy left and I paged John. I paged him over and over the next couple of hours. Finally, about seven-thirty, I got a call back. But Lil' John was on the phone.

"What are you all doing?" I asked.

"We're at Kmart with a list of things you asked Dad to buy," he said.

"I thought you were going to Odyssey I?"

"We were but we came here to pick up some things you had on the list for Dad to get."

I had given John the list months before, after he had stopped giving me money and instead asked me to make a list of the things the children needed.

"Ask your dad when are you coming home," I said.

I heard my son ask the question and I heard John say, "In an hour."

I looked at the time and said, "So that would be eight-thirty."

"Okay, Mom, I love you," Lil' John said.

"I love you, too. I'll see you later."

An hour passed. I paged John again. I continued to page him—one page after another—for the next three hours. I didn't get a call back until eleven thirty-five. It was John this time.

"When are you bringing the children back?" I asked.

"We're en route from Seattle," he said. "We will be there shortly."

I said, "Okay." As I was hanging up the phone, I felt butterflies in my stomach. Something was wrong. Seattle was forty-five minutes from our home in Tacoma. John had them in Seattle when I thought they were fifteen minutes away. If he could do this... I didn't want to think about what was possible.

I didn't sleep that night. I sat on the sofa, waiting for the door to open. I didn't tell my mother about John's last call. She was asleep. I didn't cry; I didn't want to get upset. Also, I was trying to be optimistic. I didn't know what John was doing but I figured he might bring the children home any minute. Still, I couldn't close my eyes without knowing where my children were.

Daylight came and time passed. First it was time for the children to wake up. Then time for them to eat. Then time for them to get dressed for school. I waited until school was open and the children had time to get there and be in their classes. I called Marilyn, the school secretary, identified myself, and asked her if my children were in class.

"Their dad was supposed to drop them off," I said.

She put me on hold for a few minutes. When she came back, she said, "No, Mrs. Muhammad, your children aren't here today. But you can call back anytime."

I hung up and sat in the quiet house. I did not show any emotions. I didn't call anyone. I waited patiently by the door, wondering when John would bring back the children. I was trying to remain open, not to speculate about anything.

My mother woke up. Before she said good morning, she asked, "Where are the children?"

"I don't know," I said.

I generally woke up at 4:30 a.m. for prayer at 5 a.m. It was my practice to get dressed before the children woke up. But on this morning I was still wearing the same clothes.

My mother started crying.

I called the school every day that week and received the same information from Marilyn. I called the study group coordinator in Seattle in case somebody knew where John was and could influence him. The coordinator said, "Sister Mildred, I'm sure there is an explanation. Just wait, Sister. He will bring the children back. Keep me informed."

I called my friend, Olivia, and we prayed together for the safe return of the children.

I called the school again the next morning, but I got the same answer.

The children were not there. I called the study group coordinator again.

"Brother," I said, "he didn't bring the children back last night, and they are not in school."

"Sister Mildred, why would he do that?"

"Sir, I don't know," I replied.

Finally on Friday, I walked to the school. I went to the school secretary, but she had bad news: The children were still not in school.

I went to see Lil' John's favorite teacher, Mrs. Bullock. Her class was outside and she was in the room by herself. I walked in the room and closed the door.

Mrs. Bullock looked up and smiled.

"Hey, Mrs. Muhammad, how are you doing?" As I got closer to her desk and she could see my face, her joy changed to concern. "What's wrong?" she asked.

"John kidnapped the children, and I don't know where they are," I said, barely getting out the words before I burst into tears. It was the first time I had cried since the children had left.

Mrs. Bullock came over and hugged me. She let me cry a while and then she said, "Go wash your face."

"Have you called the police?" she asked.

"No, ma'am," I said.

Her voice was calm. "Go home, call the police, and report this."

All I could utter was a whispery, "Okay."

I would have to face my mother at home, so I took the long way. I wanted to stop crying and compose myself before my mother saw my face. I had to be strong for her.

When I walked up, Mom was waiting at the door. She expected me to have the children. I had told her earlier in the week that I was going to the school on Friday to see if they were there. But now she stared at my face and let out a wail like I had never heard.

I had to hold back my tears as I was trying to keep my mother's spirits up. I would not cry until I was alone. The only word my mother could say was, "Why?" And she said this over and over, again and again. She continued to hold onto me, crying hard.

Eventually, she stopped crying, and screamed, "He took our babies! He took our babies! What are we going to do?!" Then she started crying again.

My mother could barely stand. I helped her over to the sofa.

"I don't know what I'm going to do, but I'm going to do something," I assured her. "Mom, you have to stop crying. You know how long and hard you can cry once you get started, Mama. It's not good for you."

My mother was a diabetic and she took medication. When Taalibah was around, Mom didn't dwell on her health. Taalibah became her reason for living. My mom was in the delivery room when Taalibah entered this world and the two of them had a special bond. Taalibah taught Mom how to say her name. The two took walks together. Taalibah was the only one who could burst into her grandmother's room, sit on her bed, and turn her TV channels without asking. While Mom loved each of her grandchildren, the other children and I respected the special relationship she had with Taalibah.

I had noticed that with the children gone, the light in my mom was fading. I could see it leaving her already, but I couldn't do anything about it.

Her crying slowed down. She paused and looked at me through her tears and smiled a little bit. "My poor baby," she said, "He took our babies. What are we going to do?"

"I don't know what to do yet," I replied. "But I'm not going to just sit here and do nothing."

My mom stared at me. "My poor baby," she said.

I called the police. They came and took a report. But they marked the report *"custodial interference"* since there was no parenting plan in place that actually spelled out an agreement between John and me. This meant there was nothing the police could do. These were his children too, so as far as they were concerned, he had not actually kidnapped them.

A week passed and I did not see or hear from my children or from John. Then one evening, I heard a car pull up. I ran to the window. It was my friend, Isa. She didn't know what had happened. I wasn't expecting her to come by. She was her usual jovial self. I opened the door and let her in. She was returning my sewing machine she had borrowed. As she walked in, she noticed the house was quiet.

"Where are the children?" Isa asked.

"John took them," I said, returning to my usual position, the chair by the front window.

"What do you mean, John took them?"

"He kidnapped them."

She immediately got on the phone and called a friend of hers who was an FBI agent. The friend checked and told her that the case was being handled by the local police and that the FBI couldn't do anything. I was pretty sure this meant nothing was being done to bring my children home. Isa didn't know what to say. She tried to assure me that John wouldn't do anything stupid. However, my mind was all over the place.

Isa stayed for an hour and then left. The next morning, I called the local police again, told them everything that had happened thus far, and made an appointment to speak with a detective.

On the day of my appointment, I went to the station carrying photos of John and my children, as the officer on the phone had requested. The detective told me he would put the children into the National Center for Missing and Exploited Children network. When I got home, I called the center to find out if my children were in the system. I was told they were not.

"Can I put them in the network?" I asked.

"Only the police can," the woman replied.

If the police didn't feel the children were missing, they wouldn't enter them into the system.

I called John's ex-wife, Carol, in Louisiana. "If he comes to visit, I want you to know he has kidnapped the children," I told her.

She put her relatives on alert. I reached out to everyone I could think of. But the people around us didn't seem to even know that John was gone, and they were surprised when I told them he had taken the children.

At some point, after all the calling and disappointment, I think I went into a depression, though I didn't realize it. John had emptied the bank accounts when he took the children. He had already closed the business the previous year, on December 20th, my birthday. (Later, I would wonder if he deliberately did these horrible things on dates that were special to me. After all, he took the children on my mother's birthday.)

I didn't have any savings or income, so I had to find a job. I started going on interviews. I looked for months, but nothing came through. The whole process was difficult given my state of mind, but also because I had worked in our family business for years and had been out of the normal job market.

I called the Kirby Company for an interview; I'd sold their vacuum cleaners before, during the summer before I went to college. I figured I could do it again since I was familiar with the product. I went in for the interview and was immediately given the job. I went in for training and explained that I needed to keep a low profile but did not explain my circumstances.

I began the training but one day the owner pulled me aside. He was concerned about my age, which he felt that it would be difficult for me to sell. He was also concerned with my health. I believed I was fine and wondered if maybe I looked worse than what I thought.

Some months later, I would find out that John was spying on me and knew that I was selling vacuum cleaners door to door.

I had already fallen behind in all the bills, including the rent. I wrote letters to my debtors, explaining that John had left and taken the children. I wrote my landlords and pleaded for more time to come up to date on the rent:

*"The last time I spoke to the children was on March 27th. They told me that they would be home after they left Kmart. I have not heard from them since. Not a phone call, a page, or a letter. Nothing. He drained the accounts and closed the business. He left me without any funds. I have been out of my mind trying to make ends meet. I have been trying to put things in perspective. Trying to find work and getting help for myself emotionally has been difficult.*

*I have never been without my children since they have been born. My daughter, Taalibah; her birthday is Monday. This will be the first birthday I will miss. She'll be seven years old. I have always been there for my children and this is a feeling I cannot explain. Every morning I wake up, I pray that someone wakes me up from this nightmare because this is not happening. Then I realize it is and I have to start to live that day without my children.*

*I am appealing to you for time. I just got a job yesterday and based on the pay, I will be able to maintain the rent to stay here. You see I have to stay here. This is the home the children know. They have to be able to contact my mother or me. They know the phone number and the address. I taught it to them so, in case they were abducted, they would know how to call home and know their address to tell someone. I didn't think I would be preparing them for this. I can assure you that all monies will be to you for April and May by the end of May. June's rent will be on time. I pray that you will continue to work with me. This is a desperate situation for me..."*

The landlords basically said while they empathized with me personally, ours was a business relationship and they could not extend my due date. I felt even more desperate. By the end of April, I was still calling everyone John and I knew. It was strange to me that everyone I called had no information about John. Somebody had to know something, I figured. Why wasn't anyone willing to help me to find my children? Where could I go for help?

Of course, today I know that some of those people who said they knew nothing were actually a part of the plan to take the children from me. But at the time, it was difficult to conceive of this. I couldn't imagine that people were capable of being so cruel, or that John was so good at lying that he could convince people that I wasn't taking care of the children.

Most of the people I approached for information, simply said, "Let me know if there is anything I can do."

One day I called his good friend, Robert, and he, at least, said, "I'll keep my eyes open." I don't know if Robert knew at the time where the children were, but months later I would recall his words when he became pivotal in John's capture.

Once I realized no one was going to help me, I stopped calling people. In my anguish, every single day I went over every little detail I could recall leading up to the day of the kidnapping. Was there something I was forgetting that could help me find my children? Was I missing a piece of the puzzle?

I had to find employment to pay the rent so I could keep the house and the children would know where to find me. I felt as though I was sleepwalking through my life, but still I lined up several job interviews. My first interview was on a Monday afternoon. That morning a longtime, good friend of mine asked to borrow my car and I let him. He agreed to return a couple of hours before the interview. But that time came and he was not back. I called, but he didn't answer his phone. Finally, I called the police to report the car missing.

I was without transportation for nearly a week before police called to report they had found the car and my friend who had it. Isa took me to get the car. I didn't realize my friend had a drug and alcohol problem. When I arrived, police were handcuffing him. Unfortunately, I had missed all of my appointments.

I cried a lot. On the days that I remembered to eat, I managed to eat a half of a slice of bread, just enough to sustain me. Mostly, I ate ice chips. There was something about the crunching that was comforting to me. My menstrual cycle lasted longer and longer each month, a sign that my body was turning against me. My mom ate as much as she could, probably as part of her attempt to encourage me to eat. She said very little. I suppose she was mourning in her own way. Our house, once full of activity and giggles and conversation, was silent.

On Mother's Day, the mail carrier rang my doorbell. I answered and he told me he had a package for my mother. I signed the receipt. Then everything turned black.

When I opened my eyes. I had a terrible headache. I was lying on the floor and the postman was standing over me. My mom heard the noise made by my fall and ran from her bedroom. The postman helped me up. I was wobbly. He told me that I had fallen straight back "like a tree" and had hit my head on the floor.

I stumbled to my bedroom to get the phone and brought it back to the front door where the postman was waiting. The postman called 9-1-1 while I sat on the floor. I was still dizzy.

When the emergency medical crew arrived, someone asked, "What happened?" The postman explained, and they said they wanted to take me to the hospital for observation.

I looked at my mother. I was thinking if I left, she would be alone. Right then my neighbor Brenda showed up.

"Are you okay?" she asked.

"I don't know, but please take care of my mother," I said.

Brenda went over to my mother and held her hand and said, "You know I will."

With that reassurance, I allowed the medics to put me in the ambulance. They turned on the siren.

My physician, Dr. Weatherby, met us at the hospital. He told me they needed to run some tests to find out what was wrong. Later, after the tests, he informed me that I had lost three units of blood, and he gave me the option of leaving the hospital and taking some pills or of staying and getting a blood transfusion.

"Which is better?" I asked.

"The blood transfusion and hospitalization," he said.

I couldn't believe that here it was, Mother's Day, and instead of taking my mom to her favorite restaurant, I was getting a blood transfusion. Up to that point, it was the saddest Mother's Day we had ever had. Anyway, I didn't feel like much of a mother without my children.

Isa came to the hospital. As soon as I saw her, I began crying and apologizing.

"Why are you apologizing?" she asked.

"I'm not handling this very well," I said.

"Girl, stop tripping," Isa said. "I don't know how I would be handling this myself. You have to get better. Stop crying..."

They checked me into the hospital and I was wheeled to my room. I had my blood transfusion on the day that I arrived at the emergency room. On the third day of my hospitalization, I was resting in the bed when the phone rang. I answered it and heard John's voice. I was startled. How did he know I was in the hospital? I had not talked to him since March 27th and here it was May 16th.

"How are you doing?" he said, as if nothing was wrong and we were having a regular conversation as husband and wife.

"I'm good. How are you doing?" I asked, speaking calmly.

"How is Mom?"

I was still calm. I said, "She's fine." I paused and then asked, "Why don't you let the children call me?"

"We don't always get what we want, do we?!" he yelled.

I understood what John was saying. For years, when his angry reaction was totally inappropriate, I had to read between the lines to interpret what he was really saying. So there, lying in the hospital, he was saying that I had a choice: I could go back to him and die—because he had already threatened to kill me—or I could hang up and never see the children again.

It was a choice, but not much of one. Yet, I did the only thing I believed I could if I ever stood a chance of living to see my children again. I hung up the phone—and screamed.

I was still screaming when several nurses ran into the room.

"What's wrong? What's wrong?" they asked.

"Can you trace that phone call? Trace the phone call!" I said, explaining what had happened.

They agreed to call the operator. Later, a nurse came in the room and told me that a woman had initially asked for me but then a man got on the phone. They were unable to determine where the call originated.

They called the police and shortly afterward, an officer came to take a report. I was panic-stricken. I felt totally dependent upon the police to save me now. Before, without physical scars to prove I was an abused woman, everyone ignored me. John's threat changed all of that.

"He can make a weapon out of anything," I said. "He already said he was going to kill me."

I found out that John had also called my mother that day and told her that he was going to kill me. She immediately called the hospital to report the threat and the police were notified. They moved me to another room, had my incoming calls blocked, and put a security officer outside the door.

Isa came to visit me the next day.

"Mildred, you can't go home," Isa insisted, fearful that John would kill me.

She called a transitional home for women to report that I needed a place to stay.

I was concerned again about my mother. "What about Mom?" I asked Isa.

"I'll take care of her, but you can't go home," she said.

Late that night someone from the transitional home called Phoebe's

House came to pick me up. The woman arrived with a change of clothes for me. She allowed me to take my old clothes, but what bothered me was...to help hide my identity, I could not cover my hair, as required by my religion.

As we walked out of the hospital to the car, the woman said to me in a calm voice, "You have five minutes to change your name."

I needed a new name so that no one, not even the people at the house, would know my true identity. I hadn't even considered this possibility and the only name I could think of was the name of the house. I was headed to Phoebe's House, so I chose the name "Phoebe."

The house was about five minutes away. But, in that time, my mind seemed to wander over an hour's worth of thoughts. I didn't know where this place was or what it was going to be like. I was worried about my mother not really knowing anybody. How would she fare alone without me there to help her?

Looking out the car window, bewildered with tears in my eyes, I saw some familiar streets. I was checking the rooftops and open windows. I was so scared because no one knew where John was. We ended up in a well-kept neighborhood in downtown Tacoma, near thriving businesses and the courthouse and hospital. Phoebe's House was a three-story house that blended into the community of single-family homes.

We entered through the back door, from a deck. The house was dark and quiet. Everyone was asleep. I saw a laundry room to the right. Then we went through the kitchen and a dining room, and finally, into what looked like a family room. The staff person, a woman named Sharron, asked me to have a seat while she went to prepare my room. Though I wanted to call my mother, I was told that for my safety I could not make calls for a few days and then when permitted, because of caller ID, I would only be able to call from the pay phone. And for my safety, I would have to disconnect from everyone I knew.

While I waited, I cried and asked myself, "How did I get to this point?"

Sharron returned to tell me that my room was ready. "You're in luck. You have your own room for a little while," she said, as she opened the door to my bedroom.

It looked like a dormitory room with twin beds, two dressers, and a couple of windows. I thanked her for her kindness, got in the bed, put my face in the pillow, and cried until I fell asleep.

The next morning, I woke up feeling numb, a sense that would stay with me for a few months. Everything familiar to me—including my name—was gone. I was not in my own home. I was living with women I did not know. I was scared and alone. My children were not with me. I could not call my mom. I felt totally abandoned.

I went downstairs early. There were nine bedrooms and in most there were two women. As the women woke up and came downstairs, they stared at me and I stared at them. You could tell we were wondering about each other and our personal stories.

At that time Phoebe's House was for women who were in all kinds of transitions. I would later find out I was the only woman leaving a domestic abuse situation. There were women who were recently out of prison, women who had been drug abusers, and women who had lost custody of their children but who could receive visits from them there at Phoebe's House.

There were plenty of rules. Males could not visit the house. Visitors could not go upstairs. Visitation was only on Sundays. Everyone had chores. There was only one television and on weekdays you could not watch it during the day. There were classes to attend and work to be done.

As the days passed, I seldom left the house without a staff member and I never left the house alone. Again, since I did not have physical scars, no one believed my life was in danger. But I took John's threat seriously, so I developed the habit of staying inside the house, not even to venture outside into the backyard.

I was well aware of the fact that I could have been in a much worse place, or out on the street. Phoebe's House was homey and clean and I was thankful. Throughout my stay and during the ensuing ordeal with John, I would feel as if God was watching over me and that in spite of my pain, I was living in the palms of His hands.

# CHAPTER ELEVEN:
## HOLDING THE CHILDREN IN MY HEART

While I was at Phoebe's House, my frightened mother was alone at my old home. She stayed there for more than a month before my sister came and took her back to Maryland. When my mother left the house, I gave the furniture to one of the ladies leaving Phoebe's House. Everything else in our house was put into storage.

I realized that my respite at Phoebe's House was giving me a chance to calm down and decide what to do next. I was grateful that this kind of facility existed for women who needed safety and a chance to build a new life. You could stay at Phoebe's House for up to twenty-four months. There were rooms for women with children and rooms for women without them. There were always women moving out while others were moving in.

We were like friends helping one another. I became particularly close to four women: Tami, Theresa, Oneeta, and Kathy. In the beginning, Oneeta did not like me at all. It even irritated her that I got up every morning and spoke to her. I suppose it was her way of avoiding a friendship. But in spite of her attitude, I spoke to her every morning.

Her response was always the same. "Why did you speak to me?" she'd grumble.

"I can't speak to you?" I'd say incredulously.

Eventually, I just wore her down—and she started speaking to me whenever I spoke to her. She also became my protector, making sure no one bothered me.

Theresa, my roommate, had recently been released from prison. She had two children. Her daughter was in foster care and she was trying to get her back and reunite with her other child, too. She had cleaned herself up, gotten a job, and was working toward getting her own place for all of them. She was nervous and excited about the possibility of her family being reunited. We prayed that it would happen, and finally, she went to court to regain custody of her daughter. When she came home, I was waiting for her at the door. She walked right past me and went to our room. When I went upstairs and walked in the room, she was sitting on the side of her bed crying. I asked what happened.

"They had already made up their minds before I got there," she said. "They took her from me. I don't know what to do."

She cried and I cried with her. I didn't leave her side. Finally, I was able to convince her to stop crying. I put on my favorite song, "Fragile Heart," by Yolanda Adams. It seemed to calm her down. She was so heartbroken and watching her go through that made my heart sick, too. She called her little girl her miracle child.

"The doctors told me I couldn't have any more children," she explained.

I asked for a picture of her daughter and I hung it up in our room. She thanked me for that.

Then she said, "Phoebe, what about your children? What are you going to do?"

"We have to make sure you are well," I said. "God is taking care of my children."

She began crying again. "I'm glad you're my roommate," she said.

She finally felt tired and lay down. I lay down in my bed and looked at the photos of my children, wondering where they were.

I had never been around women who had been through some of the things these women had experienced. They jokingly said, "Mildred, you would never last one day on the streets. We knew you were green from the time you said hi."

They asked if I had ever smoked cigarettes or if I had gotten high off of anything. I said, "No," and they laughed and shook their heads as if to say, "That's unbelievable," though they knew I was telling the truth.

Those women were an intricate part of my growth. When I was at that house I felt as if I was in a womb. And when I came out I was birthed into a new world. I looked at my entire life while I was at Phoebe's House. I got a chance to rebuild my life from the perspective of true reality. I was growing at a faster rate and with better understanding. I began to look at everything with clearer eyes, to reexamine life. For the first time, I saw my life for what it really was and not as I wanted it to be.

I was assigned a therapist who started out by giving me a series of "What if..." exercises that felt to me as though they were designed to help me deal with the loss of my children. I refused to do the exercises, including one where she wanted me to write a letter to the children explaining to them what I was going through without them.

"That's like giving up," I said.

I didn't want to try to adjust to not having my children. I told my therapist I wanted to know how to handle the situation with my children once they returned.

"I want to talk about who I am right now. I need to understand my feelings and how to deal with them. I need you to help me to understand my situation so that when it's time to get my children back, I will be emotionally healthy and the judge will see that," I said. "I need to know why I am so submissive," I said, offering a slew of other questions and issues I wanted to tackle. "What did I miss that could have told me John was going to take my children? Why didn't people help me? Why did law enforcement let me down? What do I need to do now?"

Just verbalizing the questions made me cry.

"We have a lot of work to do," the therapist said. "How many times a week do you want to see me?"

I stopped crying. "Every day," I said.

She said gently, "That's not realistic."

"Then you tell me," I said.

We agreed on three times a week. She gave me an antidepressant and a sleeping pill because each night I willed myself to stay awake. I told her that I felt that if I closed my eyes, it meant I was giving up on my children. I had to keep a vigil and stay awake to wait on them.

"Phoebe, you need to sleep," the therapist said. "This medicine will help you get eight hours of sleep each night." So I went back to the house and took the medicine.

On my next visit, she asked me how I was sleeping. I told her the pill only helped me to sleep for four hours. Once the therapist realized this, she doubled my prescription. "Your will is stronger than I thought," she said.

I took the pills in spite of the fact that I hated being medicated. I had to do whatever was necessary in order to be strong for my children. I had to be of sound mind and body so that when my time came to stand in a courtroom, there would be no question about my competence and the judge would say I could have my children back. I had to be strong in character and in my faith.

I returned to my room whenever it was time for prayer. Due to my depression, I had a difficult time getting up some mornings for my prayers. I beat myself up terribly, thinking God was not pleased with me. On other mornings I rose at four-thirty to pray quietly while my room-mate slept. I still did not wear my Muslim clothes; even on the rare occasions when staff members had to take me outside to go somewhere. Since I had a new name, if someone called me on the telephone and used the name "Mildred," we would know that it was John, or someone calling for him.

Generally, I only went outside for doctors' appointments. At those times, whoever accompanied me usually held an umbrella over me to hide my face. Inside, I never sat near a window. I envisioned John perched on a rooftop with a gun aimed at my head. I closed the window over the sink whenever I had to stand there to wash dishes. If I needed something from the store, I had someone get it for me.

Some people thought I was overreacting. I had gotten used to this attitude since my own family did not believe John had abused me to the degree that he had. If my own family did not believe me, how could I expect other people to?

John had such a way with words and the manner in which he spoke could convince anyone of whatever he needed them to believe. By the time I contacted his friends for help, he had already convinced them to take his side. They treated me like I was the problem and refused to believe John behaved the way I described him.

I've had a lot of time to think this through and have forgiven everyone who was a victim to his way of thinking. It was a difficult process. However, it was necessary for my healing.

Still, whether anyone believed me or not, I was cautious. I loved the summertime weather, but I was too scared to go out. I kept hearing John's threats in my head like a tape that never stopped. The women even had a tent on the deck out back and I refused to join them inside of it. I positioned myself so I could stand inside the door and see them.

But one day Oneeta proclaimed, "You are getting on my nerves." She got a jacket and draped it over my head.

"There, he can't see you," she said. "Come on."

She grabbed my hand and led me to the tent.

"See, he can't see you," she said once we were inside. "He doesn't know you are out here."

I peeped from under the jacket, paused, and then took it off. We stayed outside until dark, which was rare for me.

In the meantime, my children appeared to have vanished off the face of the earth. I was still working to convince people to help me find them. One policewoman named India got a lead on John's whereabouts and tried to set up a sting operation. John had told an undercover officer that he was a single man, new to the area, and that he was a car mechanic. India had the undercover officer call John about getting his car fixed.

The officer followed John back to a house where Tommy, the guy who used to pick up the children for him, lived. But, at some point, the officer had to leave the house. By the time a second officer arrived, John was gone. The police never found out whether or not he had the children with him.

I was devastated. I had built up my hopes and the disappointment sent my emotions reeling. My therapist asked India to stop telling me the details of their investigation. She said too much information was putting me on an emotional roller coaster and I never got a chance to recover before the ride took off again.

I called my cousin, who was a private detective in Baton Rouge, for help in finding my children. He did some research and, after some time, called me to say, "Your children are not in this country, but I don't know where they are."

He explained that he was convinced of this because their trail stopped abruptly and went cold.

I was shocked. We didn't travel overseas, other than when John was in the military and we were stationed in Germany. My cousin's summation didn't make any sense to me, but I believed him.

Next, I hired a private detective in Tacoma. I sent him a $200 down payment. He never returned my calls after he received the money. On my own I found out that John had been seen by people who said he told them different stories. He told some of them the children were in Canada. He told others the children were around the corner. His other story was that the children were in the islands. People reported seeing John, but no one reported seeing my children; that was impossible. I concluded that John had already methodically convinced these people to help him keep the children from me.

One evening at Phoebe's House, I was watching television, but not really seeing it. I was thinking. I was amazed that I was actually in such a place. I looked at the commercials and remembered the life I used to have. I never thought I would be homeless. I never thought John would treat me the way he was treating me. But people change and I have to deal with it, I thought. Allah would not put any more on me than I could stand. I was being patient and steadfast. I prayed: "Please forgive me for my transgressions. I will not participate in the pity party that Satan wants me to. I am strong, I am loved, and Allah will bless me with the strength I need to see me through to the end."

Then I saw a commercial about a paralegal course you could take by mail. Something in my head clicked: I needed to learn about the law and to find out how to get my children back. The course was only five dollars; I ordered it. When the materials came a few weeks later, I was so excited that I told everyone about the course. I read all of the introduction material, but then figured out I needed to put it aside and calm down before continuing. I decided I would study every morning from 10 a.m. to 11 a.m. As I worked my way through the course, I realized that I was on the path to getting my children back.

I made straight A's in my correspondence course, so I was aware of the proper procedures to follow to get a divorce, to get full custody of my children, and to get a writ of habeas corpus. I asked the Phoebe's House staff to take me to the courthouse with them whenever they went, so I could work on my case. I went so often that people at the courthouse began asking me if I was a lawyer. The YWCA gave the residents at Phoebe's House vouchers to get clothes and I always got suits and dresses to wear to court.

I went to my first domestic violence class at the YWCA. The counselor called me courageous because of how I was handling my situation. In class, I was thinking to myself, *Why is Allah sending me through this? Is it for me to open a house later? Is it to help women and children with legal aid, food, clothing, and shelter? Is it to be a counselor or legal aid person?*

There were so many questions and no answers. If Allah was supplying the questions, He would supply the answers. I told the YWCA that I was taking paralegal classes and they allowed me to intern in their legal department. A staff member dropped me off every morning. Not wearing my Muslim clothing gave me a level of comfort; I didn't think John would recognize me from afar without them.

I continued my domestic violence training and became a certified advocate. It was an important stepping stone toward my new dream of opening a domestic violence home for women and children. I believed this was what Allah wanted me to do.

One afternoon I came home from class to find my latest grade for my paralegal course. It was an "A." I felt very proud. I was getting my self-esteem back.

I didn't catch the bus, drive, or go walking. I only left the house if someone took me. I felt I had some control over how much I exposed myself if I was a passenger. I worked in the Y's legal department as an advocate, which meant I answered phone calls from victims, entered their names into a database, and occasionally went to court with them as their advocate.

While I did this work for clients, I did my own papers, too. I filed a new parenting plan and went to court for the hearing about custody. I dressed in a black skirt and a black-and-white blazer. I was nervous and excited; I thought everything was going to go in my favor. I had studied and prepared for this day and I was confident. I stated my case and then the commissioner said there was nothing in my file to show that John had been served to appear in court. He dismissed the case because of this, informing me that I could start the process over but I had to make sure John was served.

I thanked the commissioner. I held up my head as I walked out. I was not going to break down in public. But when I got home, I told the staff what had happened and went to my room. I said my evening prayers and broke into tears on my prayer rug. I realized God was in control, but I cried for two hours until I was emotionally drained. I was depressed. I was trying to have faith but I had to cry to get out my pain. In order for me to be well, I had to work through my emotions. Suppressing them only made me sick. So I cried myself to sleep.

I had to do something. I went to the Yellow Pages and looked at private investigators. I called one, a guy named Bob Crow. We made an appointment and he came to the house. Since he was an investigator, he was allowed to come in. Otherwise, adult male personal visitors were prohibited. At the meeting, he said that the prosecutor didn't believe my case should be upgraded from civil to criminal. I wanted to hire Bob, but he said he was expensive and I shouldn't pay for a service that I should be getting from the police for free. So he left and I started crying. The other women in the house tried to reassure me that things were working in my favor, but I couldn't stop crying.

I missed my children and I wanted them back with me. The staff tried to console me. But at different times throughout that day I burst into tears. The counselors tried talking to me. My roommate, Theresa, cried with me while trying to console me. "I just want my children," I kept saying to everyone.

Later, when I had gotten through this part of the struggle, Theresa told me she thought I was going to snap that day. A lot of the ladies felt that way; they kept coming to my room to check on me. Meanwhile, I said my prayers and went to bed crying.

A month later, I re-filed my papers and told the court I was not able to find John. This time the commissioner awarded me legal custody of my children. One of the ladies from the house was in court with me. When the commissioner said, "You have been awarded full custody of the children," and hit the gavel, I saw the law clerk wink at me.

Again, I walked out of the courtroom with my head held high, giving no hint of my emotions. I walked past people I noticed were smiling at me. Heather, the woman who had accompanied me to court, rushed out of the courtroom and hugged me. I went straight to the bathroom and started crying with joy. When I got back to the house and told the women what had happened, everyone was happy for me.

The next day I filed a "writ of habeas corpus" to try to locate my children. A warrant was issued to pick them up. I already had a restraining order to keep John from coming near me or the children. I did all this so that the paperwork would be in place once the children were located. I requested from the court that I be allowed to put a notice in the newspaper to notify John that I was starting divorce proceedings. They granted my request. I had to wait 90 days before I could file for a divorce.

Later that day I was saying my noon prayers when Shirley came up to tell me there was a phone call for me. I asked Allah to forgive me for leaving my prayers and I went to the phone. It was Deputy Ward, an officer who called every month to find out if I had located my children. He said the Gig Harbor police had stopped John but released him since they did not have any warrants on him and were not aware of my new custody decree. John had slipped away again because my custody order had not been entered into the computers.

I was angry and frustrated. How could he continue to slip away? Why was it so difficult to get him and bring my children back?

On October 6, 2000, at 9:30 a.m., the court granted my divorce from John. I felt free from his grip in one way but still in his grip in another. While I was at the courthouse, Cindy, the facilitator, told me about a new ruling in Washington State that allowed a victim of domestic violence who feared for her life to remove the children from the state without getting the permission of the abuser. With the help of the YWCA, I filed the necessary paperwork to be able to do this. Between my paralegal courses and learning by doing, I became pretty comfortable with working my way through the court system.

The other women in Phoebe's House took notice and, occasionally, they asked me to look over paperwork and advise them. I accompanied some of them to the courtroom and showed them what they needed to do. The more I did this, the more confident I became. The women told me I should become a counselor.

I was the first resident chosen to participate in a program that let residents work with the staff and get paid. I started helping out in the office on the evening shift and eventually began working as the executive secretary when she was out.

Meanwhile, there were several incidents at Phoebe's House that confirmed my suspicion that John was looking for me and might even have an idea where I was. People in the house could recognize him; they had seen my photo of him and the children. One day one of the women saw him standing in the parking lot across the street.

Another time, someone from the outside called the fire department and reported a fire in Phoebe's House. It was at night, and when the fire department arrived, they put a spotlight on the front door of the house and ordered everyone to evacuate. I panicked. I told the staff I couldn't go out. Thank goodness, one staff member told me to get a blanket and hide under a bed. Like me, she honestly believed John was behind that phone call.

On another day, I was upstairs cleaning when I saw a truck outside. I recognized it as the truck John used to drive sometimes. I ran downstairs and hid under a desk in the office. Some staff members had to pull me out.

"Are you *that* afraid?" one of them asked.

"Yes, I am, and you all aren't taking me seriously," I said.

Shortly after the fire incident I was in my therapy session when we began discussing anger and abandonment. I expressed to my counselor that I was angry with John for giving up on our dream. I started crying, which surprised me. I was feeling anger, abandonment, betrayal and loneliness, a flood of emotions.

"What are you thinking?" the counselor asked.

"All the things I needed John to be, he wasn't any of it. He was not even the father for our children that I wanted and needed him to be. The reality about John is that he's a jealous, envious, self-centered, abusive, backstabbing, low self-esteem, controlling man that I no longer want in my life."

"Where do you think your abandonment issues are coming from?"

"My abandonment issues come into play with all the people that knew us and did nothing for me. They were not supportive and left me to die by John's hands."

Then I cried harder.

The counselor told me it was a good session. "You are learning to let go. Your expectations were not met and you have a right to be angry," she said.

My grief for my children was intensified by my disappointment in people who did not believe me when I said John was going to kill me. Some people blamed me for my predicament. Some said that it was my fault since I let John walk all over me; others said it was my fault since I didn't let him walk over me enough! Some people said I should have been tougher and should not have allowed him to take the children on weekends; others said I should go back to him and give him one more chance. Everyone had a different idea about how I had brought this on myself and what I should be doing.

I was depressed. I was trying to hide it but I was not successful. I finally told her what was going on with me; that I was frustrated with people who claimed they wanted to help me but didn't follow through.

"Just say what you mean and mean what you say," I said. "I've had so many inconsistencies in my life. No one knows how to keep their word."

Praise God that I strive hard to do this right, I thought. Since the Qur'an says, "Why do you say that which you do not, it is most hateful to Allah?" So, I went upstairs and told my dark secret.

"I am afraid that my children have forgotten about me," I said. "I really worry about that."

On another day, I listened to the other women talk in domestic violence class. I recognized their pain, but I felt extremely happy that I had made it through the external pain they were speaking of. My journey was focused on me preparing for my children emotionally. I wanted to be ready when God returned them to me.

In my journal that day I wrote: *"I've learned so much, being here at Phoebe's House. I've learned so much from my therapist. I've learned to truly take responsibility for my actions. Thank God for the teachings of the Honorable Elijah Muhammad as taught to us by the Honorable Minister Louis Farrakhan. I have never understood God as much as I do now. I've never loved God as much as I do now. I truly believe that I was on the wrong path before coming into the Nation of Islam. No one can take me off this path. I am here by Allah seeing something within me."*

The weekends were the hardest. I felt vulnerable. When Fridays came it seemed to me everyone was enjoying their lives and I was left there in the shelter. I prayed, "Oh Allah, please allow John Jr., Salena, and Taalibah to continue in their worship of You. Please allow John to give them that. Keep my children safe from harm and keep their mental health intact. Please allow them to remember how much I love them, in spite of what John is telling them. Help me to find them. It will happen in Your time, Allah. And as the Qur'an says, 'When it does happen, it will seem as if I've only tarried for a day.' Bless me to be a witness for You and appreciate the little things You do for me. Help me continue to submit my will to do Your will."

My time at Phoebe's House allowed me to reflect on exactly what had happened and to come to peace with what I did or didn't do. I felt ashamed of my condition. And I had not tapped into the emotion of shame enough to understand why I felt this way or where it came from. I had worked through all my other emotions—guilt, betrayal and abandonment—which was hard work. I didn't know I had so many layers of pain. I found out more and more about myself. Phoebe's House gave me the space and time to become more committed to my spiritual practice. I learned that I needed to become still and be patient. I learned that I needed to increase my faith and stay in the word of God. I turned more and more to Allah for guidance and wisdom.

I was sitting in my room on January 17, 2001, when I realized it was my son's birthday. I began crying and singing happy birthday to him. He was eleven years old that day. I wondered if I would miss Salena's birthday, too, February 1, and perhaps Taalibah's birthday, May 1st. The thoughts became so overwhelming. I had to start thinking only in the moment. I had to catch myself before I spiraled into a depression. I would enjoy the day, since it was Lil' John's special day.

After I had been at the house for seven months, my sister called to say my mother was ill and that she needed help taking care of her. Suddenly, I had to choose between my mother and my children. I had to leave the one place my children might come back to. I was worried about my mother, but I was also comforted; all my legal paperwork was in order. There was nothing else I could do in Tacoma, so I decided to leave to take care of my mother. I thought: *Why are these life-altering decisions coming at me so fast? My mother or my children... What a decision to have to make.*

The women of the house, who had become my sisters, did not want me to leave. I had developed a bond with them that neither time nor distance would ever destroy. It was a special and hard time for me, leaving the known for the unknown.

I left Phoebe's House on January 20, 2001. It was a bittersweet departure. For years afterward I would look back at my stay and some of the months were blurry. The days were like video, shot by a camera, held by the unsteadiness of my life. I recalled receiving so much there and I had some memory of giving what I could. My memory was helped by an email I received from my caseworker at that time, after I asked her to write me a note about my stay:

*Hi Phoebe,*

*Girl, once you got your strength back, you went online and enrolled in paralegal courses, you did your divorce, you got the lists of all of the schools around Washington State, stuffed envelopes and mailed them everywhere looking for your babies. It breaks my heart, just thinking about everything, but you held on. I know you had your moments up in your room; I think that even made you stronger, the unconditional love and faith that you have in God, who heard and answered your prayers. You became resident staff; you were soooo inspirational to the clients. They all loved and had much respect for you. I believe you started a lot of them journaling each day. When Phoebe's House was going through hard times and Mrs. East was out ill for a long period of time that year, especially during the holidays, it was you, Red, and I think Pat, that helped keep things going. You put on your sunglasses and disguised yourself to speak to the City Council at the public meeting downtown. I wish I had that tape. You helped me more than you know, even with what you were going through. You have such a kind and peaceful spirit. Even though I was a case manager, we could still talk about any and everything. While you were doing your classes, I remember your grades were always good and you started working at the YWCA as an advocate using my maiden name, Rozell. (SMILE) I LOVE you, Phoebe. You are stronger than you know. Even looking at the picture of you passing out the gifts during Christmas, you didn't care much about yourself. It just made you happy seeing them so happy.*

*God Bless You and Your Family,*

*Doris*

On the day I left Phoebe's House, seventeen women—every person except the one who had to stay behind to watch the house—accompanied me to the airport. It was a parade of affection.

On the way to the gate, an elderly white woman, floored by the sight of such a goodbye committee, asked me, "Are you someone special?"

"No, ma'am," I said.

"Then why are all these people with you?" she asked.

I said the first thing that came to my mind. "I guess because they love me."

We hugged and wiped tears. I tried to smile as I waved to them for the last time. On the plane, I couldn't stop crying. I was leaving the city that had been home to me and my children for six years. How would they find me now?

I felt a level of safety at my sister's. John did not know my brother-in-law's last name, nor did he know where they lived, so I believed he couldn't easily find me. I also felt blessed that my sister and brother-in-law were open-hearted enough to offer me a home. My mother did not know I was coming, so she was surprised. She was sick with pneumonia, but her health had also been compromised by the broken heart she suffered from the children being taken by John. When I walked into her bedroom, she looked surprised to see me and, at the same time, disappointed since she did not see the children behind me.

She told me she was glad to see me and then she asked, "Where are the children?"

"I don't know. I'm still trying to find them," I said. She hugged me. I was happy to see her and felt disappointed I did not have what she wanted the most...my children.

My friends Isa and Olivia continued to correspond with me. Isa sent e-mails telling me that John had called her trying to find out where I was. She tried to get him to tell her where the children were, but he wouldn't. John seemed to find it easy to talk with Isa. He didn't know she knew where I was. If he found out, he would look at it as a sign of betrayal. I asked her to be careful when dealing with him.

Meanwhile, John threatened Olivia; he believed she was the reason I asked for a divorce. He didn't think I could come to that conclusion on my own, but that I needed someone else to tell me. He believed that since I was attractive, I was not smart. He thought I was pretty and stupid. I warned my friends to be careful and that John knew how to tap phones.

In Maryland, I found work as an administrative assistant through a temporary agency. I used some of my salary to continue to try to find my children, saving to hire another private investigator.

Time kept passing. It was February 1st and I was missing Salena's birthday. She was turning nine years old that day. I had to do something so I wouldn't spiral into a depression. It was really a lot of work, handling all of my emotions alone. I sought refuge in Allah. Praying calmed my spirit. I prayed for peace within myself.

I wrote letters to a variety of public officials—from governors to the Department of Social Services. I wrote to television shows like *The Oprah Winfrey Show* and *The Montel Williams Show*, but I didn't send the letters. I could not take the chance of John finding me through some fluke of my own. I had to keep my location a secret. I had to continue searching under the radar.

I was upset that I got so little support from the police in Washington State. A detective at the Tacoma Police Department told me that he would put John in the National Crime Information Center (NCIC) and put my children in the database of the National Center for Missing & Exploited Children. But I found out later that he didn't.

I called the FBI in Washington, D.C. to report my children being kidnapped and taken out of the country. An agent named Jensen Jordan came to my home. I told him about John's threats and that he had kidnapped my children. I told him my cousin, a private investigator, had tried to locate John and the children and concluded they were out of the country. I gave him copies of my divorce decree, writ of habeas corpus, pictures of John and my children. He took the paperwork and told me he would be in touch. Weeks later, I received a letter from him stating that since this was an open case, I needed to go back to Seattle, and file a report that the children were missing. However, I called the FBI in Seattle as he suggested. The FBI agent in Seattle, Washington had another plan. He suggested that I fly back to Tacoma. He said, "Ms. Muhammad, since we know he's looking for you, we can put you in the middle of a parking lot, as a decoy so we can lure him out."

"Excuse me; you don't understand," I told him. "This is going to be a head shot. HE IS GOING TO SHOOT ME IN THE HEAD! By the time you figure out where the bullet came from, I will be dead and where will my children be."

"Well, Ms. Muhammad, we're only trying to help you out," he said.

I hung up the phone in amazement. How in the world was this happening? What is he thinking? I wondered. Why is it difficult for me to get help?

Meanwhile, I worried about John doing something purposefully to hurt the children. I worried about where they were and whether they were being taken care of. I worried about my little girls' safety and I worried about my son's asthma. I worried about what kind of ideas John was putting in their heads. I even thought that because he hated me so much, he would wait until the children were asleep and shoot them in the head to punish me for not coming back to him. It had happened before to other victims' children. Some-times it felt like I wasn't a mother, that I didn't have children at all; I had such a yearning for them but they weren't around. I missed them so much.

I dreamed about them many nights. One particular dream seemed so real that when I woke up, I thought they were beside me. I thought I was losing my mind. Since they were so young, I worried that they would not remember me. My head was full of questions. Do they know I'm looking for them? Are they scared? Is John really taking care of them? So many questions and no answers. I prayed every night for God to return them to me with sound minds and bodies. I prayed every night for patience, for strength, for peace of mind, for joy even in the midst of it all.

Time would not stand still. The days without my children continued one after another until it was May 1, Taalibah's birthday. She turned eight years old that day—and I missed it.

# CHAPTER TWELVE:
## MY CHILDREN ARE SAFE

E arlier in the week of August 2001, I had received a phone call from Mrs. East, the executive director of Phoebe's House. She had informed me that my children might have been found in Bellingham, Washington. She gave me a fax number to the Bellingham police department and asked me to fax all my legal paperwork to them. She told me to call and ask for Detective McCarthy and talk with him about my children. I called him and explained the situation. He stated he had received the faxed paperwork. He indicated to me that they were on the Canadian border, and once John crossed the border, it would be virtually impossible to get my children back. He asked me to fax him pictures of the children as well. He would call me once everything had transpired. I didn't mention this to anyone. I was so nervous and excited at the same time.

John had gone to social services requesting food stamps and cash in Bellingham, Washington. It is an automatic red flag for a man to come into social services to request those items. He had our children under assumed names; John Jr. was "John Thomas," Salena was "Theresa," and Taalibah was "Lisa." He had to give them their legal names to get the assistance requested. They did a cross check and found the children had already been in the system and flagged as kidnaped because I had been receiving assistance and had them entered into the system as that. They stalled John by telling him to come back th next day for the food stamps and cash. The person taking the information informed the authorities of what had occurred.

It was 4:35 p.m., August 31, 2001. I was sitting at my sister's house in Maryand and writing in my journal when the phone rang. I answered. It was Detective McCarthy. He said the words I had waited eighteen months to hear: "Ms. Muhammad, we've got your children."

I began screaming. My brother-in-law came downstairs to find out what the problem was. I said, "They got my children! They got my children!"

At that moment, I was incapable of saying anything else. All I could do was scream, so I handed the phone to my brother-in-law. "Can you talk to him?!"

I hollered and ran throughout the house, then up and down the stairs, crying every step of the way until my brother-in-law called me.

"Mildred, the detective wants to talk to you," he said.

When I took the phone, I heard the detective laughing. "Ms. Muhammad, would you like to talk to your children?"

I tried to take a deep breath. "Okay," I responded, but honestly, I was scared. I didn't know if the children would remember me or even recognize my voice. I didn't know if they wanted to talk to me.

Taalibah got on the phone first. "Hi, Mommy," she said.

It was like a dream. I couldn't speak. I hadn't heard her voice in eighteen months.

"How are you doing?" she asked.

"I'm good," I said.

"Is Grandma there?"

"No," I said, figuring I would tell them later that their grandma had moved to Texas to live with my older sister.

"You want to talk to my sister?" Taalibah asked. I said yes and she passed the phone to Salena.

"Hi, Mommy, this is Salena. Guess what?"

"What, honey?"

"I'm nine years old."

"I know that, honey," I said.

"What are you doing?"

"Eating cheese pizza," she said.

She sounded as happy as the little girl I remembered.

The detective got back on the phone. "Your son doesn't want to speak to you."

"That's okay. Is he well?" I asked.

"He's well, *physically*," the detective said.

"Well, what's the next step," I said, alluding to the mental healing we all needed, which would take time.

"They're keeping a close eye on your son. He has the potential of running away," he said.

Then the detective told me that I had to return to Tacoma, Washington as soon as possible for an emergency custody hearing.

"They'll put the children in child protective services until the judge decides who gets them," he explained.

I had to move fast. But I didn't have the kind of money it was going to take to buy a last-minute plane ticket, so I got online and told my friends that my children had been found and I needed to raise money to go to Tacoma. People were generous, and before the night was over, I had raised enough money for my ticket.

I left on Labor Day. I cried all the way to the airport and then I continued crying on the plane. I was excited—and nervous. I was finally going to see my children's faces. Later that same day, I arrived at Sea-Tac Airport in Seattle.

The next day I was in Tacoma, heading to court for the emergency custody hearing. It was September 4, 2001. I went to court accompanied by one attorney—Anita, the lead attorney at the YWCA, and Heather, the advocate from YWCA. Marisol, the paralegal from the "Y," and my friend, Isa, were also with me.

When we arrived at the courthouse, the substation was on the right just past the front door. I was looking around for John; he was going to be there. I didn't know from which area he would be coming from, but I had my eyes and ears open. I was sitting in the substation when I looked up and spotted John at the pay phones across the hall. I panicked. I was petrified. I could barely speak but I managed to tell Isa.

"Switch places with me so he can't see you," she said.

I saw Deputy Ward, an officer that had searched hard for my children. He went over to John—and then when I looked again, John was gone. We decided to head upstairs to the courtroom to wait on the proceedings to start.

As soon as we entered, I scanned the room and saw John sitting in the back. He hadn't spotted me yet. I was so frightened, I thought my knees were going to buckle.

I squeezed Marisol's hand. "He's here. He's here," I uttered.

"Where?" she asked.

I motioned in his direction, so as not to be noticed.

"Don't look," she whispered. I said, "You don't understand, he can move fast enough to come up here and snap my neck."

We all went to the front row and sat down. I was shaking. I sat in the middle of Heather and Marisol now, squeezing both of their hands. John was seated at the back.

"It's okay. It's okay," Marisol said.

I appreciated her attempt to comfort me, but my mind kept saying, "They don't know what I know." I wanted to look back at John to make sure he wasn't headed toward me, but I willed myself to keep my eyes up front. There was only one security guard in the courtroom and he was too far away for my comfort. My hands sweated. My legs trembled.

The court reporter called our names. My advocate, Heather, and I went first, then John, who didn't have an attorney, followed. We stood before the judge. While we were standing, my thoughts turned to thinking about getting past John to get to my side of the bench. I couldn't exit without going past him. I felt boxed in. My heart raced, thumping madly.

My legs shook so hard I thought people would hear them knocking. Actually, I shook all over. I had to move around to make it look like I was fidgeting; I did not want John to see me shaking. The only thing separating John from me was Heather, who stood between us.

"This is an emergency custody hearing. We are here to decide where the children of John and Mildred Williams will reside," the judge said.

"Judge, what is going on?" John asked.

He was talking in the voice that I had heard so many times over the years; the sweet, innocent voice that convinces people he does not know what is happening when he knows exactly what is going on.

"We are only here to decide who will have custody of the children," the judge said.

"Judge, I don't understand," John said again. "She told me to take the children because she didn't want them anymore. She knew where I was. She could've contacted me at any time."

I couldn't believe he had said that. But I shouldn't have been surprised at all. Why would I expect him to be honest now?

The judge explained to John that I had obtained a writ of habeas corpus to have the children picked up when they were found.

"The court will decide today who will have custody of the children," he said. "Mrs. Williams has completed all of the necessary paperwork pro se and it is in perfect order."

"Are you telling me I'm not going to see my children again, Judge?" John asked.

"Mr. Williams, you have to file your paperwork because the only thing we are here to decide today is who gets the children and, according to the paperwork, I am awarding custody of the children to Mrs. Williams," the judge responded.

The judge told John to sign the document from the clerk to release the children to me. John looked extremely angry; however, he signed the paper. And it was over. When it was time to leave I didn't want to pass in front of John. So, I waited until he left the courtroom. I also hid my emotions; I didn't want to do anything to upset him. He glared at me and walked out of the courtroom.

I jumped up and down and ran over to the other women who had come with me. We hugged each other. I was so happy. I was laughing and crying. We were all laughing and jumping up and down. Heather and Marisol left the courtroom first. Anita, Isa, and I left the courtroom and went into the hallway.

While in the hallway, Anita called the social worker for the State of Washington Child Protective Services (CPS) to let them know I was awarded the children and to get directions to where we were to meet them. The women surrounded me as we stood in the hallway but while we were talking, I had a strange feeling. I looked over my right shoulder and saw John rushing toward me. He was staring straight at me and walking real fast, like he was coming to get me. I took off in a full sprint down the hall, losing my shoes along the way. Anita and Isa saw me running, looked back and saw John, and took off running behind me. When we got to the end of the hall, we stopped, but we peeped around the corner.

He saw me and he turned to mouth the words, "Got cha."

Anita and Isa said, "Did you see that?"

"Yes," I said. "Don't let him kill me, don't let him kill me," I continued to say. I was terrified.

His expression was so menacing that Isa called her daughter and told her to lock the windows and doors and not to let anyone in the house. Isa knew John. She knew that he felt betrayed by her when he saw her in court with me. She also knew that his wrath could easily extend to her.

"Okay, that's it," said Anita. "You're leaving Tacoma tonight. We have to get you out of here."

We took the stairs down to the sheriff's lounge and asked if there was another way out of the building, perhaps through their offices.

"Only the front door," someone informed us.

We were all scared. We watched everything, carefully, and walked very fast to the car and got in.

Marisol and Anita took me to the Social Services office in Tacoma because we were told that that was where the children were being held. Isa followed in her car. We went to the wrong side of the building at first. Anita called for more directions. I was anxious. As we pulled up, I saw a man and a boy get out of a car. At first I didn't recognize Lil' John. He was so beautiful. He was taller than he was when I last saw him. He was skinny and he stared at me hard. I ran to him and hugged him. He did not hug me back. He just looked at me. I laughed and cried.

"I've been searching for you for such a very long time," I said.

John had his pants sagging and even though I was crying, and happy to see him, I pulled them up and said, "This isn't going to be an issue, is it?"

He smiled and shook his head.

"Where are Salena and Taalibah?" I asked.

Right then, I heard two high-pitched voices scream, "Mommy!" I looked at the building and saw my girls running out of the door toward me. I was crying so hard. I tried to see them, but I couldn't clearly see through the tears. I wiped my face and scanned the area. The employees of Social Services were watching while on break. I thought: *If they realized that they were witnessing the return of children to their mother after eighteen months, they probably would have been crying, too.*

In tears, Isa came over and told the children how long I had been looking for them. The girls cried and both kept saying, "We missed you, Mommy. We missed you."

I hugged them and cried. "I love you," I said.

"We love you, too, Mommy!" the girls screamed.

We hurried to get into the car. We wanted to get to the shelter at the "Y" before John found us. I could not help but notice that Lil' John did not state that he loved me; that was cause for concern.

In the car Taalibah said, "Mommy, Daddy said he was looking for you and couldn't find you."

Now I was beginning to understand how John had manipulated the children. I spoke directly to them. "Can I ask a question?"

"Yes, ma'am," they answered. I could see they were hanging on to my every word. "If your dad had wanted me to find you, why did he change your names?"

They looked at me and then at each other. I could see the thinking going on inside of their heads. They were quiet for the rest of the ride. They sat back and stared at me. I imagined that, to them, I had also changed a lot.

We went to the YWCA shelter. As soon as I got there, I called my mom.

"Mom, I got 'em!" I said into the phone.

She started crying.

"Hold on," I said.

I told Taalibah her grandmother was on the phone and she smiled from ear to ear and jumped up clapping.

"Hey, Grandma. It's Taalibah," she said.

After Taalibah finished, Salena spoke to her grandmother, and then John reached for the phone. When they finished talking to her, I spoke to my mom again.

"I'm proud of you," my mother said to me, and I beamed even more than the children.

I explained to Mom that we had to leave Washington quickly and had to go and make arrangements.

I turned my attention to the children's hygiene. I made sure they took a shower and I washed their hair. They had old suitcases with metal fasteners and when I popped them open, I found clothes that told me the children had lived on the run. Their clothes were too little; their shoes were too big. They had more toothbrushes, toothpaste, and dental floss than they could possibly have needed.

Some of the ladies in the shelter saw me looking at the children's bags and they asked me what had happened. I told them my story and they started yelling, "You go, girl! You go, girl! She found her babies! I know that's right!"

Once the children were clean, I let them call three of their friends that would want to know they were safe. One friend, Anthony, was only ten when the children left. When his school had a contest to sell candy, he won a television set. But he took the TV back to the school and asked for the money so he could give me the money to help get the children back. I called a few other people to let them know that I had gotten the children back. I called Shirley, my friend who worked at a travel agency. She asked how I was going to pay for the tickets and I told her other people had promised to help. Even though I didn't have the money at that time, she booked me on a flight into Baltimore-Washington International that same night.

The "Y" staff allowed me to go through the clothing closet to get clothes for the children. There was a birthday pizza party going on for one of the residents and they let us join them and eat. Late that night, it was time for us to go. We went through the basement, around the swimming pool, through the clothing closet to a door that opened to the street where a car was waiting for us. The executive director of Phoebe's House, Mrs. East, was driving and Isa was with her. It was the first time Mrs. East had met my children. As we rode, she said, "Mildred, I'm proud of you."

It was ironic to me that I was flying out of the airport called Sea-Tac late at night. I had flown into that airport when I came to join John to start our life together and now I was using it to flee from him to save my life.

When we arrived at the airport, Isa explained our situation to the airport security guards and they took us upstairs to their office until it was time for our flight to leave. They gave the children soda and chips and brought them coloring books, crayons, and games. I laughed and joked with the children. Taalibah sat in my lap the entire time. She would not let me get far away from her.

It was a good time for us to get to know each other, while playing. We stayed in the office until the pilot from the airline called and said it was time to board. The two security guards walked us down to the flight and an attendant took us to the back of the plane. It was a huge plane, but there were only a few passengers. We went to the back. I did not know where to sit. Should I sit in the middle or near the window? I wanted all of my children around me, within touching distance. I sat down with Taalibah next to me at the window and John and Salena behind me.

As the plane was backing up, Salena asked if she could hold my hand.

"Yes, honey," I said, putting my hand through the seat to hold hers.

"Mommy, can I tell you something?" she asked.

"Yes, Sweetie, what is it?"

She started crying between her words. "Mommy, I missed you so much. I prayed and I prayed that you would come to get us. Please, Mommy, don't go away again."

Taalibah started crying, too, and holding onto my shoulder. John was silent, just staring straight ahead. I wanted to cry, but I didn't. The children were relying on me for strength.

"Salena," I said. "I will try my best, Insha'Allah, for us not to be separated by force again. I give you my word. Okay?"

"Okay," she whimpered.

I asked her to stop crying.

"Okay, Mommy," she said.

She held my hand throughout the flight. Then it was my time to cry. I cried quiet tears of joy and realized that, for the first time in months, I felt alive again.

I watched over the children for the entire trip. It was my opportunity to study them. At first, every time I moved, Taalibah and Salena woke up; they were still holding onto my hands. But after they sank into a deep sleep, I was free to move and I stood several times so I could have a view of all of them. While we flew to our new life, I studied the peaceful faces of my children. I was amazed to see how much they had changed. They had gotten older without me watching. I was thankful for sameness, such as the way Salena still slept with her eyes half-open, the way she had done before she left me. John would snore and Taalibah would sleep quietly.

I thanked God for returning them to me. I didn't sleep. I needed to stay awake to protect my babies.

When we arrived at BWI, it was morning. We waited for my sister Adele to pick us up. It was her first time seeing them and their first time seeing her. We picked up our luggage and headed for the car. I sat in the back with them. It was a tight squeeze—and I enjoyed it.

# CHAPTER THIRTEEN:
## REALITY CHECK

W e arrived in Maryland on September 5, 2001. The children spent their first few days at home, staring at me a lot. We talked about what had happened. I told them their dad kidnapped them. For the first time, they understood that they had been kidnapped.

I showed them the website that I had made, with their photos and descriptions of them on it. I showed them the different responses I had gotten from people who were helping me find them. As they put these details together, they understood clearly, for the first time, that their father had essentially stolen them from me.

They were not the same children who had left me eighteen months earlier. They were scared. They sat on the sofa or in a chair and followed me with their eyes. If I left the room, then one of them—as if they designated a person—came to see where I was. That person didn't necessarily come into my space, but sat as a lookout, watching my movements. We ate dinner together, which was something they were not used to doing. They explained to me that each of them ate at different times, whenever they wanted to, and they wanted to continue that practice.

"No. We'll have meals together like a family," I said firmly. "We're going to do things together."

This was what we used to do, but the disarray that was their life for so many months had erased the memory of our together times. I spent my days reintroducing them to how we used to do things as a family.

I took them shopping for clothes; the clothes they returned with were not presentable. The YWCA had given me a few items that would last a while, but they needed more. Salena still proved to be my little helper. She helped me cook and clean. She was the first to let down the barrier that time and myths had built between us.

My children, who used to be active, outgoing, playful, and inquisitive were now very, very quiet.

"How are you doing?" I would ask them.

"Good," would be the reply. They did not follow with the customary, "How are you doing?" When we went out, they stayed close to me and seemed shy. When I went to the bathroom, they stood outside the bathroom door to make sure I came out. I stepped out of the bathroom many times to find them waiting and watching. As soon as they saw me, they would leave to do something else.

It hurt me to see them going through so much emotional pain and mental anguish. All I wanted to do was to gently nudge them through it—to be encouraging and supportive. I didn't spank them or punish them or force them to tell me what happened to them. I felt the best possibility we all had for healing was for me to keep my heart open; I did not know what they had been through and they were not talking about it. I did not know if John had threatened them and instructed them not to tell me anything about what had happened. They did not talk and I did not ask.

We seemed to be inching along in the right direction, so I didn't seek advice from a professional at first. I didn't have friends that I could ask for advice; I didn't know of anyone else who had gone through this. I prayed and asked God to send people to me who had the experience to help us through this and to allow me to recognize them when these people were present.

On the morning of September 11, 2001, we were all sitting in the living room watching a movie when my sister called, her voice filled with urgency. "Turn on the news," she said.

I stopped the movie and turned on the news, as she requested. I saw the World Trade Center on fire.

"Is this a movie?" I asked.

"No, girl. This is the real thing."

The children were amazed and baffled also.

"Mommy, is that happening right now?" John asked.

"Yes," I replied.

Then, the news switched to a fire at the Pentagon. I was frozen in my seat. In New York, I saw parts of the buildings falling into the streets, people hanging out of the windows, and others running for their lives. Someone had run planes into the buildings, we found out.

As I watched in horror, I thought about how close I had come to being in the section of the Pentagon that was destroyed. I had recently been offered a position there, but I turned it down. I had just gotten my children back and needed to spend time with them. Later, as events unfurled, I thanked God that I had gotten my children before all of the airlines shut down.

That night, I wrote in my journal: *So many people died today. Oh Allah, have mercy on all those people and their families.*

With so much sadness and confusion going on, I was happy my children were not in school yet. Getting them registered was more complicated than normal; we didn't have their birth records or any of the papers they needed. I wasn't even sure that they had attended school while they were away. They hadn't mentioned it and I hadn't asked.

In the D.C. area, everything felt different after 9/11. People seemed more afraid, more guarded. My children were already terrified of losing me and the occurrences of 9/11 made it worse. If I was even five minutes late coming home from work, my daughters panicked.

Then, as the weeks passed and we fell into a routine together, the children became more at ease with me. They even started joking. I cooked and we sat down to eat together, without anyone complaining about the time.

One evening, as we ate, I noticed there was one dinner roll left.

"Does anyone want it?" I asked.

They said no, so I reached for it. I broke it and was putting it in my mouth when John started crying.

"Mommy, you took the last piece of bread," he said.

I felt so bad. "Oh, my babies, I'm sorry."

John laughed. I said, "Oh, it's like that, huh?"

Then we all laughed.

"No more jokes," I said, still smiling about how I had been fooled.

That joke was the ice breaker between us all. I think they relaxed with me once they saw that, instead of getting upset when John played a joke on me, I laughed with them. I was determined to remain open with them, to always keep in the forefront of my mind that I was dealing with children who, without warning, had been taken from what they knew and plopped down in the middle of what they didn't know. And here they were, now, in another place they did not know.

I had to be patient with them and still have boundaries. As gently as I could, I reminded them of the reality we were living.

For example, Taalibah wanted me and her daddy to reunite.

"Mommy, are you and Daddy going to get back together?" she asked.

"Your dad loves all of you very, very much," I said. "But he and I will *never* be together again."

Taalibah looked awfully sad. I wanted to make sure that all of the children understood the situation, so I called a family meeting.

"Taalibah brought up a question that I'm sure both of you are probably thinking about, too," I said to John and Salena. "We need to talk about this."

"What is her question?" John asked.

"Her question is will me and your dad get back together again. Is that something you and Salena are thinking about?"

They both said, "Yes, ma'am."

"Although I understand how important it is for children to want their parents to be together, there is no possible way that your dad and I will ever be together again," I said.

Taalibah cried immediately. John had tears in his eyes.

Salena put her head down, but she also asked, "Why, Mommy?

I spoke as gently, but as firmly as I could. "Number One: I don't trust your dad. Number Two: Your dad has threatened to kill me and I don't know anyone that can love someone who has threatened to kill them. So I have to move forward with my life with you. Your dad and I are divorced. And that is the way it is going to stay."

Tears welled up in their eyes. All three of them cried.

"Any more questions?" I asked gently.

They each said no. And after that day, the question never came up again.

I constantly had to deal with John's dishonesty with the children. I didn't know what he had told them or taught them while they were with him. But I knew what he was capable of. He could mingle truth with falsehood so efficiently that it was almost impossible to know what was real and what wasn't. Often he wanted to appear more important and bigger than he really was, and so he told stories with this exaggeration in them. Sometimes he didn't want people to know what he was doing or thinking so he changed the facts. He was so convincing that even the smartest people had to think long and hard to figure out what he was really saying.

Not only could John lie about anything, but he was also strategic in the words that he used. He wanted to make sure his words had an effect on people. He was precise in his language and this precision helped him convince people that he was telling the truth. The way he spoke impressed people and blinded them to the truth.

I wanted my children to know reality and to be truthful.

"Honesty is an act of trust," I told them.

They had so much to sort out in their heads. They had just realized they were kidnapped, and that I was looking for them. They were dealing with a lot of new information. This is why I figured they were so quiet.

Before my son was taken, he had this get-up-and-go spirit. When he came back he was real laid-back, even lazy. It nearly drove me crazy. He didn't move fast for anybody. If he had to run, he just walked faster. If he had to walk, it was at a snail's pace.

He presented me with my toughest parenting challenge. Prior to him being taken, Lil' John was always up under me. We did a lot of things together. He talked to me about everything.

When he came back, he was distant, which worried me. It seemed as if he was tolerating me, going through the motions of a mother-and-son relationship. But I didn't feel his love for me. He was emotionally detached. I could see the difference in how he treated me and how he treated his sisters. Sometimes he behaved as if he was protecting the girls from me or didn't want them to get close to me.

One evening, when we were in the kitchen, I said, "John, you need to take out the trash."

He was seated at the table and he didn't move.

"John, you need to take out the trash," I repeated.

He didn't move, so I repeated myself again. When he still didn't move, I went over to him. He stood to meet me. He was eleven years old but we stood face-to-face. We were so close now that, if one of us had leaned slightly, we could have kissed

"Who do you think you are talking to?" Lil' John asked.

In a flash, I prayed, "Lord, help me." I was not intimidated. The prayer was to keep me from hurting that boy. I grew up in a household where you said, "Yes, ma'am" and "No, ma'am" and I expected my children to be respectful.

"John, you need to back up and get over there and do what I told you to do," I said.

He stood in place and said, "What did you tell me to do?"

I spoke firmly. "Do I have to repeat myself? Go over there and do it now."

He glared at me, but he got up and took out the trash. When he came back, he said, with sarcasm, "Anything else you need me to do?"

"If I have something, I'll let you know," I said.

He went over and sat back down. I went outside and prayed, "Lord, give me strength."

On another day, John told me he wanted to be with his dad. His words pierced my heart, yet I understood. He thought I was responsible for taking him away from his dad.

"John, I want you to be honest with yourself," I said. "You were with your dad for eighteen months. In all that time, was your dad there for you the way you wanted him to be?"

He looked at me, with tears in his eyes, and said, "No."

"Did you like moving around all the time; not being able to stay in one place or not being able to make friends and have a place to live?" I asked.

"No."

I said "That is what you came from. Do you want that again?"

"No," he said.

"We are going to deal with the truth here—not the way we want it to be, but the way it is. No sugar-coating, no what-ifs; just the truth. If we do that, then we can build our lives upon truth, and falsehood will not play a part in our development."

He agreed.

The girls were the opposite of John. They didn't give me any problems and seemed to do everything they could to help make this transition we were living through smooth and easy. They did what I asked them to do. They helped me in all the ways they could. In fact, they were angry at John for the way he talked to me. I heard them telling him, "If this was Dad, you wouldn't be doing that. Why are you treating Mommy like that?"

They were all trying to learn me and I was trying to learn them. I was thinking: I have three different perspectives and personalities to deal with. They only have one individual to learn: me. I was careful to treat each one of them the same, to be balanced in how I dealt with each of them so no one would feel I had a favorite.

I would go to bed every night, praying and seeking advice. "Lord, am I doing this thing right? Am I putting on the right emotions? Am I firm enough? Am I not firm enough?"

The one thing I had going for me with Lil' John was that he liked to eat. So I figured he would probably show up for meals; he didn't have any place else to go and didn't yet know anybody in Maryland. I didn't think he would run away; he didn't know anything about where he was and, without me, he didn't have any food. As long as I was cooking and had the right snacks, he wasn't going anywhere. At the time, I didn't realize how much food really meant. Months later I would learn that, at times, their father went away on trips, leaving them without enough food to eat.

As my children became accustomed to being with me, they began to trust me with more information about the time they had spent with their dad. We were watching television when a commercial about the Caribbean came on and someone said, "Mommy, that's where we were—in Antigua."

"Was it pretty like that?" I asked.

"No, not where we were," said Taalibah.

"We were on the native side. Way back in the woods," said John. "We didn't have running water. We had to haul water from a pipe."

"You know those gallon milk things. We had to go get those and fill them up before we went to school," Taalibah said.

I just listened.

"Daddy got arrested and was in jail, but he escaped," John said. "He came out and he told us we had to move. That's when we came back to the States."

From the information they dropped here and there, I discovered that John was arrested for illegally falsifying documentation for people coming to the United States. He was in jail for two weeks, but managed to escape. He and the children had to leave in a hurry.

I learned that, when John had traveled from Antigua to the States to look for me, he had left the children with some adults who hit them with wooden spoons when they tried to eat some of the food. The adults knew the children did not have any food and yet they ate without offering to share their food with them.

The more I learned, the angrier I got at John. I hated what he did. I struggled to not hate *him*. I blamed him for the challenges my children now faced. I was trying to help them work through challenges when they should have been carefree and outside playing like regular children. They should not have had to worry about whether they had food or clothes or even someone to play with. He took away their childhood and made them grow up too fast. They went from Washington, where they lived in a nice home with plenty of food, to a country where they had to fight children every other day just because they were from the United States.

We talked to my mother nearly every day. Sometimes I called; sometimes the children called; sometimes Mom called us. I promised the children we would go to Texas to visit her for Christmas. Mom was doing well, in spite of having diabetes, glaucoma, and high blood pressure.

One evening my sister yelled from upstairs. "Mildred! Mildred!"

There was a desperation in her voice that let me know something was wrong—but I didn't expect what I was about to hear. She was on the stairs when I got up.

"Mildred, Momma's dead," she said.

"What?" I couldn't believe what I was hearing.

I was emotionally numb. My mother had been in bad health for some time, but I still didn't expect her to die. As I faced the reality of the moment, I had one overwhelming thought: Momma never had a chance to see the children.

My sister and I sat up all night, talking and crying. She went back to her room. I decided that I would stay awake and tell the children when they woke up.

John awakened first. I told him in the kitchen. He put his head down and rubbed his face. He didn't say anything. Taalibah woke up next. I told her and she cried a little. I was expecting more from her. Salena was last and when I told her, I wasn't expecting her response. While crying, she said, "She was supposed to wait for us, Mommy."

We made arrangements to go to the funeral and I kept my emotions in check so I wouldn't upset the children. But, later that week, I drove to the store and, on my way home, I started thinking about my mother and I could feel the tears coming. I went to my favorite park, rolled up the windows—and finally, I cried uncontrollably. At times, I screamed out my grief. I don't know how long I sat there, but I stayed until I was too weak to cry any more. Then I drove home.

We flew to Fort Worth. I had gone to talk to my minister before leaving. He listened and then he told me we only have a certain amount of time to grieve and after that, we have to get up and go to work. I remembered Joshua after Moses died. And the Lord said to Joshua, "Have I not commanded you to be strong and of a good courage."

So I dealt with all of my grief before the funeral. I grieved over the fact that I would not see my mother again, that she would not be there for any of my children. I grieved for the talks we would no longer have. I grieved for her presence in my life.

By the day of the funeral, I'd had ten days to grieve.

When I saw my mother in the casket, I did not cry. I was looking at her shell. Her spirit was in all of us, I thought. Since I had already grieved, I was able to help my girls when they started to cry. John didn't shed a tear. It was the first time I looked at him and saw that he was trying to protect me, to be strong for me.

If Momma's funeral had been in our hometown of Baton Rouge, Louisiana, a lot of relatives would have been there, but most of them couldn't make it to Texas. I was happy to see that my cousin, who is a minister in Baton Rouge, was there and delivered the eulogy. The choir sang Momma's favorite gospel song, "His Eye is on the Sparrow." Salena and Taalibah cried throughout the service.

When we walked up to view the body, Taalibah said, "Mommy, that's Grandma, right?"

"It's the house her spirit lived in," I said.

This confused Taalibah. "That's *not* Grandma?"

"Yes, that's Grandma. But the spirit that was there has gone," I said.

I'm not sure she understood, but she didn't ask any more questions.

After the service we went to the repast at my sister's house, where my mother had been living. We flew home the next day.

I heard from my advocate friends who had gone to court with me that John had filed a motion to have me brought back to Washington State since he didn't know where I was. I was nervous. It seemed to me that John was able to do whatever he wanted; regardless of the law. Since, at the time, he didn't know where I was, I never received any documents.

Meanwhile, the children adjusted to school. John was in sixth grade, Salena in fourth, and Taalibah in third. The girls made the honor roll. John did okay, though not as well as he used to do in school. He was dealing with an identity crisis, trying to figure out who he was and whether he should be with me or his dad.

That winter, in January, Lil' John had an asthma attack and, though I wanted to take him to the doctor, he repeated what his father had taught him: "Real men don't have asthma."

The asthma attack brought me face-to-face again with my ex-husband's effect on the children. At another time, my son's asthma was so severe that it appeared that he might need hospitalization; nonetheless he resisted treatment, saying again, "Real men don't have asthma." He refused to take the medicine that could possibly save his life. So, the doctor and I came up with a plan. I told the doctor that we were dealing with thoughts in his head that his father put there. We had to come up with a plan to counter those thoughts. The doctor told Lil' John, if he took the medicine for a week and it didn't work, he wouldn't have to take it at all. However, if it *did* work, then he would have to continue the treatment. Lil' John thought it over. He said it was fair, and we moved forward with him taking the medicine. Within the week, the medicine began working. At the end of the week, Lil' John could breathe normally and continues to take his medication.

I had medical issues of my own that required hospitalization; we had so little money that I sometimes had to make a choice as to whether I could take a bus to work or eat lunch. And, of course, as always, I was worried and fearful about John's threats against me. My Seattle lawyer called to tell me that John filed a restraining order against me and that he now had a lawyer. I later learned that, before I had boarded the plane with the children, John had asked the court to stop me from leaving the state, to vacate the default divorce decree, to appoint a parenting investigator, and to enter a new parenting plan. After everything I had gone through, I could not believe that I might end up married to John again. I was also beginning to worry that he would somehow discover where we were living. I still avoided open spaces and checked the tops of buildings. I knew if he found me, it would be a head shot.

Among the new friends the children made was a boy in the neighborhood named Ravaughan. He was the first child to visit me when I moved in. He came up and sat on the porch with me the first time he saw me.

"Do you have children?" he asked.

"Yes," I said.

"Where are they?"

"I don't know," I said, explaining that their father had taken them away.

Ravaughan looked at me with sympathy in his eyes. "I'll be your son until you get your children back," he said.

I was happy to introduce the children to Ravaughan and they quickly became best friends. He showed them around the neighborhood, introduced them to friends, and spent the night at our house. He was more like a member of the family than a friend—and he loved my cooking.

We settled into a comfortable daily routine. The children got up at 6 a.m. and started getting ready for school. I generally spent the morning cooking dinner so they would have something to eat when they got home that afternoon. I watched them catch the school bus, then I left for work. They got home first and let themselves in with their keys. I usually got home about 5:30 in the evening and helped them with their homework. We spent a lot of time laughing and joking and getting to know each other. We watched our favorite television shows and I listened to old school songs. And I proclaimed every Friday pizza and movie night; a tradition that we still have to this day.

One evening, while the music was playing, I started dancing. I was pop lockin', doing a popular dance that involves short, rapid movements of the neck, arms, and legs. The children got excited.

"Hold up, Mom," Lil' John said, laughing. "I didn't know you could do that. Teach me how to do it."

My son stood beside me, watching, and then he tried the steps and was able to do it right the first time. In fact, he took the dance to a whole different level. He put me to shame.

"Teach me!" the girls said.

I did the best I could, first teaching them how to swirl their necks. We must have been quite a sight, laughing, and jerking our bodies around the room.

John joined the school basketball team and we all went to games to cheer him on. I was happy he had found something he loved. His team did so well the first season he played that they were in the state championships. The night of the final game John was nervous and excited and I was thrilled for him. I sat in the bleachers, a proud mama wringing her hands. But John's team lost and as I went down to meet him afterward, I tried to think of the right words.

He was already crying as I approached.

"John, are you okay?" I asked. Then I hugged him and he crumpled, falling on me with all of his weight. It was as if I was the only thing holding him up and stopping him from hitting the floor.

"It's not right, Mom," he said. "People cheated. People cheated."

I could tell from his reaction that he was crying for more than the game. His body shook with sobs.

"I'll never trust people again," he said between his weeping. "They lie. They cheat. You have no say-so on the matter. You get what you get."

"That's not true, John," I said.

"We were supposed to win," he said.

"That's the way you felt. But the other team won," I said, hoping to encourage him to move on and accept the reality of the loss.

"Why do people say things they don't mean?" he asked. "Why do people do things they don't mean?"

His words only confirmed what I had been thinking. He was not simply crying over the basketball game. He was grieving for all of his losses, for the change in his relationship with his father, and for the disappointments this relationship had brought him. I comforted him because I was sure I did not know—and might never know—all of the losses Lil' John was thinking about.

On another night I remembered a time when the children were still away and a terrible feeling had come over me. I thought something bad had happened to one of the children. When I could not shake the feeling, I called Olivia.

"Let's pray and Allah will reveal what happened," she said, before leading me in prayer on the phone. The feeling seemed to leave me and I forgot about it for months.

But on this night, I asked them, "Was there a time around June or July when something happened to one of y'all?"

The children all looked at one another.

"That's when John almost drowned," Salena said.

"Can you tell me about that?" I asked.

"We were at the beach," said Salena. "Dad threw the ball into the water. John went out to get it. He didn't see he was stepping into the deep side. He went down." John said, "I screamed and called Dad and he didn't hear me. I called again. I called a third time and Dad heard me and came out to get me."

My heart was beating hard now, but I tried to speak calmly. "Did Lil' John have to be revived?" I asked.

"No, he was just coughing up water," Salena said.

"Okay," I said. Then I left the room, went outside, and cried. I was crying out of relief for my son's life being spared and how God allowed me to have that feeling. Amazing.

It was almost springtime when I got sick at work one day. I was feeling horrible. I looked in the mirror and noticed I was pale. They made me go home, but I still went to my son's football game. That evening, when I didn't feel any better, I went to the emergency room. They told me I had lost three units of blood, a dangerous amount. With tests, they discovered I had fibroids the size of grapefruits. I had to be hospitalized immediately and given a blood transfusion. I thought *This is my second one. What am I doing wrong for my body to respond this way?*

My sister brought the children to visit me. I was hooked to an IV and I could see the worry on the faces of the children. I tried to assure them that I was fine and would be home soon.

"I want you to be strong. We're going to go on with our plan," I said. "The Lord wouldn't take me away from you after He gave you back to me."

# CHAPTER FOURTEEN:
## "WHEN WAS THE LAST TIME YOU SAW JOHN MUHAMMAD?"

I received an email from Isa that broke my heart. She said her niece, Kenya, had been killed and that Kenya's boyfriend, who had abused her in the past, was a suspect.

It happened when Isa and her daughter went down the street to the store. When they got back, they found Kenya in the middle of the floor, a teakettle still on the stove, and Kenya's baby, crying but fine, upstairs.

We had just celebrated a new year—2002—and I couldn't imagine that Isa already had such tragedy and grief to deal with. The thought of this murder filled my mind for days. It was Lil' John's twelfth birthday.

He thought he wasn't going to get anything because we didn't have much money. He told me he didn't want any gifts or any kind of party. But I could tell that he was only saying that to be considerate. So I decided to surprise him.

When he and the girls came home from school, they saw the house looking the same way they had left it that morning. However, shortly after they arrived, I pulled out a cake, decorated the table, and put out presents, including a stereo.

I called the children into the kitchen and as soon as I saw Lil' John, I led the girls in singing "Happy Birthday." What happened next was a gift to me: I saw a glimpse of my son that I hadn't seen in a long, long time. He was smiling. His face was bright and he looked at me with such tremendous joy in his eyes that I started crying.

I had touched that tender, innocent part of him I had been trying so hard to reach. We had a great time. We took pictures. He put his favorite CD on his new stereo. I put on Michael Jackson's song, "P.Y.T." and Lil' John started moonwalking, something I didn't even know he could do.

Then I started pop lockin'. I waved my arms, snapped my neck and jerked my body to the beat.

"Go, Mommy! Go, Mommy!" the girls shouted in unison.

We all laughed, hugged, and danced some more. We had ice cream and cake and took more photos. It was the best time we had all had together since the children had returned home.

After we settled down, John came over to me and stared at me, lovingly, for a long time.

"I love you, Mom," he said. "Thank you for this day."

"John, always remember that I love you and I've got your back," I said.

We hugged each other and I thought he would get up, go back to the stereo, and maybe dance some more. But he stayed nestled up next to me. At one point, he rested his head on my shoulder and neither of us spoke, letting the shared silence between us say everything. Then the girls came over and sat next to us. Salena sat next to John and Taalibah sat next to me. We stayed like that until they fell asleep. I didn't dare move. I was thanking God the whole time and eventually, I fell asleep also.

Two weeks later we celebrated Salena's birthday with another party. I prepared it the same way I had done John's. I pretended I didn't have anything planned and then just pulled out the decorations, cake and gifts. She had fallen in love with accessories so I gave her some bracelets and other jewelry and barrettes.

We played music on John's stereo and he served as the DJ. We all danced and had another memorable day of fun.

As the months passed, I was happy for the normal days and events, for the opportunities to fill our family albums with the kinds of photos that some families take for granted. Lil' John's asthma medication was switched to something not as powerful as what he had been taking before, and we were all happy about that.

My son and I also had a breakthrough one night. I caught him cheating while we were playing checkers.

"Your dad taught you that. Didn't he?" I asked.

He got angry, stood, and went to his room.

I felt I had blown the opportunity to teach him in a way that would allow him to accept the lesson. I followed him to his room.

"Lil' John, I'm sorry. I shouldn't have said that," I said.

"Dad never said anything bad about you," he replied.

"I don't believe you," I said. "Your dad took you all from me. He took all the money and had me and Mom evicted. If you want to be angry for something, then be angry because of that."

I tried to say this as calmly as possible. Lil' John just stared at me. I was willing for him to be upset with me, but I wanted him to think about the truth. I left the room.

Shortly after that, he came downstairs.

"Can we talk?" he said.

I looked in my son's eyes and saw hurt and fear. Here stood before me a small, scared boy. He explained to me that his dad did say bad things about me and that he wasn't going to tell me because he didn't want to hurt my feelings.

"I'm a big girl, I can take it," I said, smiling. "You can tell me whatever your dad said and we will handle it together."

I paused. "Your dad taught you that move because he had done that so many times to me. The way you did it, reminded me of how he had done that exact same move."

Lil' John said he understood and he admitted that his dad had indeed taught him that move.

"I need to spend more time with you," Lil' John said.

I was stunned. "What do you mean?"

He was quiet for a while but then he explained as best he could that he just wanted to be with me more. I was able to figure out that this meant that my son wanted to know the real me. He needed to be assured that I was who he was beginning to think I was, or the mother he had remembered in his head for the eighteen months he was away. Also, both Lil' John and I had been changed by our separation and by our mental growth, our maturing.

We decided I would spend more time with him and he would tell me the truth, no matter what. That night I prayed that my son would be honest with me and that I would be able to handle it in the best manner possible.

The months passed and we worked at our healing as a family. We marked my mother's birthday by forming a circle and singing "Happy Birthday." Then Taalibah read a letter she wrote to Mom, we told "Mom" stories, and we all cried.

I had started having abdominal pains and, at times, felt miserable enough to go to bed and stay there for a while. But I prayed, "Oh, Allah, thank You for the love You have for me. Allow my body to heal so that I may become stronger. Help me to be a good example to my children. Please forgive me for my transgressions. Amen."

I had hoped to get a driver's license and then a car. But I found out that I was liable for a lot of tickets that John had gotten. I would have to straighten out that mess before I could get a license. I was undaunted. Allah would help me find a way.

I went to an awards ceremony for Salena and Taalibah and when the choir began singing "I Believe I Can Fly," I started crying uncontrollably. It was just another sign for me that I was still carrying invisible pain. That song echoed my feelings at the time.

Most of the time, my children were more than enough company for me, but occasionally I felt sorry for myself—and lonely. I would think: *Who wants a woman who doesn't have her own place and who has little money and three children? And once a man gets to know me, will he stay with me?* I still saw myself as damaged goods. But mostly, I missed the companionship and tenderness of a man—and some days were harder than others.

On September 5, 2002, the children and I celebrated a year of being together. We ordered pizza, watched television and enjoyed an evening of fun together.

Later that month, I was watching the news when I heard that someone had shot the owner of an Italian restaurant about a half-mile from our house in Maryland. The owner was shot six times; it was amazing and wonderful that he survived. The shooter took his briefcase, a laptop computer, and several thousand dollars in cash.

A little over a week later, on September 15, another man, Muhammad

Rashid, was shot and wounded in Brandywine, Maryland, at a liquor store some two miles from my house. I paid more attention to these crimes than I normally would, simply because they occurred near my house. But I certainly didn't think they were unusual.

Then came a string of shootings, more than we were used to, even in our huge metropolitan area. First, on the evening of October 2, somebody shot out the windows of a Michaels crafts store in Aspen Hill, Maryland. Nobody was hurt in that incident, but within an hour, a man named James Martin was gunned down in the parking lot of a grocery store in Wheaton, Maryland.

The next morning, four people in Maryland were shot to death within a span of approximately two hours. A man was killed while cutting grass at an auto dealership; a taxi driver was killed at a gas station; a woman was killed outside a post office in Silver Spring; and a woman was slain as she vacuumed her van at a gas station.

These shootings got the attention of everyone, including the police, since there were so many and happened within a few miles of each other. The police were amazed to discover there was a pattern to the shootings, that each victim was killed by a single bullet fired from a distance. The thought of an anonymous sniper, hidden from sight, terrified everyone in our region.

The shooter struck again on the night of October 3, adding a fifth victim in less than two days. This time it was a seventy-two-year-old man who was gunned down while standing on a street in Washington, D.C.

The sniper was taking aim at people with no thought to race, gender, or age, which terrified all of us. We were used to personal incidents that ended in violence between two people or groups who knew each other. But the randomness of these shootings made every resident of the area feel as though he or she could be next.

There was a brief lull in the shootings, a few days without terror, and, like thousands of others, I hoped for a return to what had been considered peace. Then on October 7, a thirteen-year-old boy was seriously wounded outside his suburban Maryland middle school. I remember thinking, *Oh no, not a child. What kind of person could do this?*

I began crying when I heard about the shooting. For some reason, this affected me to my core and I didn't understand why. Perhaps it was because a child was shot and I was thinking of how his mother would be feeling. I was already emotionally fragile; I had just gotten my children back and I imagined how I would feel if something like this happened to them.

Many parents started picking up their children early from school or they didn't allow them to take a school bus or to walk home alone. Schools stopped having outdoor activities—games, recesses and gym classes. My neighbor, Tommy, waited for the school bus with the children from my area. I instructed my children to call me as soon as they got home in the afternoon. I did all I could to see that they were safe and then I prayed and left the rest to Allah.

While I dealt with the same fear as other parents, mine was compounded by the fact that I was also afraid that John was out there somewhere looking for me, too. I was looking for John and the white box truck with two Caucasian males as the media instructed us to. It never occurred to me that the sniper and John could be the same person. In fact, the sniper shooting and wounding a child made such a thought impossible.

The police chief of Montgomery County, where most of the shootings had occurred, suggested parents talk to their children to find out how they were handling their fears. I called a family meeting.

During the meeting, Lil' John said, "I'm not going to be afraid of someone rolling around with a gun. If that bullet is meant for me, it's my time. I ain't ducking."

I concluded that if my son felt that way, then I also needed to demonstrate courage.

The police collected more and more evidence and soon, they added to the list of sniper victims, the earlier shooting of Paul LaRuffa, the owner of the Italian restaurant near my home. Each day I passed that business, I thought of going inside to meet him to let him know he was in my prayers.

On October 8th the children ran into the house, frightened, after getting off the school bus; they had seen a white truck parked near our house. Taalibah said to run from the truck and they had ducked in between houses and cars. I called 9-1-1—and we waited. And waited. And waited.

The police never came. After that I started walking to the bus stop to meet the children and accompany them home.

A few days after that initial incident, the children saw the white van again, parked within sight of our house. A white man was sitting in it, reading a newspaper. I dialed 9-1-1 again and this time we saw a police car drive by a short time later. But the policeman didn't ring our doorbell or stop to check out the van. Taalibah was so scared, she asked me to call the police again, so I phoned 9-1-1 a second time. The original operator forwarded me to somebody else, but no one picked up.

I was frustrated. Taalibah was scared.

On October 11, shortly after 8 a.m., my coworker came to pick me up for work and, as soon as I got into the car, she said, "Do you see that dark-colored car?"

She pointed to a car that was parked on the street at the end of the cul-de-sac where my house set. "I'm getting a really bad feeling from that car," she said.

We were running late. "Okay, let's just go to work," I said.

But as we passed the car, we both saw the driver staring at us. He was a young black man that I didn't recognize. The person in his passenger seat quickly raised a newspaper to hide his face so we couldn't see it.

Now I was nervous. "Did you see that? Oh, hell no, do you have a cell phone?" I said. She said yes. I said "Let me use it to call the police." I dialed 9-1-1 and reported a suspicious, dark-blue car in the parking lot near my house.

The operator asked me to describe the car and I did the best I could.

"Late-model Caprice or Chevy Impala with New Jersey plates," I said. "Two black men in it."

The officer promised to send someone to check it out. And my coworker and I dismissed it. But the next day, on my way to the bus stop, I saw a neighbor who was noticeably upset. When I asked him what was wrong, he said that his car had been stolen. I told him about the dark-blue car. Later, I discovered that several of my neighbors had spotted the same car parked in various spaces, always facing my house.

I was scared, but I didn't let my fear stop me from going about my daily routine. I still walked to the bus stop, though I was always looking around me. My fear actually fueled me to do what I needed to do. The drum in my head beat the message: *"I have to keep going. I can't stop; I can't give up."*

Even while I was on a lookout for the sniper, the thought of John hunting for me was always in the back of my mind. I was standing at the bus stop one day when Olivia called to say, "John is looking for you."

I panicked. I stood there, scared, crying, and praying for God to protect me from John. Thinking to myself: *Why won't anyone help me? Why won't anyone believe me? Why is he terrorizing me like this? I just want to be left alone to raise my children.*

When I saw the bus was coming, I pulled myself together. *Never let them see you sweat, never let them see you sweat,* I was thinking as I stepped onto the bus. There had always been background nervousness to every move I made, and now Olivia's call had heightened my fear. Whenever I walked to and from the bus stop, I was constantly looking around, checking the rooftops and trees, my eyes scanning the houses and cars to make sure no one was hiding or sneaking up on me. It was a terrible feeling and I wondered when I would get my sense of balance back again.

We were eating dinner and listening to the television news on October 22, when we heard that a bus driver named Conrad Johnson had been shot while working. I heard the newscaster talk about how Mr. Johnson was in his mid-thirties, with a wife and children, and each bit of information seemed to strike my heart deeply. When they showed his picture, I dropped my fork and started weeping. The children stared at me. I was upsetting them, so I went into the bathroom and cried into a towel.

The next morning on the news and in the paper, I heard more about Mr. Johnson. I got sick on my stomach as they talked about how devoted a family man he was. I thought about his wife and her having to raise her children alone. I thought about the hardship that comes along with that and coming to terms with such a loss. *He's dead for no reason,* I thought. Each time I repeated in my head how his wife had lost a husband and a best friend and his children had lost a father and a best friend, I wept. I was thinking about how often the news reports were about black men who didn't care about their families and how this news was about one who was gunned down while working to provide for his family.

The evening after Mr. Johnson was killed, on October 23, the children and I were having dinner when someone knocked on the door. I went to answer it and the children trailed behind me. I opened the front door and saw a tall, husky black man in a dark suit.

"Is Mildred Muhammad here?" he asked in a calm voice.

"Who is speaking?" I asked.

"ATF agent Purvis Smith." He showed me the badge that hung around his neck. I sent my children back to the table to finish their dinner. Not knowing what this was about, I didn't want them to be alarmed at what would take place.

The agent immediately began asking questions. "Are you Mildred Muhammad?"

I first ignored him. "I'm Mildred Muhammad," I said. "How are you today? I'm fine."

He responded with another question: "When was the last time you spoke with John Muhammad?"

My body shook. My hands began to sweat. "Why are you asking me that question?" I asked.

"We need an answer to that question," the agent insisted, in a polite, calm tone.

"The last time I had any contact with John Muhammad was on September 4, 2001, in Washington State."

"Have you seen him since?"

"Why are you asking me these questions?"

"We need for you to come down to the police station to question you," he said. But he did not raise his voice one decibel.

"I'm not going anywhere until you tell me what you want. You don't understand. If you want me to identify John Muhammad, I can't go near him because he is going to kill me," I said.

Agent Smith still spoke in a soft, peaceful voice. "You can come with us to the police station or we can question you here," he said.

"Bring your boys because I'm not going with you," I said.

I stood at the door as he walked back to his car to speak to someone who was sitting inside. Then he came back to face me.

"We really need you to come with us to the station," he said.

He was such a calm man that I did not feel threatened, even though I felt scared. I decided I needed to get what seemed to be the inevitable over so I could find out what was going on.

"Let me talk to my brother-in-law first," I said.

I went upstairs to get Chester's advice. I didn't have a clue what could be happening beyond them wanting to question me.

Chester advised me to cooperate with the police, and he would watch my children.

I was coming downstairs from talking to Chester and told the agent I needed to get my scarf, but had to go down another flight of stairs to the basement to get it. As I was getting my scarf I wanted to call someone. I phoned one of the sisters at the Mosque. I needed to let somebody else know that I was being taken to police headquarters and questioned about my ex-husband. I told her I needed legal advice. Before leaving, I told the children I was going to the police, however, I would be right back.

In the car Agent Smith asked me about the Nation of Islam. He asked about my experience as a Muslim and about the diet. Then, after chatting for a while, he asked, "What do you think of John?"

I became guarded and wondered why he was asking me such a question.

"He's a man of his word," I said. "He means what he says and says what he means."

"Sounds like you're proud of him," the agent said.

"I understand him," I said.

"I'm only asking questions, so I can understand him better," Agent Smith said.

My cell phone rang. It was a sister from the Mosque named Melinda, an attorney in the Nation. She asked if I was okay and what was going on.

"I don't know, but you can talk to Agent Smith," I said, passing the phone.

They talked briefly. He didn't say much. I didn't listen because I was busy looking out the window trying to figure out where he was taking me. I was in survivor mode. Listening to their conversation was not my priority. I had to know where I was going in case I needed to jump out and get back to my children. For months I had been protecting myself when no one else would because they didn't understand or wouldn't listen to my warnings of the danger that I was in. After the conversation, he returned the phone to me.

Before Melinda hung up, she advised me to cooperate and told me to call her if I needed anything else.

We rode a long time and I tried to figure out where I was. I had been in hiding for so long that I never ventured out to learn the area. I was so used to being afraid and, even though I went about my daily routine, I never went for a walk, or to the movies, or the mall, or did any of the outdoor activities that require you to explore new territory.

I thought about my children. They were worried when I left the house. They still had their fears of being abandoned again and they were used to knowing where I was.

When we got to the police station, I was surprised to see Jenson Jordan, the FBI agent who had taken the first missing persons report I had filed in Maryland regarding my children. At the time, he had advised me to talk to the police back in Seattle since it was an ongoing case.

Now Agent Jordan joined Agent Smith and another man as they started questioning me. "Why am I here?" I asked. They began with a series of questions about the 9-1-1 calls I had made about the white van. I answered their first questions but it was obvious this wasn't why they had brought me to the police station. "I know you didn't bring me all the way out here to ask me about three phone calls to 9-1-1. What is going on?"

They looked at each other and then one of them said to Agent Smith, "You didn't tell her?"

He didn't respond. Instead, he started asking more questions. I don't know how much time passed but it seemed like a long time before they got to what I could see was the point of my being there.

"When was the last time you saw John Muhammad?" Agent Smith asked again.

I repeated the first answer I had given him.

At one point, they had me listen to a CD with a voice on it.

"Have you ever heard that voice before?" one of them asked.

"No." The voice didn't sound familiar at all.

They showed me a letter. "Do you recognize the handwriting?"

"I don't know the handwriting," I said.

I could tell they were getting frustrated with me, as if I was supposed to know the answers to the questions they were asking. Agent Jordan kept walking in and out of the room as the others questioned me. Each time he came back, he seemed more anxious. He was talking on his cell phone when he paused, turned to me, and said, "Ms. Muhammad, we're simply going to have to tell you."

The other two agents were silent. They looked at him, waiting.

"Ms. Muhammad, we're going to name your ex-husband as the sniper," Agent Jordan said.

"What?" I leaned over and dropped my forehead to the table. "Oh my God!"

"Do you think he would do something like this?" one of the men asked.

I raised my head from the table, looked up at the ceiling, and around the room. I focused on a corner in the room and, for the first time, everything seemed to come together and make sense to me, so I said, "Yes."

"Why would you think that?" one of them asked.

For some reason, for the first time, I remembered something that happened in Tacoma when John and I were watching a movie. I couldn't even recall the movie's name, but I remembered him saying to me, "You know I could take a small city, terrorize it and they would think it would be a group of people. But it would only be me." I recalled that John was really confident when he told me this. I asked him, "Why would you do something like that?" He looked away and changed the subject.

"Ms. Muhammad, didn't you know he was shooting people all around you?" an agent asked.

I was operating on automatic pilot. "I didn't know the area. How would I know that?" I said.

They recounted the sniper shootings.

"The man shot at the restaurant was right up the street from you," someone said. "The man shot in Brandywine was only two miles from you."

I was stunned that I had never even considered the possibility.

"Did he ever bring a weapon home?" an agent asked.

"He was in the military. I thought they all did that. He brought home his M16 rifle and cleaned it and took it back."

"I don't think the military does that," an agent commented.

"I don't know what they do, but John did," I said.

They showed me photos of guns.

"I haven't seen this one, but John had a gun," I said.

"Where was it?"

"In the shed."

"What kind of gun?"

I told them it was the kind of gun that you opened the barrel to put in bullets.

They showed me more photos of guns. I pointed to one.

"Was it in the house?" one of the agents asked.

"No, outside in the shed."

When we were evicted, I had gone out into the shed to clean it out, and I had seen the gun and rounds of bullets.

Finally, the agents were finished.

"Okay, Ms. Muhammad, we want to put you in protective custody. Do you want to go?" someone asked.

My only question was, "You have to ask me that?" Of course, I wanted to go.

They explained that some people would not want to go.

"Have you caught him yet?" I asked.

"No," an agent replied.

"Do you know where he is?"

"No," the agent replied again.

"And you still have to ask me do I want to go into protective custody?" I asked.

"Yes," the agent said.

"Then, yes, sir, I want to be put in protective custody."

I told them they had to place my children and sister and brother-in-law in protective custody also. At first they balked at taking my sister and her husband, but I insisted.

"If he goes to the house, he will kill them," I stated.

It was still light outside when they picked me up but now, as we left, it was dark. I still couldn't tell where I was and it was clear to me that I would never know. My cell phone rang. It was Melinda, the lawyer. I told her what was going on. She wanted to come to the station to meet me, but I told her there wasn't time. "We are leaving to pick up my children, sister, and brother-in-law. They are putting us in protective custody."

When we got to the house, my sister was watching the television. They were already showing a tree trunk in the yard of a house in Tacoma, where they said police believe the sniper had gone to practice his marksmanship. The media had not gotten the information yet that John was named as a suspect.

My sister looked up when she saw me. "What's going on?" she asked. She looked angry.

I went over to her to explain. "They named John as the sniper," I said. "We have to pack up and go with the police."

I gathered up things for me and the children. Agent Smith remained his calm self, even while encouraging me to hurry.

I took Lil' John into the bathroom. "They have named your dad as the sniper," I said. He went limp. I caught him before he collapsed. "Honey, you can't break down on me now. You have to be strong. I have to go down and tell the girls and we have to get our things together and go with the police."

I went downstairs and told the girls about their father and they started crying. I didn't have time to think about how to tell them, so I just said it, the same way I had told John. They asked questions, but I told them I didn't know anything yet.

My children and I were put in one car. My sister and her husband were placed in another. An officer told me that just as we left the station, the media had pulled into the lot. I held my children close. They were scared. I was also but, as usual, I tried to remain composed and in control for them.

In the car, I could not believe what was happening to us. We went from being a family struggling to make ends meet, to a family on the run. Still, I was thinking about the appointment I had with a homeownership program. I had worked hard and long to meet the requirements and now I had an appointment scheduled that I did not want to miss. I also thought about my job at Southern Maryland Hospital. When would I be able to go back to work? How long would it take for them to catch John? Why was this happening to us? Why didn't people listen to me? What did I do wrong: Did I scream long enough? What would people think of me and my children?

I had always wanted a simple life, to be a good wife, to be a good mother, to be a good servant of God. I wanted a home that the children could come to when they were old enough to have their own families. I saw my upcoming appointment as a closer move to that dream. And now this.

I had so many questions and so many confusing thoughts. But it came to me in that car that I had to let all of it go and turn it over to God. After my mind rested on this thought, I realized that I needed to turn my energy toward my children instead of to worrying. I looked at them and realized that all of them were clinging to me. Even John was holding me tighter than usual. They were looking to me for emotional strength. Therefore, I could not cry; even though I wanted to scream.

I wanted someone to hold me and tell me what to do. I wanted someone to ask me what I wanted. I wanted someone to talk to me with compassion and understanding. I needed someone to hug me and tell me that everything would be alright. I was confused and hurt, but there was no one there for me. I was not who I used to be, a woman dependent upon a man for self-worth or even strength. I had to figure out how to do all of this on my own. So I said a prayer, *"Oh, Allah, give me the strength to bear all of this. I know You would not put anything on me that I can't bear. I ask that You give me the wisdom to make the right decisions as they come up. Help me to care for my children as they struggle to understand. And most of all, Lord, help me to care for myself and to remember Your word that You will rescue me and protect me. I need You, Lord, because I have no one else to call. Amen."*

We went into protective custody that Wednesday night, October 23. They escorted us to a Maryland hotel. The children and I were in one room and my sister and brother-in-law were in another.

I was exhausted. I don't even remember whether or not they placed a guard at the door. As soon as we got into the room, I turned on the television and saw John's picture. The children started crying. I walked up to the television, put my hand on the screen, and whispered, "What happened to you?" My son got in one bed and began crying; the girls went to the other bed and did the same.

I could not imagine what had happened that caused John to reach this point. It was unfathomable.

I consoled the children until they were no longer crying. They finally went to sleep. As they were sleeping, I went into the bathroom. I took a pillow with me. I needed to cry. I turned on the water in the bathtub and the sink. I sat on the closed toilet, put my head in the pillow, and screamed. I cried so hard I had to sit on the floor so I wouldn't fall. I don't know how long I was in there before my cell phone rang. It was a woman.

"Ms. Muhammad, this is Nicole. Do you remember me?" she asked.

"No," I said.

She told me she was a victim advocate I met when I went to the domestic violence office in D.C. Then I remembered that I had met her when I registered my restraining order.

"How are you?" she asked.

"I don't know," I said.

She reminded me I had her card and told me to call if I needed anything. Then she said the words I needed to hear: "Ms. Muhammad, you will be alright."

After we hung up, I washed my face, turned off the water, and went back into the room with my children. While they slept, I sat in a chair, watching the news. I finally dozed off.

It was daylight when I heard a small voice trying to awaken me.

"Mommy, are you okay?" Taalibah said.

John and Salena were looking at me as well. And then the questions began.

"Mommy, what did Daddy do?" Taalibah asked.

I looked at her; it was as hard for her to believe as it was for me.

"They are charging your daddy with being the sniper. They say he killed many people," I said.

"My daddy wouldn't do anything like that," she said.

"I wouldn't say that if I was you," John said.

"Why did you say that?" I asked.

He turned his head away from me. I wondered what else he was thinking; he was the quietest of my children.

They told me they were hungry, so I ordered breakfast. We ate and continued to watch the news. We saw on the television that they had caught John and his seventeen-year-old accomplice Lee Boyd Malvo that night. We were still eating when my sister came in with her cell phone. ABC News was calling and they wanted to talk to me.

I answered and a woman explained that ABC was willing to put me and my family in a hotel for six months if I gave them an exclusive interview. She said they would fly my relatives to Maryland also, so we could all be together during this time.

"I don't know what exclusivity means. I can't promise that. I only want to go home," I said, giving the phone back to my sister.

I was not thinking properly. I did not know it then but later I would realize that I was suffering some sort of post-traumatic disorder. I was in denial. To survive, my mind got busy, turning to other matters, anything other than the crisis at hand. All I was thinking about now was going home and my appointment at the housing agency to talk about getting my own home.

Melinda, the lawyer who had spoken to me earlier, called to say I could not return home; the media was waiting. She told me to expect a call from another lawyer and that a car was coming to the hotel to get me and the children.

When the other lawyer, Andy, called, he said the Nation had obtained him to represent me.

"What do you want?" he asked.

I had a quick answer. "I want my life back. I want my home. I want my children to be in school. I want a normal life."

"We will work on that," he assured me. "It looks dark right now, sister, but there are two things I need you to do."

"What?"

"Make Allah sufficient for you—and pray," he said.

"I'm doing both of those, sir," I told him.

I thought of the verse in the Holy Qur'an I read daily: *"O, my son, keep up prayer and enjoin good and forbid evil and bear patiently that which befalls thee. Surely this is an affair of great resolution.*"

I thought of how this verse, which I began to read while in the shelter, had even greater meaning for me now.

The attorney told me to check my messages and write down all the media organizations' names and phone numbers. All kinds of media organizations were calling me.

"Meanwhile, someone will come and pick you up and take you to a safe place," Andy said. "Then we will talk."

Agent Jordan came and announced that we could leave. "Now that the threat of imminent danger is over, you can go," he said. "But before you go, you have to pay for room service."

I was surprised. "I don't have any money," I said. "You said *you* were putting me up."

"We asked if you wanted police protection," he said. "We didn't say we would pay for the food."

"How will I get money?" I asked.

"I don't know, but you can't leave until you pay the bill," he said.

My sister paid the bill and ABC took her and my brother-in-law to the Mayflower Hotel in D.C. (Later, my sister from California and her family were flown in as well.) The children and I got into the car sent by the Nation. Melinda was waiting inside. We were driven to a beautiful townhouse in the District owned by some members of the Mosque.

The home was stocked with food. The new attorney came to get basic information and left. Later, the officials from the Mosque came to check on us. Before they left, we held hands and prayed. I felt my spirit filling and my strength growing. I put the children to sleep and watched the news until I fell asleep.

In the morning, I cooked breakfast while listening to the "Tom Joyner Morning Show." I'd listen to this show each morning before going to work. It was good to have some normalcy about the day. It was good to hear their jokes. I needed to laugh so I could greet my children in a cheerful manner.

I learned more about John from watching the news. I found out that the warrant for his arrest was based on the order of protection I had gotten two years earlier. But the order was not entered into the data file when I originally filed it. Instead, it was only entered when police were looking to find a way to hold him while they collected enough evidence to charge him in the sniper case. I speculated that someone did some research and discovered the order of protection and finally, put it in the data file. Having a gun while a restraining order is against you is a federal offense. The fact that John owned a gun meant he was violating that order and gave them a reason to hold him.

I learned on the news that John had multiple identities and that he used to help people from the Caribbean get into the United States illegally. I was blown away by the information coming out about John. It was as if I was trapped in a movie, watching scenes unfold around me.

One report had something in it that made me think of Isa's niece and I told my attorney, "I bet tomorrow we'll hear John was responsible for her death, too." Still, when the news came out the next day, linking him to this dear young woman's death, I was devastated. I felt that somehow her murder was my fault. Isa had helped me through my ordeal, even accompanying me to court—and because of that her niece had been killed.

I called Isa. "Why didn't they listen?" I cried.

She comforted me. "You did everything you could do. You can't blame yourself."

"If they would have listened, no one would have died," I said.

Isa continued to comfort me. Before we hung up, she said, "Call me if you need me."

At times, remembering her words was a comfort. At other times, I cried myself to sleep, asking again, "Why didn't they listen?"

*All of these murders are my fault.* This is what my mind repeated over and over, until it wound me so tight I had to think my way out of it—or suffocate. I had to remember that no one could help me when I tried to get help. Because no one saw what I saw when I looked at John.

Then I heard on the news that John's best friend, Robert Holmes, was the person who called the police to report him. He had called the FBI in the middle of the shooting spree and recounted how John had visited and shot his rifle into a tree stump in the backyard. Holmes remembered conversations about constructing a silencer. He stated that John had said, "Can you imagine the damage you could do if you could shoot with a silencer?"

I thought that sounded so much like John. His personality was all about going the extra mile to dazzle people and he liked to play "What if?" games. He wanted to be noticed. He wanted to be the go-to person.

Holmes knew about John's threats to me; I had told him about them when I was in the shelter. I recalled his response. "He threatened to kill you, Mildred? Girl, if I were you, I wouldn't let him scare me like that," he'd said.

At the time, his response was like so many others. Nobody even entertained the thought that John could actually take his anger to the level of killing a person, unless it was during war. But I knew the John that no one wanted to accept. People were much more comfortable believing that I was inventing another John than they were with trying to see the truth.

I found out on the news that John had told Holmes that I was in the D.C. area, but that he had not pinpointed the exact location.

I called Holmes to thank him.

"Thank you for saving my life," I said.

"You don't have to call me for that, Mildred," he said. "Don't get it twisted. You and I both know John came over there to kill you. He told me that he had found you. I asked him if he was going to hurt you."

"You asked the wrong question," I said. "You know John is specific about words. You should have asked him if he was going to kill me."

"You're right," Holmes said.

After we hung up a few moments later, I thought of the day I saw the dark-blue car outside my house and of how close I had come to being killed.

# CHAPTER FIFTEEN:
## THE AFTERMATH

The children and I stayed at the townhouse for two months, from October through late December. While we were there, the girls went to the school at the Muhammad University of Islam. John stayed home with me since the school didn't have his grade level. Every day someone picked up the girls and dropped them back at home.

I didn't leave the house; I never felt safe.

After I was released from protective custody, more than anything else, I wanted to go back to my sister's house. But everyone told me that I shouldn't since the place was surrounded by the media. I couldn't even go to my job.

When I called my supervisor, of course she asked, "When do you think you are coming back to work?"

I gave her the only answer I could: "I don't know."

I had fought so hard to have a life free from abuse and now it was on hold again. I wanted to go home, to go to work, and to go to my homeownership program appointment. I wanted my children to attend their regular schools where they had friends and knew the teachers. But my lawyer and everyone else advised me that all of that would be impossible for a while.

Still, I was obsessed with the thought of getting my own place. I wasn't willing to allow any situation or person to get in the way. I kept thinking: *They caught him, so leave me alone. I have to get a house and take care of my children because no one is trying to help me do that.* I wanted us in a safe and normal home where we could grow and thrive and heal as a family. While every media organization was hounding me for an interview, I simply wanted to act as if we were regular people; not at all connected to someone called "The D.C. Sniper."

I didn't want to feel obligated to give an exclusive interview. I didn't think my head was clear enough to talk to anybody about what was going on; I didn't even know what I was thinking. I needed time and perspective.

In the evenings the children and I stayed inside the townhouse, cut off from the rest of the world. We didn't even use the telephone in the house. Andy, the lawyer who had been sent by the Mosque, told me to write a timeline of what had happened up to that point. He said he was going to help protect me from all the newspapers and television stations that might try to take advantage of me. He told me to trust him, and then he instructed me to check my messages and give him all of the names of the newspapers, media organizations, and reporters who were calling. I guess he felt he needed to say this to me again after telling me earlier.

Understandably, the children were having a difficult time dealing with what was happening to their father. They were also upset about Lee Malvo, who had been like a brother to them when they were in Antigua.

As the story went on and on for months, I would change the way in which I handled all of the news stories about their father. But in the beginning, we watched the news together every single day. In fact, I made it a point for them to watch the news; I wanted them to know what was going on with their father. I thought it was necessary that they understood how their father was viewed by the public so they would know how to deal with the situation once they went back to school.

I explained that we had to watch the news together, so if they had questions, I could answer them as best I could. And I promised that if they ever asked questions I could not answer, I would get the answer and bring it back to them.

They questioned me like attorneys. Once Talibaah said, "So, Mommy, they said that Daddy made false documents to bring people to the United States. Did they say who the people were?"

"No, ma'am," I replied.

"Did they say how he got the papers?"

"No, ma'am."

"Did they say how he made them, when, and whose names were on them?"

"No, ma'am."

Talibaah did not hesitate before saying, "You need to find out those answers for me. When you get the answers can you come back and tell me?"

"Yes, ma'am," I said.


I prayed and asked God to direct my path. It was a very difficult time but I was so happy we had each other. When we got up in the morning, we hugged and kissed one another. We did the same thing in the evening before we said good night. It was a habit I had started when they were small and we easily fell back into it and it comforted us. It was our family practice that would forever remain a ritual.

Still, each morning I saw the pain in their eyes. They looked at me achingly and I could tell they were looking to me for something. I was their personal, living gauge who told them with my smile, or lack of it, whether or not they should be worried or sad each day. If I cried, they would cry. If I was belligerent or confused, then that's what they would be. They looked to me for direction. Therefore, each morning I thought about their future before I thought about anything else and this gave me the ability to have a smile on my face, to play with them, and to laugh in the face of great sorrow. They needed to see a strong mother—and they got what they needed.

Sometimes they cried and I comforted them. I told them it was okay to cry, okay to be confused, or to not understand. But after we hugged and kissed good night and they were sleep, I did my crying. By morning I was spent from the grief I kept stuffed inside my chest during the day. By the time they woke up, I was empty of sorrow and ready to smile again.

I didn't even realize I had this kind of strength or courage, if these are the right terms for how I acted. I am not sure what I was operating on. My children needed courage; they needed to be strong; and I thought the best way to teach them was to show them.

My son, who was just twelve, became troubled about his father's relationship with Lee Malvo. He started asking questions that indicated he was jealous: "Why are there so many photographs of Dad with his arm around Lee? Why did Dad call Lee his son? Why is Lee also called John?"

I can only imagine how difficult the news reports were for Lil' John; the media did portray my ex-husband's relationship with Lee as a father-son relationship.

I did not know what to say to Lil' John, so I winged it. "What was the relationship between them in Antigua?" I asked.

He thought a moment. "Dad said he was our big brother and he was to take care of us when he left to come back to the States to look for you."

"Why are you jealous?"

"I'm jealous because *I'm* his son; not Lee. I should be there with him," he said.

"Wait, hold up," I said. "Do you understand what you are saying? I understand that you are jealous and he is your dad. That's a territorial thing. You want people to know that Lee is not John's son. But I need you to look at what is going on before you get jealous because someone else is saying who this boy is. You know you are his son. You know he is not. You don't have to have anyone to validate who you are to your dad."

"What is validate?" Lil' John asked.

I smiled. "You don't have to have anybody's approval for you to know you are his son. They are going to say a lot of things you won't like. It doesn't mean you should be jealous. Look at what they are saying. Is it true? You have to say what is true and move on. It doesn't matter what anybody else says."

Tears formed in my son's eyes and he came over and gave me a hug and said, "Thank you."

I had to think on my feet many times. I had to have an answer to a question right away, even if the answer was, "I don't know but I'll find out." I didn't have the luxury of sitting and looking bewildered when we were dealing with issues that were the foundation of their lives. Their emotional status was based upon me, how I acted, what I said. And I had three sets of eyes watching me.

As strong as I was trying to be, it was an emotional strain on me. It is stressful to hold in emotions or deny feelings, even if it is just the hours from morning to night. They watched me like a hawk. If I got up to go to the bathroom, my children walked behind me and waited where they could see the door until I came out. If they saw me with my head down, they said, "Mommy, are you okay?"

As we were watching the news one evening, Lil' John said "I don't want them to find out about my dad. I don't want them to look into everything like that." I told Lil' John that we should let the investigators do their job and inform the public on everything that they found.

"Don't you want to know the truth?"

"Yes, ma'am," he said.

"Then we'll let them do their job and we'll watch it unfold."

Lil' John agreed. "Okay," he said.

He would remain the most protective of his dad. I do not know if it is because of the bond they developed or because he was a man-child himself. They all loved their father very much, but John was the most protective.

Andy set up an interview for me with the *Washington Post*. I assumed they contacted him first.

"Does the leadership in the Nation know?" I asked.

He assured me that they had given their approval.

We met the reporter, the producer who was going to record the interview, and the photographer at some downtown hotel; we did not want them to know where I was living. The story was on the front page of the paper the next day. Then I saw the reporter on CNN talking about what I said and how I looked, which angered me. I still didn't understand the magnitude of what was going on. In my mind, I was giving a little interview to the local paper.

Next, Andy told me the *National Enquirer* had offered to pay me $65,000 for an interview. My children and I were barely making it financially, so I was excited about the possibility of receiving that much money for an interview.

"It would help you get back on your feet," Andy said.

This time they said it would be an all-day interview so I took the children with me to the Four Seasons Hotel on the edge of Georgetown. The *Enquirer* had reserved a room for us and sent up room service so the children could eat while we went downstairs to start the interview.

However, it didn't take long for me to realize that the reporter interviewing me wasn't pleased with my answers to her questions and I didn't understand why.

"Do you think he was coming here to kill the president?" she asked me.

"No," I said.

She asked this question again and again, sometimes in a different way, sometimes using the same words, as if I had not understood her the first time.

"Do you think he's part of a militant group?" she asked. "Do you think he's part of a black military Islamic group?"

My answer was always the same: "No."

"Do you think he was ordered to do those murders?"

"No."

I could tell the reporter was frustrated. At one point, she said, "Stop the tape. She's not cooperating."

I could understand her frustration but I was baffled by this remark.

My attorney walked over and sat next to me. "You're doing really good on the questions. I'm so proud of you. However, they need you to say that Minister Farrakhan ordered John to do the shooting."

I glared at him. I couldn't believe those words had actually come from his mouth.

He stood and walked over to the *Enquirer* people. I heard the producer say to him, "Do you think she will say that, knowing they are taking care of her?"

"She will say what I tell her to say," he said.

The reporter resumed questioning me. "Was he ordered to shoot anyone?"

"No," I said.

The attorney rolled his eyes.

"Why do you think he came here?" the reporter asked.

"I know it's hard for you to understand," I said. "But he didn't come to kill the president. He wasn't part of any Islamic militant group. He came to kill me. In his head he figured that if he killed other people, then when he put a bullet in my head, it would be blamed on a random sniper. That way, he would regain custody of our children and nobody would be the wiser."

But they didn't want to hear that this was a case of domestic violence. Domestic violence is rampant in this country. Statistics were on my side. Still, they couldn't accept my answer.

They stopped the camera again. The producer said to Andy, "Maybe you need to talk to your client."

Andy suggested we go for coffee. "They need you to say Minister Farrakhan ordered him to do the killings," he said once we sat down in the restaurant. "I'm not going to do it," I replied. "No way am I going to say that because it's not true. I'm not going to put the head of a man who is helping me on a silver platter. I won't do it. I came here broke; I will leave broke."

Andy must have known from the look in my eyes that he didn't stand a chance at persuading me otherwise. "You're right. You're right," he said.

I said good-bye to the reporters and went upstairs to the room to be with the children. I figured we'd check out in the morning and that would be the end of it. But later, Andy came back. He said when I was talking to the reporters, I had mentioned that one of the reasons why I felt certain that John was going to kill me was because he made a point of following through on his words. I told them, "His word was his bond." When he said he was going to kill me, he planned to do just that. Andy said, after some back and forth, the people from the *Enquirer* said that they might be prepared to do a story from that point of view, if I also handed over the keys to the storage bin I had left behind in Tacoma. If I let them go rummage through my old sofa and pots and pans back in Tacoma, I could still get some money. In other words, they would give me $5,000 for the keys to the storage bin.

"Why are you trying to make me do that?" I asked Andy. "I've already told them that 'my word is my bond' is not something that is said only by people in the Nation of Islam. I'm not giving anyone permission to go through my things. I'm not doing it."

Nevertheless, we returned to the room where the reporter was. I started to answer a question but, for some reason, I could not thoroughly explain how John used, "My word is my bond." So Andy jumped in and started to explain it. I sat quietly looking at everyone in the room. When he was finished, he walked me to my room.

"Since you would not say the minister was responsible, they could not pay you sixty-five thousand," he explained. "They will pay you five thousand for what you said about my word is my bond."

That didn't sound so bad to me. It was five thousand dollars for the truth versus sixty-five thousand dollars for a lie. I'd take the lesser amount any day, given those terms. That was my thinking as I got the children ready to leave the hotel. I never received a penny of that money. I don't know why I didn't, or if Andy received it or not.

As I was leaving the hotel, one of the producers came up to me and said, "Ms. Muhammad, I am proud of you. You showed integrity and not many people would do that."

He gave me the contact information for an old friend of mine who was trying to get in touch with me. "I wish you luck in whatever you do in the future. Be strong for your children."

Andy took me and the children back to the house. The next day I told the leadership of The Nation what had happened and they said they were not aware that my attorney was setting up appointments with the media. I retreated after this incident. It appeared people were trying to use me as a cash cow, or to make a name for themselves.

I needed to step back to get a better perspective on what was going on around me. I still didn't understand the magnitude of the situation. I couldn't put my mind around the reason why what John had done had to affect me and the children so deeply. Why couldn't we have our lives back?

Even years later, when I would think about it in retrospect, I'd think of it as if it were not real. For years, I would chastise myself. *I should be farther along than what I am*, I would think. *I should be in a better financial state. I should have protected my children better.*

It's sad that people forget about the family of the people who commit a crime. In my case, people seemed to forget there were children involved. They didn't consider the struggle of my family as we tried to create a better life, or how their overwhelming curiosity about us seemed an insurmountable challenge on some days. My life was affected by the evening news. What a reporter did or did not say meant I had issues to address so that my children could have any kind of chance in the future.

This was an extremely difficult period. I saw John's picture in the news all the time. Every time I heard his name, I felt as though somebody had hit me in the chest. I was trying to sort out my emotions. One moment I felt sorry for John; the next I remembered how he was when I first met him and we went fishing. Then I thought about the years when he was cold and hurtful. Finally I thought about his wanting to kill me. Then I started all over again. I had all these pictures in my head. I wondered if I would ever be free of all these thoughts. I wondered if I would ever again be in a relationship. Would I be able to love again? Would my past stop somebody from loving me?

I was also still questioning myself about everything that had happened. What could I have done differently?

In late December the heating system in the townhouse started leaking and needed to be repaired. By this time the media had died down. We moved back to my sister and brother-in-law's house. I called the homeownership program only to find out they had closed and I'd lost the $2,000 I had paid the program as a down payment on a house. I have not been able to find this company to retrieve my money. That money is gone.

For a victim of domestic violence, having your own place is the first step to freedom. Although my sister and brother-in-law allowed us to live in their house, the children and I needed our own place. We had mixed emotions about leaving the townhouse. We wanted to return to the place we called home but the townhouse was our first experience at living in our own place as a family. The pleasure it gave us made me more determined.

# CHAPTER SIXTEEN:
## GIVING TESTIMONY

We went to Waldon Woods Elementary to check on getting Salena and Taalibah back in school one Thursday afternoon. I had an appointment with the principal, Mr. Brickhouse, but when we got there he was busy and we had to wait.

As the time passed, we all became restless. The girls begged to go to their old classrooms, so eventually I said okay. We went to Salena's class first. Everyone was happy to see her. Some of her classmates ran over and gave her a hug. They jumped up and down and made such a fuss that I had a hard time holding in my tears.

"Can I stay?" she begged.

"I guess so," I said.

Of course, then Taalibah wanted to go to her old classroom. Lil' John and I walked with her and her classmates greeted her with great enthusiasm, too. Consequently, Taalibah wanted to stay with *her* friends.

"Okay, okay," I said.

At that point, I couldn't hold it in. As soon as I walked out of the room, I cried; I was elated about how the children were received. I went into the bathroom to get myself together and when I came out, John was shaking his head and smiling at me.

"Mom, you're crazy," he said, giving me a hug.

"I know," I said, wiping away my tears.

Finally, it was time for my meeting with Mr. Brickhouse. He was happy that I was putting the girls back in school. I let him know that I hadn't kept any of the news about their father from them.

The next day, the children and I visited John's school, Stephen Decatur Middle School. Taalibah asked the principal, Mr. Newsome, so many questions that he told her that she should be an attorney. We all laughed.

When the laughter stopped, John said to Mr. Newsome, "I feel comfortable about coming back to school. I just want to be treated like everyone else. Like nothing happened."

I was so proud of him for speaking up and for his courage. I felt everything would be fine for him. Yet the mother spirit in me noted the sad look on his face.

In addition to getting John back in school, I had a party that day to celebrate my forty-third birthday. Instead of adults, I invited the neighborhood children who called me "Miss Mildred" and had comforted me while my children were gone. Ravaughan was my special guest. We had cake, played video games, and laughed a lot. I couldn't help but reflect on everything that had happened to me over the past year. According to John's plan, I would have been dead but, instead, wonderful things happened throughout the day, as I whispered, "Thank You, God, for allowing me to be here to see it."

In my journal, I wrote: *I'm striving to remain steadfast with my duty to Allah. I am relying on the promises of Allah. Every time I look at my children, I know those promises are true. I have to remain prayerful and not allow any weaknesses to display. To me, that is Satan trying to show he has some play and, in reality, he doesn't. So, my praises will only be of the wonderful blessings God has bestowed on me. And whatever discomfort I have, I will complain only to Allah since He is the only one who can do anything about it anyway. I thank God for sparing my life.*

As Muslims, we do not celebrate Christmas. Instead, as a family, we choose to celebrate Kwanzaa, which begins the day after Christmas and ends New Year's Day. There are seven principles and, each day that week, we discussed the principle of the day. After being apart for eighteen months, we had particularly amazing conversations; we were getting to know each other. We all brought new perspectives that we did not have the last time we celebrated. I would always listen carefully to what they had to say, but that year, I seemed to hear them in a profound way. I was overwhelmed by thankfulness.

I also thought about their dad sometimes; we had always celebrated

Kwanzaa as a family. I wondered what he was thinking. I also thought about what my future might be. I wondered: Who is the man coming into my life? Although I know that nothing is guaranteed, I asked God to help me to discern between those coming to me. I trusted Allah that things would work out according to His will.

On the Sunday before the children were to start school, I was up early. I did my prayers and my rakahs. I watched Creflo Dollar and listened to his message that said if you are sorry for your sins you must truly repent about what you are sorry for, so that the goodness of God can flow through. It was a powerful message and I began checking myself for the chains that might be holding me back from God's goodness. Time would tell me if the chains were still there. Later, I said my noon prayer and read the Qur'an and the Bible. I was trying to return to a routine of studying.

As I cleaned the house, I thought about telling my life story and decided I didn't want to do it at that time. I wanted to get my life together first, go back to school, and raise my children. I wanted to return to my first desires—to make a life that is safe and happy for me and my children, to fade away from the public. I thought also about giving lectures to help women who were in my situation. Yet, I wanted to be considerate of the children's feelings, which might mean being quiet for a while. "Help me, Allah, to change my life so that You will be pleased with me," I prayed.

The children started back to school the next day, stepping out into a world where everybody knew they were the children of "The D.C. Sniper." But if anyone ever taunted them or made them feel bad, they didn't let me know and I didn't see any signs. Instead, I remembered how ecstatic their classmates were when they saw them, and the children returned home from school with stories that backed this up.

Salena became a cheerleader and played the violin. John played football at his school and took drama. Taalibah sang in the school honors chorus.

That week in my journal I wrote: *Everything that is for me, by the grace and mercy of Allah, will be given unto me. I will strive, very hard, to remain steadfast in prayer, keeping my duty to Allah and giving in charity. I know that the promises of Allah are true every time I look at my children. So, at the appointed time, He will deliver His promises to me.*

Since I was back at my sister's house, the FBI knew how to reach me and agents started calling me regularly, to ask questions as they pieced together the case against John and Lee Boyd Malvo. The calls were aggravating, although I understood they were necessary. I was angry that they wanted to talk to me or use me to build a case against John, but they had ignored me when I called them for help. Now they were persistent and yet, I kept thinking that if they had listened to me in the beginning, none of what we were going through would be necessary.

Most of the time, although John's name was in the news every day, the children and I kept a low profile, trying to have as normal a life as possible. It helped that there was no media hounding us. They were concentrating on John. The story was John; not us.

I searched for work and started taking a mail correspondence study course to become a court reporter. I didn't talk to anybody about my feelings or my concerns about my life. I did not confide in people; my experiences had taught me not to trust anyone. The only person I talked to was Olivia and she was 3,000 miles away. I had our friendship, my prayers, and my journaling to help me through. Writing took me to another place and then I would explore that place with my thoughts and my writing. Through journaling, I came to understand myself and everybody else, without having to feel someone was judging me or that I wasn't doing the right thing.

Journaling made me reflect on my life. I would read over my journal writings of a year ago and see how much I had survived. It was *only* by the grace and mercy of Allah that I was able to make it through. My worst fear—that John would kill me—almost came to pass. But angels truly were camped out around me.

In one of my journal entries from the previous year, I pondered the question: When was the last time I had felt safe and secure? Writing about this prompted me to recall that, even as a child, I did not feel secure, and I realized this had always been a big issue for me as an adult. I had stayed with John for twelve years and, at first, he made me feel secure. But after he returned from Saudi, things had changed. I wrote my way into remembering when I was sixteen years old and someone broke into our home and attempted but did not suceed in raping me. My brother was present and too high to help me. I journaled until I remembered that it was my brother's friend who had broken into the house, a friend who had come over earlier to visit him, only to unlock the window so he could get back in later. He had never been caught. I remember the police coming over to take a report. I was scared. It had taken me six months to sleep in my room again. Until then, I had slept with my mother.

I kept writing until I wrote, "Security for me went out the window! And it appears I've been looking for that ever since."

Meanwhile, Taalibah had to face "newspaper day;" a part of current events studies at school. This meant she had to face a show of front pages with photos of their dad on them, as well as coverage of his trial. I always gave my children a summary of the news, but I only told them enough for them to know what was going on. I edited out what I thought might be too upsetting. We didn't watch the news together any longer. If they were passing a television and they saw some news about their dad, they stopped and looked and then moved on. But they didn't deliberately turn on the television to watch the news.

John became the first teenager in our family when he turned thirteen that January. The girls went to school on his birthday, but I allowed him to stay home. It was a beautiful snow day. By God's grace, I was able to get John the PlayStation 2 he had asked for. My children had lost everything and they asked for so little that I wanted to try to get them whatever they asked for. I didn't want to be another person who failed them.

Salena celebrated her eleventh birthday on February 1. She invited girls from her cheerleading squad to her birthday party. We had a good time and it occurred to me that finally we were all growing together.

About this time, I found out Taalibah was having some anxiety about my health and about her dad being in jail.

"I don't want you to die and leave me alone," she said, and in the next breath she added hesitantly, "I miss Dad."

"Insha'Allah, I won't die now," I said. "And it's okay to miss your dad. Have you written your letter yet?"

"No," she said.

The children knew that one day I was going to have to go to court and testify at their father's trial. They had asked me if each of them could write him a letter that I could deliver when I went. I said, "Yes."

Now I told Talibaah, "After you write it, put it in an envelope, and seal it. I don't want to see it. That's between you and your dad."

On March 27, I was in a melancholy mood. It was my mother's birthday and my mind was a flash of memories—my mother as a young woman bathing me; my mother older, laughing with Taalibah. I was in the middle of my memories when a reporter from the USA Network stopped by. She asked for Mildred Muhammad, which let me know she didn't know what I looked like.

"She's not here," I said. "Would you like to leave a message?"

"I want to let Ms. Muhammad know the network is making a movie. Someone will be playing her and we want to get information on how she dresses and her mannerisms so that the portrayal will be correct."

"I am not at liberty to give out that information," I said. "Do you have a business card?"

"No, I don't," she said. "Thank you."

She turned and left. What I thought was odd is that she backed her car out of the cul-de-sac, so I could not read her license plate number. I was definitely going to call the police if I had gotten her tag number. A little later on the same day, a reporter from Japan came to the house. He didn't recognize me at first, but before we finished talking he did. He asked for an interview. I told him no.

"Please leave," I said, closing the door.

I had had my fill of living under a spotlight.

Taalibah's birthday came and we had a party for her also. I looked at her and her friends playing games and thought of how such happy occasions seemed to be zooming by while, at other times, days filled with questions by the police and media made time appear to drag or stand still.

It was decided that John's trial for the first victim, which had happened in the Virginia suburbs of Washington, would be held 200 miles away in Virginia Beach. The trial began in October 2003 and I kept up with the daily accounts by reading the paper, watching the news, and listening to the radio at work.

I read a *Washington Post* article online about writings found in the cell of Lee Malvo. The article said he apologized to John, Salena, and Taalibah. I didn't know how to feel about Malvo. I kept remembering that Isa's niece and many other people were killed by him. But I also thought about how, because of John, this child's life was over before it ever began.

At some point, my mind became consumed with thoughts of all the things I had gone through. My thinking kept me awake at night. I prayed to Allah to quiet the voices in my head so I could rest. I had to be strong to go into that courtroom to testify. The idea of seeing John again, even in a courtroom, terrified me, and that thought crossed my mind a countless number of times while I waited for the day to come. Soon, I developed an ache in the muscle of one shoulder. I took Aleve and put a heating pad on it, but it still ached.

One night I took the children to a dance at Salena and Taalibah's elementary school. After John was allowed to stay with the girls, I returned home to rest. Later, I would remember opening the door for the children and feeling dizzy and lightheaded. I remembered John walking me to the sofa and Taalibah holding up her fingers and asking, "How many fingers do I have in front of me?" and "Who am I?"

The next morning the children told me that I had passed out, which was why Taalibah was testing me. I only remember seeing a frightened look on her face. They all stayed around me the whole evening; when I woke up that next morning, they were sleeping near me.

At times, I was weepy. I was walking to the shopping area when I remembered how many times people turned their backs on me when I needed help. I thought of all the other women who have gone through domestic violence and been rejected by friends and family. I began crying. As I walked, I said to myself, "Don't turn your backs on us. We need support, love, and understanding."

Right when I desperately needed a vacation, my cousin Taliba called from Baton Rouge to say she and some of our other relatives would pay for me and the children to come there to visit them. I was ecstatic. I hadn't been to Baton Rouge since 1989, and the trip couldn't have come at a better time.

Before we left, I saw John on TV. My heart hurt for him. I could not figure out what turn he made to get on the path that had led him to where he was now. When they showed the picture of him with his face in his hands, I felt so sad. I was thinking: *We went through so much to be together to end up like this with so many broken dreams and promises.* But even as I thought this, I was also praising God for allowing me to love myself enough to not use alcohol or drugs to get through this. I needed to keep a clear head.

It was good to return to Baton Rouge, where I had been raised. The days were as hot as I remembered them. I visited relatives and looked around—at homes we used to live in and schools I used to attend. I bought a T-shirt at Southern University since I had attended the school for a brief time. I saw new places that had been built since I was last there. I was surprised to find that things looked smaller to me. But I laughed at the realization that I had grown, that I now thought of myself as bigger, and so that was probably why Baton Rouge seemed smaller.

I really needed to reconnect with my family. I saw my favorite cousins, Michael and April, and found that we still understood each other after all this time. It was like time had stopped for a minute and then we were grown. The children enjoyed meeting relatives and learning about their family. Taalibah wanted to stay longer, to spend more time with her cousins. John had a great time with his brothers.

We had a family meeting after returning from Louisiana. We talked about the teachings and about discipline and our future. We all agreed we were different since visiting Baton Rouge and that visiting other people in their homes made us want our own home even more.

John and I had a long talk about his behavior. Our problems rose from our eighteen months of being apart. I didn't have to discipline Salena so much. She was more like me in terms of caring for herself and others. John and Taalibah were different. Taalibah desired to change when mistakes were presented to her. She apologized, meant it, and tried to change. John would do this only when it was beneficial to him. When his mistakes were brought to his attention, he blamed me. I wanted to help him understand what he was doing.

"You need to take responsibility for your actions," I told him.

My relationship with John had been strained since his return. Whereas Taalibah and Salena were happy to be with me, John wasn't and there was nothing I could do to change that. It was hard for me to handle the truth—that if his dad wasn't in prison, John would go with him. He loved me on some level, but I wondered on what level was that. Would he protect me should anything happen? There were times when he should have defended me and he didn't. There were times he should have protected me, but he didn't. I believed his friends were more important to him than his sisters and me.

I got into a conversation with a neighbor about the sniper case. He suggested that any monies that I received should be donated to the families of the victims. I was finally brave enough to say that I was also a victim and I was not responsible for John's actions.

"Yeah, but they died and you are still alive," he said.

I thought to myself: *Another person minimizing my victimization.*

I came home and told my brother-in-law about the conversation.

"Dismiss that talk and don't allow it to affect you," he said.

I explained my reasoning. I would be taking responsibility for John's activities if I pretended not to be a victim and accepted some responsibility for what he had done. Over the months, I had to repeat this reasoning to myself because, occasionally, others blamed me also. People were so cruel and rude to me, making comments such as, "If you had stayed with him, he would have only killed you," or "If you had stayed on the West Coast, he would have killed people there and the people on the East Coast would still be alive." To these people, I am not a victim because I didn't have physical scars, am not dead, and I didn't lose anyone to the violence. For months, I heard comments like this all of the time.

I had to protect myself and my children from these kinds of hateful remarks. It was such a difficult time in my life. As a surviving victim, I presumed people would embrace us. Instead, their behavior reminded me of what my ex-husband once said to me: "I don't mind, because you don't matter. And I'm going to fix it so that no one will ever believe you or want you."

John's oldest son, Travis, called to tell me that John's attorneys wanted me to give them information that would help with his defense.

"Ms. Mildred, are you going to help my daddy?" Travis asked. "Are you going to let him die?"

I felt my anxiety level go up. I took a deep breath. I could hear the pain in Travis's voice. I told him to give John's attorney my attorney's phone number and we would go from there. John also sent a message through Travis to our children.

Travis said, "Dad said, 'Tell John, Salena, and Taalibah that he loves them, and to take care of their mother.'" I didn't give them the message.

All of this sent my mind into a whirlwind. I began thinking about how I was being asked to help a man get out of prison who had threatened to kill me.

While I was still processing John's message, two investigators for Lee Malvo came to my house to ask me to help in his defense. I left them at the door, standing in the rain while I called my attorney again. He told me to have them call him. I went back to the door and apologized for leaving them in the rain.

"I am Mildred Muhammad," I said, and I gave them my attorney's name and number.

There were times that I felt compassion for John. Since we had children together, it is difficult for me to think of him in a cage for the rest of his life. He was missing so much of their lives. Olivia and Isa were concerned that I would testify to help John. My thinking was puzzling to me at times. Here was a man who was trying to kill me and I was thinking about what he was missing with his children. Was that normal? I was not sure, but it is a scary thought. It made me wonder about myself. I didn't love him. I didn't understand him at all. How was I supposed to feel? I was still confused on this issue. But I always returned to this fact: He is the father of my children.

When Lil' John played his first game of tackle football, I watched, thinking that his dad should be there to see him. They both were missing so much of each other. I was afraid to pray for John; I didn't know what I should say and praying for him would have made me envision him before me.

I accepted a position as an administrative assistant for the Pennsylvania Coalition Against Domestic Violence. For safety reasons, I decided not to use my real name and my new employers agreed. With an income, I felt hopeful about the chance of getting a house for us, so I contacted United Home Buyers to begin the process. *First a house and then a car*, I thought. Within a few weeks of working there, I was able to get an SUV. The independence this brought to me and my children was great. The first day I brought the car home, my children and I stayed out longer than usual. We were able to go and come as we pleased. Next…our own place.

The prosecutors in John's case decided to go with the motive that John killed all those people so that when he shot me, it would look like another random shooting. I was elated that the world would finally know that he was hunting for me. I called the children's schools to warn them that the media had begun calling us at home so they might try coming to the school.

Some days I felt disappointed in myself for putting too much confidence in other people, who in the end hurt me. John always said, "You expect people to treat *you* the way you treat *them*." Now I was wondering if I was really that gullible. I didn't want special treatment. I simply wanted people to be fair.

I began to withdraw from the people around me who seemed to always cause me pain. I could feel myself pulling back, emotionally. Many days, I gave in to crying over my disappointment in the other people and in myself.

Shortly after John's trial began, the judge said that he wouldn't allow anyone to speculate that John came to the East Coast to kill me. That was very disappointing. It meant my issues of domestic violence would not be addressed. The newspapers were also providing me with details about John's life. I learned, for example, about two relationships he had had while we were married.

When they showed a photo of one woman, Lil' John said he remembered her since I used to drop him and his father off at her house. I didn't recognize the woman but I did recall that his dad was supposed to fix a woman's car and that he had taken Lil' John along to play with her son.

I read one article that quoted John as saying he should have stayed with his first wife. The article also mentioned two relationships he was having while he was with me, including a seven-year affair with a white woman. None of this news bothered me; I had suspected he was having affairs long before reading it. Also, I was more secure within myself than I had been when I was with John. I was stronger and I was proud of myself for how I was handling my life now.

The article was so thorough, it explained how John had looked for me. I figured there were questions only John could answer, but I did believe he was going to kill me so he could get the children back. He didn't care about me.

The daily news sparked memories for the children and as we talked, I learned more about their life during our separation. One night, I realized how different Lil John's perception of his experience during our separation was from that of his sisters. He said he did not like the people his dad left them with when he traveled.

"I hated being there so much I could have slept on the street," he said.

I was at the Mosque one Wednesday night when my son called me on my cell.

He was excited and breathless. "Mommy, don't come home," he said. "The police are knocking on the doors all over the house and they are scaring us. They're saying, 'Mildred Muhammad, we know you are in there. Mildred Muhammad, we know you are in there.' Mommy, what shall we do?"

I used my voice to calm him. "Take the girls and go to the basement," I said, knowing that my sister and brother-in-law were in the house with them.

John agreed to follow my instructions. "Mommy, don't come home 'cause if they take you, we won't have anyone," he said.

I assured him I wouldn't and told him that I was going over to a girl-friend's and to call me there later. When the children called, they all asked the same question: "When will we see you?"

I told them I'd be home soon, but we had to find out what the police wanted first. The next day, the children called to say there was a car sitting outside of the house. "When are you coming home?" they asked again.

My new employers instructed me to stay away from the house until they found me an attorney who would take the case pro bono. They knew I did not have any money, so they put together a care package for me with clothes, a calling card, and snacks. But I needed to have my children with me, so my girlfriend and I hatched a plan. We knew the police were watching the front of the house but we didn't think they were watching the back. So we told the children to put on backpacks containing clothing and items they needed for a weekend stay and then to go outside and play.

They played around in the front yard first and then one by one, eventually they went around to the back yard, where they walked across the lawns to the street behind the house. My girlfriend waited there in her car and, once she had them all, she brought them to me and we had a nice weekend together.

By this time the people at work had found me an attorney named Martha "Marty" Rogers, who was with the Ober, Kaler, Grimes & Shriver law firm. We had found out the police were trying to serve me with a subpoena the night they had come banging on the doors. Since they couldn't find me, they wound up giving my sister a subpoena to appear in court so they could question her regarding my whereabouts. Marty told the prosecutor to drop the subpoena against my sister and that she would arrange our meeting.

I dressed in a disguise, left the children at my friend's house, and caught the subway to Marty's office, where she had arranged for the prosecutor in John's case to meet me.

The prosecutor, Paul B. Ebert, arrived with two detectives.

"Ms. Muhammad, do you know Isa Nichols?" he asked.

"Yes, I do."

"She tells me this is the worst case of domestic violence in the history of the United States," he said.

That didn't make sense to me; I was still alive. To me the worst cases were when the victim was killed, disfigured, or mutilated.

"We thought that since he had done all of this to you, you would be willing to help us," Ebert said.

I was infuriated by the prosecutor's approach. "Why would you think that? You didn't help me."

"We didn't?"

"No, sir. When my children were kidnapped, I called your FBI agent and they said, 'We're going to put you in the middle of a parking lot and use you as a decoy to lure John out since we know he is looking for you.' How was that going to help me?"

He sat back in his chair with his mouth open. "An FBI agent told you that?" He paused. "Yes, he did," I said.

One of the detectives jumped in. "When is the last time you saw John Muhammad?" he asked.

"It was September 4, 2001."

"What was that for?"

"An emergency custody hearing."

He and the detectives continued to ask questions while I gave answers without elaborating. After some moments, they became frustrated.

Several times, Marty objected to the tone and manner in which they were asking questions, as if they were blaming me for something. She reminded them I was there in good faith and said that there was no way she would allow them to continue to ask questions in that manner. For the first time in years, I felt protected.

"Ms. Muhammad, we're going to just sit here and let you talk," a detective said.

"Why would I do that?" I asked.

"Because it doesn't appear you are answering our questions," the man said.

"I'm answering. I'm just not elaborating."

He stared at me. "Perhaps you can elaborate."

"No, sir. I'm not going to talk frivolously."

The other detective seemed overwhelmed by his frustration. "Here's a subpoena," Ebert said. "You will have to testify in this trial."

With that, the prosecutor and detectives left. After they left, I began crying. My attorney said she never knew about this side of the case.

My children were so happy and relieved when I returned home. I explained to them that I would have to go to court to testify at their father's trial. I looked up a map of the courtroom online to find an escape route just in case John was able to get loose. I found that there was a door behind the witness stand, so I thought I might ask to go through that door instead of walking past John. They asked me if they could write letters to him and if I would take them, and I said yes. I agreed to give the letters to Marty, who would pass them on to John's lawyer.

As the police continued to gain evidence against John, they had my storage bin flown to Maryland from Tacoma so they could go through it to look for evidence. As I waited with a police detective for the bin to arrive, my attorney Marty and I were in the lobby of the storage facility. The detective came over to us and began talking about John. He said to me, "You know, Ms. Muhammad, when we were questioning John we asked him why did he do these shootings. The first thing John said was, 'It's Mildred's fault.'" Marty and I looked at each other, then looked at the detective. He said, "What do you think of that?"

I said, "I don't know what to think of that."

That comment opened a dam on my emotions and the tortuous thoughts flowed. I thought about all those victims and their families. I worried about my role in causing so many deaths. I was also still upset about how my relationship with John had begun. If I hadn't started what amounted to an adulterous relationship with him, what would have happened? There were a lot of unanswered questions and I spent a great deal of time reflecting and praying on them.

On Sunday, November 9, Marty rented a car and drove my sister and me to Virginia Beach for my court appearance. I was still petrified at the thought of being so close to John. Marty and I met with the attorneys that evening and left, not quite sure of why I was there. It appeared that they thought my testimony would help John.

We arrived promptly at the courthouse the next morning. After being checked in, an FBI agent escorted us to the witness waiting area. I was nervous. I asked to see the courtroom. As I entered, I began praying. They showed me the way I would come in and where my sister would sit. After we returned to the waiting area, I asked for a Bible. I wanted to read the 20th Psalm. I had already read passages from the Holy Qur'an before leaving the hotel. I needed more than my own wisdom to make it through the day.

I couldn't see John from the witness waiting area, but I still trembled in fear. I looked out the window and was astonished at the number of reporters, trucks, and equipment from the media around the world.

It felt like an out-of-body experience. *This cannot be my life. This cannot be happening to me. I'm in someone else's nightmare*, I thought.

While we waited, I saw some of the family members of the victims who had been killed. I was afraid to go over to speak to them. Everybody else blamed me for the tragedy, so I wondered if they would also blame me. I was conflicted. I wanted to apologize but, if I did, I would be apologizing for something John had done. Being his ex-wife did not make me responsible for his actions. And yet, I wanted to say something to these family members each time I thought of the pain they had to be experiencing.

I wasn't ready to test those emotional waters, though, so I stayed in the corner and Marty stayed with me. Sometimes, when I was overwhelmed by the sadness of everything, I put my head down on the table and Marty patted my back and said, "Mildred, it's going to be alright." I prayed silently, asking God to give me the strength to handle what was going on and to hold my head up regardless of what anyone said, but being surrounded by the families of John's victims was difficult. We waited in that room for over an hour. In the end, I was happy to be told I didn't have to testify that day but might be called back for the sentencing phase.

As we were leaving the courtroom waiting area, an investigator for Malvo gave Marty a subpoena for me to testify in that case. I was conflicted about helping this child. I believed he needed to be punished for his part in the crime, but I didn't think he should be executed for it.

When the day came for my testimony in John's trial, Marty and I flew to Virginia the day before my scheduled court appearance. We checked into our hotel room, then went to meet the prosecutor, Mr. Ebert, at the courthouse to go over my testimony.

During the questioning, Mr. Ebert asked me about John. "Did he hit you?" he asked.

"No," I said.

"Did he threaten to kill you?"

"Yes. He said, 'You have become my enemy and, as my enemy, I will kill you.'"

It seemed to me that they did not think that John's verbal or mental abuse, or his stalking of me, or the kidnapping of our children, was enough to portray the image of him they needed. When the questioning ended, Marty and I returned to the hotel to wait. Later, someone came and told us I wouldn't have to come to court.

John's trial lasted for a month and as it turned out, I did not have to testify. I was at work watching the television on November 17, the day the jury announced their verdict. We all expected the verdict to be announced that day and we gathered around the television. Of course, I expected the outcome of guilty, but it was still startling to hear that John Muhammad, the father of my children and the man who had swept me off of my feet two decades ago in Baton Rouge, Louisiana, was found guilty of capital murder, conspiracy, and firearms charges. This trial had been for the victim Dean H. Meyers, but the prosecution said that his death was an act of terrorism, a violation of Virginia's anti-terror law. I could only imagine what would come next for John. But I did not have time to be concerned about that; I had to rush home to my children.

I got off early to beat the children home. I was standing in the doorway when I spotted them walking up the hill and I smiled. I always smile when I see them because any day is a good one; even if we have something difficult to face. Now, I wondered how I would tell them their dad had been found guilty. They had already asked me if I thought he was guilty.

"We will allow the police to do their job and allow the jury to make the decision based upon the evidence presented to them," I said. "Whatever they decide, we will discuss it, accept it, and move on."

They agreed with that. And standing there waiting, I was glad I had laid that foundation. As they each walked in, they spoke.

"Hey, Mom," they said, one by one.

Then each child gave me a hug and went to the kitchen table to do homework. They were happy to find out I already had dinner fixed. I decided to go through our regular family rituals.

After they completed their homework and ate dinner, we went downstairs to discuss our day. They went first, each describing a different situation at school. We all laughed.

Finally, John said, "Mom, you are home early."

"Yeah," I said.

"How was your day, Mommy?" Salena asked.

"It was good."

"Tell us what happened with you?" Taalibah said.

I started describing my day. Then I said, "The verdict for your dad came in today."

Their faces turned serious.

"Okay, what was it?" John asked.

"They found him guilty of all charges," I said.

They all asked the same question, "What does that mean?"

"Well, he is guilty for the shootings. But they have not said how long he will be in prison," I said.

They wanted to know when the court would decide that. I explained that they had to have a sentencing hearing and then they would determine what his sentence would be. This answer seemed to relieve them.

A couple of days later I was called by the prosecution to testify during the sentencing phase of John's trial. The morning of my court appearance I put on a blue suit and a blue scarf, which looked simple and professional to me. Before leaving home, I read again the 20th Psalm from the Bible. Then I read Chapter 113, known as The Dawn, from the Holy Qur'an: *Say, I seek refuge in the Lord of the daybreak, and the plain appearing and emergence of truth.*

The prosecution wanted me to bolster their argument that John should be put to death, but what I hoped for was much simpler. I wanted my testimony to serve the truth. My children's opinions had become the driving force that colored my feelings about John. My children loved their dad and prayed for him. They had a right to do this.

I was traumatized by the thought of seeing John in the courtroom. I mentioned the door behind the witness stand to the detective. He stated that I could not go into the courtroom through that door. I was disappointed. My attention went toward the security guards inside the courtroom.

"How many security guards are in the courtroom?" I asked the detective accompanying us.

"Five," he answered.

"Can you add three more?" I asked.

"Ms. Muhammad, these are big guys, they have their weapons, and there is no way anybody is going to get to you."

"They may be big, and they may have guns. However, we both know they can't fire a weapon in a courtroom. And we both know their guns are set on 'safety.' I know John; you are *getting* to know him. Before anybody can even react, he could get to the witness box and snap my neck. So could you please humor me and give me three more guards?"

"Okay, Ms. Muhammad. You will have three more guards," he said, smiling.

He had a police officer escort me into the courtroom, down the aisle, and through the well to the witness stand. Two guards stood near me at all times.

I got on the stand just after 9:30 a.m. and was there until 1 p.m. The questions centered on the history of our marriage and divorce. The prosecution wanted to show that John Muhammad presented a danger to me as well as others and should receive the death penalty. The defense wanted to show that he was a loving father whose life continued to have some merit.

In the courtroom, I was asked to describe the reactions of my children to John's guilty verdict. I told them Lil' John was stoic.

"John said that he knew he would be found guilty, and he is just going to handle the rest of it," I said. "Salena asked me what would happen next."

I told them that Taalibah, my youngest, was afraid for my safety. "She said, 'I know if Daddy gets out, he's going to kill you, and I don't want to live the rest of my life without a mommy.'"

I testified that John said, "Mom, if Dad takes you out, I'm going to have to take him out."

Under cross-examination, I explained that I believed John had experienced something that I did not know about as a result of his service in Operation Desert Storm and I agreed with the defense that mental health assistance wasn't made available for him. His defense attorneys wanted to put on experts to say that John suffered from Gulf War Syndrome, but John wouldn't let them examine him.

I talked about how John had abused me, his training in explosives, his target practices, and the "night rides" he and one of his friends had taken, riding black bikes and dressed in black clothing.

I avoided John's face and eyes and spoke of his abusive treatment of me and how he abducted the children on my mother's birthday and I did not see them again for eighteen months. I told the court about the time we talked in the garage and he said, "Just know this: You have become my enemy and, as my enemy, I will kill you."

I had to tell strangers the intimate details of my life, circumstances I had not fully reflected on myself, things I was still ashamed of: that John did not support me; how me and the children were evicted; of my losing blood stressing over the disappearance of the children; and ending up in the hospital. And of John calling the hospital to threaten me while I was there.

I talked about living in a shelter and my campaign to find my children. Several times in my testimony I expressed, in various ways, my fear that John would one day kill me. Of course, now everyone realized how dangerous John is. Even in the courtroom, when John approached the judge's bench with his attorneys for conferences, the judge ordered me in the corner while two sheriff's deputies stood in front of me to shield me from him.

On cross-examination, John's lawyers showed blown-up photos of my family during happier times, including one of John, his face glowing with pride, holding John and Salena when they were toddlers. I was surprised to see the pictures. I had not seen those pictures in years. My mind wandered: *How did we get here, to a courtroom where John was standing trial for murder?* I wanted to cry but I didn't want to give John the satisfaction of thinking that he'd gotten to me. So, I held everything in. I wanted to appear strong and in control but inside I was screaming for someone to please take me out of that courtroom.

"He was a good father at that time," I said.

The jury was shown videos of John playing with the children.

One of the things that most concerned my children during John's trial was whether or not it was okay for them to love him. They heard so many horrible things about him that I believe they questioned their right to love the kind of person the media called "a monster." Someone had been quoted as actually saying John should be tarred and feathered. My son, John, especially, wondered why others said such mean things. I tried to explain to him that people say some pretty cruel things when they are angry. And I told the children that, yes, of course, they could still love their dad. They had written their letters to him and sealed them in envelopes and I had given them to my lawyer, as I promised, so that she could pass them along to John's attorney.

But I found out during the sentencing trial that John never opened the letters. He was suspicious of me and said I had enticed the children to write letters to convict him of the charges.

In court, the defense attorney handed me the letters, still in sealed envelopes. I was shocked. The attorney questioned me about the contents of the letters and I told him that I had not read them. He asked me to read them aloud. As I did, they projected them onto a screen in the courtroom.

John, who was thirteen, wrote:
*"Hey, Dad, this is your son. Doing good. Wish you were here with me. So I have been doing good. I play full contact football. I am in a play at school called* The Wiz. *And I weight lift. I've made new friends and you were right. I would have more female friends than male friends. Dad, I love you so much and nothing will ever change that ever. I'm in eighth grade. That's pretty much it. I love you, Dad. Peace. Love, John, Jr.*

My eleven-year-old daughter, Salena, wrote:
*Dear Daddy. How are you doing? I play the violin like Minister Louis Farrakhan. I am in the sixth grade and have good grades. I am happy that I get to write a letter to you. I am in the chorus and am in the honors chorus.*

*I am in the patrol at my school and I made friends also. I pray that I can write you a letter again.*

Taalibah, age ten, wrote:
*Dear Daddy. How are you doing? This is your baby girl, Taalibah Muhammad. I miss you soooooooooooo much. And can I ask you some questions:*

*1. Why did you do all those shootings? 2. And did you tell Lee to say, "Call me God?" 3. And did you say my name on T.V.? 4. Did you do most of the shooting? And I thought that it will be a long time until I visit you. So I will be 16 years old.*

*And I love you Daddy and I always will. NO MATTER WHAT!!!!!!*

*And John and Salena are sending you one too!!!*

As I was reading the letters, I was surprised at how many details they were giving their dad about them. I was glad I had done the right thing by not talking badly about him to them. I was glad to read how careful they were in selecting the words to describe their lives at the time.

Later, when my son, John, saw his letter in the paper, he said, "If I had known it was going to be in the newspaper, I would have spelled everything right."

I laughed. "That's why I always say do your best, even when no one is watching."

But Taalibah was upset the most. When she saw her letter in the paper, in black and white, she second-guessed the way she wrote it. She thought her dad was upset and wouldn't understand why she asked the questions she did.

"I just wanted him to know I loved him, Mommy," she said.

I was relieved when I answered the last question and the judge proclaimed it time for a recess. As soon as my testimony was over, the guard escorted me out of the courtroom. I was glad. I had survived yet another unbelievable twist in my life.

On my way out of the courthouse, one of the female guards asked me a curious question.

"Since John mistreated you as a Muslim, why don't you leave Islam?" she asked.

I was intrigued by the question but it didn't take any thought for me to answer it. "In Islam, I have a better understanding of who God is and I love being a Muslim," I replied. "I didn't get into Islam because of him. He took something peaceful and used it for evil. That's him, not me."

For the next few days, my emotions were in flux. I wrote in my journal: *I want to cry and then don't. I have to make it through this ordeal in one piece. I know that God is in charge and I have to accept what is presented to me and make decisions that are pleasing to Allah. I really have no control over any of this. I'm thankful my life was spared, so that I, with the grace and mercy of Allah, can raise my children.*

One day, I got in my car and drove to the park. I looked around to make sure I was alone in the area. I rolled up the windows, turned on the radio loud, and screamed to the top of my voice for what seemed like a long time. And then I cried. I called Olivia, who helped calm me. I told her my biggest fear, 'What are my children and I going to do now? I do not have a plan.' I listened to Yolanda Adams sing "Open My Heart" and went to the Mosque and clung to the words of comfort I heard from the Minister.

I decided to go on *Good Morning America*. My children and I flew to New York. We were all excited. It was a bumpy flight. The wind was blowing pretty hard. The girls were making funny noises when the plane dipped. John slept the whole way. The show sent a limo to pick us up at the airport and we stayed in a nice hotel.

The next morning, I was interviewed on the show. Charlie Gibson was the host of the segment. Only one question was asked from the list we had gone over. Realizing what was happening saddened me to my core. Now I had to think before answering each question. The agreement was to have information for victims of domestic violence posted at the bottom of the screen. I was supposed to be asked questions regarding domestic violence and I wasn't. I was trying to maintain my composure as I answered each question, trying not to burst into tears. It was a "live" show and I felt everyone was watching to see if I would cry or show some type of emotion to indicate I had not recovered from the ordeal. I had not recovered, but I wasn't going to let the world witness that.

As soon as my part was over, they signaled for me to leave the set and then I started crying. I wasn't even sure why I was crying. People at the studio kept telling me I did great—and I kept crying. I didn't feel great; I had added to the madness. Nobody wanted to hear about domestic violence; they wanted to promote the sensational side of the story instead of the abusive side. It is an issue that has been ignored for years. There has to be a public outcry for this issue, just like breast cancer, drunk driving, and other issues that center around human tragedy. It was really sad how much the issue was overlooked and downplayed. No one was interested in *my* story. They were only interested in what I had to say about John.

I was really hurt and disappointed. And the interesting part…as the limo was taking us back to the hotel, the TV was on and they were reporting a story of domestic violence. A woman was saying how her sister was killed and she needed help. She was crying and I was crying with her. That made it worse for me since that was the reason I was there, to talk about domestic violence and to give resource information. I was wondering if this show could have helped her had we spoken about domestic violence. When I saw the taped version, the hotline number for domestic violence was not displayed. I dropped my head in tears.

There was little time to recuperate before I was subpoenaed again to appear in court; this time for Lee Boyd Malvo's sentencing trial. I didn't think I would be called but often, in the silence of my heart, I heard a call for me to help him. Also, my children had said several times, "Mom, you have to help Lee. He's our friend and he should not be in there, Mom."

Malvo's attorneys wanted me to speak about John's ability to manipulate and control others, particularly children. I wanted to help Lee avoid the death penalty. I did believe that he had been manipulated and asked to prove himself to John in ways that are difficult to comprehend.

When I told the children I had been called to testify, Lil' John did most of the speaking.

"You have to help him because if it wasn't for Dad, he wouldn't be there," he said. The girls nodded in agreement.

"I will have to say negative things about your father," I said.

The children were adamant that I do all I could to help Lee.

When Marty and I arrived at the courthouse, I saw Lee's family in the courtroom lobby. We sat at a table in the court waiting area and talked.

There was a couple there who were related to his mother who could not get a visa to travel to the United States. They were hurt and angry with John for manipulating Lee. They described how Lee had changed when John was around.

My heart ached for them and for one of Lee's little friends, who spoke of how he missed Lee.

"He's my best friend. It's sad to see him in jail," the boy said.

I could tell they were all mourning. They all spoke of the exceptionally smart Lee who loved school and dreamed of being an attorney.

"All of his hopes and dreams are gone," the woman said.

I told them that my children loved Lee and had spoken of his playfulness and kindness to them.

I was called into court fairly late one afternoon, so I had to return the following day to complete my testimony. When I walked into the courtroom and took the stand, I saw Lee at the defense table, doodling on some paper. I thought, *This little boy.* The judge ruled that I could not testify that John had threatened to kill me because they considered that "hearsay." I did, however, tell the court about seeing a car near my house that was similar to the one John and Lee were eventually found in. I explained that John was a magnet to children. He was that father figure they were looking for.

I called John a "controlling parent."

"He was the disciplinarian sometimes, but his tactics were that he had to have complete control of them," I testified.

The prosecutor was irritated that I was there. I will always remember his statements: "Your Honor, what possible reason does Ms. Muhammad have to be here? She's not dead. He didn't come here to kill her. What does her testimony have to do with this case?"

I put my head down, thinking, *Wow, he is blaming the victim. I'm glad I'm not dead. He is so insensitive. But what does sensitivity have to do with me being a victim and getting the death penalty?*

I was watching Lee during that time. He looked like a scared little boy writing on paper. During the testimony, Lee's attorney asked me did I recognize him. I answered no. He said, "Ms. Muhammad, John sent Lee to knock on your door so that he would know he had the right house." He said, "You answered the door and you don't remember him?"

I said, "No sir. I didn't remember," but at that point, I truly realized how God was protecting me.

When I returned home, I told my children about Lee's relatives and friends that I had met. They told me that a few of the people I mentioned were the ones who treated them badly. I got angry. But the children told me not to worry; I was with them now.

"You will protect and care for us," one of them said.

I was really surprised and happy to hear that. They now understood and saw for themselves how much I loved and cared for them.

I was watching the news when the verdict for Lee was reported. The verdict was guilty. Days later, a judge decided Lee would serve a life sentence without possibility of parole. The public reaction varied. My primary concern was for my children. They were not home when the verdict came in and I wanted to be prepared to tell them. I watched for them and did the same thing I'd done when I found out the verdict for their father. I waited until they finished their homework and ate their dinner. When we sat down to discuss the day's events, I told my children about Lee's verdict. They were sad to learn he would spend the rest of his life in jail. However, they were glad he did not get the death penalty. They agreed he should be punished for his part and that he should spend time in jail. But they did not want him to spend the rest of his life behind bars because of what their father had done to him. They thought the sentence should have been lighter.

John put down his head and began blinking really fast; he was holding back tears. Salena and Taalibah watched John, attempting to receive a clue from him on how they should react. John asked to be excused and the girls followed. I could hear them crying. When they composed themselves, they came back in the room and cried in my arms. John said, through his tears, "I lost my dad *and* my best friend."

I held them.

"Mom, do they think Lee is a monster?" John asked. "They think he did this on his own? He didn't, Mom, he didn't." He paused. "I miss my friend. I miss the fun we had together. Why did Daddy do this to him? Why did Daddy do this? Why did he want you dead so bad?"

The tears continued to flow from his eyes. "We love you, Mom, and we're glad you're not dead. This hurts so much. When will the pain go away?"

All of them were crying hard.

I spoke to John, but what I said was for all of them. "Honey, time is the only remedy for this. You will learn to live with it and I will always be here for you to talk to." He was crying so hard he didn't clearly hear me.

"I don't want to go to a counselor, Mom," John said. "They don't want to help us; they want to know our business. I can talk to you, right?"

"Yes," I said.

"About anything, right?"

"Yes, John."

"You won't lie to me; will you?"

"No, John. I will tell you the truth, even if it makes me look bad. I will be honest with you and the girls."

He hugged me tighter and said, "I love you, Mom, and I'm thankful to Allah that you're not dead."

Finally, four months after he was found guilty, John Allen Muhammad, my ex-husband and the father of my children, was given the death penalty. John was sentenced to be executed on October 14, 2004. In court, John's response was, "I had nothing to do with this. You do what you have to do and let me do what I have to do to defend myself."

When the sentence came, it would be big news and would be announced on television, so I took the children to work with me. We were together when we heard the sentence. No one cried, but they all looked shocked and confused.

I explained that, although they had given John an execution date, there was an appeals process and it could take years before he would be executed. Inside my mind, I dealt with my own mixed feelings. I would have to forever live with this: John is the father of our children and he came to Maryland to kill me. I am alive only because Allah interfered with his plan and allowed me to live.

# CHAPTER SEVENTEEN:
## LOOKING FOR ANSWERS

When it was time for John to be tried again, the children came to me and said they did not want to be in the area when the trial started. Summer was coming so I asked our longtime friends, Stanley and his wife, Pam, if the children could visit them in Houston. In addition to offering them a reprieve from the news, they could tell the children about the John they knew before he was labeled "The D.C. Sniper."

The children were excited about the trip; except they wanted me to go also. It would be the first time we were apart since we had been reunited. But I had to work, so I explained that it would be good for all of us to part for a while and look at this issue from our own perspectives and then get back together and share our feelings. They seemed satisfied with my explanation.

Before they left, Salena and I were sitting on the stairs talking about relationships and the importance of being a family. All of a sudden, she burst into tears.

I said, "Salena, what's the matter?"

"Mommy, Daddy lied to me," she said through her tears.

"What do you mean?"

"He said he would always be here to protect me. And he's not. He said he would always be here for me and he's not. My faith in men is gone," she said. "I am not going to believe anything a man says to me again. They all lie."

"Whoa, Salena. That's a pretty harsh statement to make," I said. "It is not fair to judge all men by your father. Are you saying you don't trust any man?"

"Yes, ma'am. Not even Uncle Stan." She paused and looked at me. "Well, I don't know about Uncle Stan."

"Okay, then let's take this one step at a time," I said. "Salena, I'm here to protect you."

"I know, but not like a father would. He lied to me, Mommy. How can you fix that?"

"Honey, I can't fix that. I can tell you that all men are not like your dad. I believe by going to Texas and being around Uncle Stan, you will see that he will protect you and be there for you when you need him. Is that what you need?"

"Yes, ma'am," she said.

I immediately called Stan to tell him about our conversation. I told him that the state of all men for Salena rested upon his shoulders. He laughed and said sarcastically, "No pressure, right?"

A few weeks later, we were at the airport. At first we laughed and had a good time while we waited on the flight to be announced. But when the time came for us to say good-bye, we all got teary-eyed.

"Look out for each other and remember, we watch each other's back," I said. "Stick together. We are family; regardless of where we are."

We said a prayer, hugged each other, and then they boarded the plane. I waved until I could no longer see them. I watched the plane take off. Then I went into a bathroom stall and cried.

When I got to my car, I sat for a minute and cried some more. I asked myself if sending them to Texas was the right thing. But I determined it was better for them to be away from this area for a while.

I decided to take a journey within myself while the children were away. I no longer had the excuse that I was putting my "stuff" aside to help my children. Now I had to go to work on myself. I went on a thirty-day juice fast to purge myself of the impediments that may have been hindering me from getting closer to God. I had never fasted for this long a period. But I needed to go deeper inside myself to recognize my true feelings, so I could move forward.

I started with shame, an emotion that was the most compelling one for me. I wanted to know why I felt ashamed. Then I dealt with rejection and fear. I journaled, furiously.

When my fast was over, I liked the Mildred who had evolved from the trauma. It was the beginning of me falling in love with myself. I pledged that what I had allowed into my life would never, by God's grace, occur to me again. I would not be abused, ignored, dismissed, or overlooked.

By the time the children came back from Texas, we were all different people, but this time it was a peaceful reunion. I had a direction in my head and a way of how we were going to get there. My thoughts weren't scrambled. The children were stronger and more stable in their attitudes and behavior.

We went through a brief period of getting to know each other again. The one thing I noticed was that they didn't eat as much as they used to. They were also more mature, more focused and more responsible for their actions and how they related to me.

I pulled Salena aside.

"How did you enjoy your trip?" I asked.

"I had a good time. Uncle Stan told us about a side of Dad we didn't know. He restored my faith in men," she said, smiling as she gave me a big hug.

She said Uncle Stan would always be there to protect her.

John and Taalibah had enjoyed themselves also. They all liked how Uncle Stan spoke of their dad. He had them laughing about different things he remembered about John and reminded them of other things they had forgotten.

I was looking for books to read regarding my victimization and how to come to terms with it. Most books centered on physical violence; not many spoke to the issues that I encountered. Finally, I found the book *Trust After Trauma* by Aphrodite Matsakis, Ph.D., which taught me about "triggers" and how to handle them in my daily life. A calm came over me as I read this book and I would continue to use it throughout my life.

Unfortunately, John's trial didn't start while the children were away. When it finally started, it was in a suburban Maryland county near us—Montgomery County—where six people had been killed. Since Maryland didn't have the death penalty, if convicted, John would get life without the possibility of parole. Surprisingly, the judge allowed John to represent himself; despite evidence he might be mentally ill.

John had no legal training but he got what he wanted: a chance to defend himself. Knowing John, I figured he thought that since he could convince his prior defense attorneys that he was innocent, he had a chance to convince the jury and the public. I also thought John might be capable of handling this case. I remembered his court-martial case at Fort Ord. The attorney they had given him was new and John had to learn some of the law to help her. *Once again, the authorities are underestimating him*, I thought.

John's defense was the same one he had used many times during our marriage: If you didn't see me do it, then how can I be charged with the crime?

Just as I expected, my children began experiencing some anxieties during the trial. For one, they could not understand why another trial was needed. Lil' John became rebellious again.

One evening, he and I were sitting on the sofa, settling down after an argument.

I said to him, "Honey, I'm trying to help you through this ordeal and I need you to understand that."

He looked at me with a piercing, frightening look that reminded me of the girl from the movie, *"The Exorcist."*

"You can't save me," he said. "Go on with your life."

I looked at him and said out loud, "Oh hell no, Satan! You are not having my son! I'm going to fight for my son!"

The look on Lil' John's face went away. He leaned over and hugged me.

"Honey, I'm fighting for you. I'm fighting for you," I said. "Do you understand?

Through his tears, he said, "Yes, ma'am."

During this time, I was trying to get counseling for my children. The school counselor, Mrs. Johnson, told me about a program for boys and girls from ages thirteen to eighteen. John entered the program, but sometimes all of us went to support him and, as a byproduct, we learned also. He had to wear a suit to his sessions and he liked that. Eventually, he felt comfortable enough to let the group know who his dad was and the information was well-received.

However, some weeks later I saw a change in my son. I noticed he became anxious when it was time for him to go to counseling. There were times he didn't go. At other times, he insisted that I go with him. That was strange since he never insisted that I go anywhere with him. Then one day, when we went into the office, a counselor met us at the door. As soon as John saw him, he moved closer to me. The counselor asked John did he write down the information that he had asked him to. John fumbled over his words, speaking fast and unclear.

"What's going on?" I asked.

"I asked John to write down what he had been through and I asked if he could call Lee Malvo and ask him his thoughts as well," the counselor said.

He explained that he wanted to help John write a book since we needed the money. He said his son was a publisher. I was furious. But it was not right for me to say what I was thinking, so I cried instead. I told the counselor how disappointed I was in him and that we would not be returning.

As we were going to the car, John looked at me and said, "I'm sorry, Mommy."

I looked back at him as tenderly as I could. "Why are you sorry, honey?"

"I let you down."

"Oh my God, John, you didn't let me down," I said. "They let *us* down. We trusted, yet again, others who said they could help us, only to find out they were trying to make a dollar off our pain. So that's it, honey. We're going to the library."

"Why, Mommy?"

"I'm getting a book on how to counsel you, me, and the girls. No one will ever hurt us again, by God's grace. I promise, okay?"

He smiled. "Okay," he said.

"Are you okay with this?" I asked.

"Yes, ma'am. If they can do it, so can you."

The second trial appeared to focus more on the relationship between Lee and John. My children were paying close attention to the news about the trial and I was paying close attention to them. In his opening statement, John actually stated the reason he had come to the area was because he had lost his children in a custody battle with me. He called Aug. 31, 2001, the day the detective picked up the children from him, his "September 11," and said he had launched a nationwide search for his children. He learned that the children were in the Washington, D.C. area, and drove to the region with Lee, who he acknowledged treated him as a father figure.

I had mixed feelings about John. One minute I was scared for him, the next minute I remembered what he had done to me, our children, and the innocent people who were killed. I tried working through these feelings by getting to the root of them. But I found out this would be a long and continuous process since my feelings kept changing throughout the trial.

My children wanted their father so badly. I tried to find a way to comfort them—with a word, a gesture, or some activity that would help them through this process. As the trial unfolded, I constantly prayed to God to give my children peace of mind and allow me to handle this situation in a manner pleasing to Him and my children.

I recalled that when I spoke with Lee's attorneys, they spoke of how he was transforming into a different person than the one he had been when he was under John's influence. I could identify with that because of my son. When I was blessed to get my children back, I realized that our reunion was the beginning of our process. I understood that we had to get to know each other again. However, I didn't expect it to be so difficult.

My daughters were easier to get to know than my son. The girls welcomed me back into their lives, but John was constantly pushing me away. Giving up was not an option for me, so I kept trying. His dad had worked on Lil' John's thoughts regarding me more than he had worked on my girls. I believe John was jealous of my relationship with my son. We were incredibly close and John often called Lil' John a "mama's boy" because he spent so much time with me. John would pull him away from me when he needed comforting, saying, "He has to handle it on his own."

But I felt Lil' John was too young to handle emotional issues on his own. Often John and I argued about this. And my son seemed to hate me when I got him back. We were constantly at odds with each other. The more I showed him that I loved him, the more he resisted. I got him back in September 2001 and it took him a year to embrace me. It took him another six months to tell me what his father had said to him that kept him from getting closer to me. I was still waiting to hear him say, "I love you."

One evening, as I sat on the sofa reading, John came in the room, sat down, and said, "Do you want to know what Dad said to me about you?"

I was shocked to even hear the question, though I tried not to show any emotions. "Yes, John, I would like to know," I said.

He took a deep breath and looked at me, his eyes filled with tears. "Daddy told me that you didn't love me. He said you loved the girls more than you loved me. He said that you wanted to go on with your life without me and that you told him to take us away from you because you didn't want us anymore."

By this time, my eyes were welling up; I was thinking of all the pain my son had gone through, all that time thinking that I didn't want him or love him. I wondered why John would put this into our son's head. Did he hate me so much that he would harm his own son like this?

After Lil' John stopped talking, I asked him if there was anything else he wanted to tell me.

"Yes, but it will hurt you too much," he said.

"Honey, I'm a big girl. I can take it."

"No, Mom," he insisted.

I respected his decision and didn't push. "Can I respond to what your dad said?" I asked.

"Yes, ma'am."

"John, I have always wanted *three* children since I was a child myself. You are my first born. I prayed that God would give me a son first and He blessed me with you. I have wanted you from the time you were conceived in my womb—and to this very day. There has never been a time that I did not want or love you. I've shown you how I've looked for you since your dad kidnapped you, right?"

"Right," he whispered.

"I've been patient with you since I've gotten you back, right?"

"Right," he said again.

"I have sacrificed my own comfort to make sure that you were comfortable, safe, had enough food to eat, clothing, and a place to sleep. Honey, there is nothing you could say or do that would make me turn my back on you. I realize your dad worked on you the most and I knew he would try to turn you against me. I looked for all of you and knew my hardest time would be to get you to understand that I love you. I will always want you, love you and need you in my life. My life was so empty without all of you. You, John, are my only son. And I love you from the depth of my heart.

From this point on, please don't ever think that you are not loved, wanted, or needed by me. I love you, I want you; I need you in my life for it to be whole. And don't you forget that, okay?"

He looked at me and said, "Okay, Mommy. That is what I needed to hear. I love you, Mommy."

I had waited so long to hear those three words that tears began trickling down my face. I kissed him and hugged him tightly, imagining that as we embraced, the love I felt for him was being passed from my heart to his.

As the trial went on, our lives moved forward. John injured his knee playing football outside the house. The doctor diagnosed it as a torn ACL and he had to have surgery and rehab. He was disappointed since he was unable to try out for the team. Salena and Taalibah went to Orlando to perform with their school chorus and had a fantastic time, going to a water park and an amusement park also.

Finally, the day of the verdict arrived. John was found guilty on all six counts. Although the children were expecting the verdict, it was hard. I could see the grief on their faces and I realized that while the pain might one day be easier to bear, they would also mourn forever in some way or another.

Since Maryland doesn't have the death penalty, John received life without the possibility of parole on all counts. He was returned to prison in Virginia while his other appeals regarding the death penalty were processed.

In the days that followed, the children and I talked more about how they felt and how much they wanted to be normal children.

"We need to find a way to live with this instead of ignore it," I advised. "It would be healthy for us to live with it."

"How do we do that, Mommy?" they asked.

"The best way we can do this is when you are thinking about your dad and you want to talk about it, come to me or talk to each other," I said. "We can't pretend this didn't happen and we can't pretend we don't feel anything."

They asked me what did I feel and I told them I was angry with their father for taking us through all that we had been through. "It didn't have to happen like this," I said. "I didn't keep you all away from him. He could have seen you whenever he wanted. He actually wanted me dead and that is so difficult for me to come to terms with. I'm praying that Allah will help me with it, but it is a difficult thing to understand."

"Well, Mom," said John, "I feel that Dad was wrong for wanting you dead. You're our mother and I don't know why he would take you away from us. That's selfish."

Salena and Taalibah agreed. They all hugged me.

At one time, I blamed myself that there was a "D.C. Sniper"; perhaps I hadn't done enough in articulating how dangerous John was. But here's what I know now: I told others that John Muhammad was dangerous, and nobody did anything. I went to the authorities and the Tacoma Police Department lied to me, saying they had put John's name in the National Crime Information Center (NCIC) and the names of my children in the database of the National Center for Missing & Exploited Children. Even though I told them he had military training and he could *"make a weapon out of anything,"* they had placed nothing in the system to protect me, or others.

I followed the law in executing the procedures that were supposed to help me. I've come to terms with the fact that I did my best and that was all I could do. I strongly believe that since I did not have the physical scars to prove that I was a victim, no one believed me then—and some still don't. But victimization is more than physical scars. Only twenty percent of domestic violence is physical; eighty percent is verbal, emotional, spiritual, mental, stalking, and economic. I can say that God put people and resources in place to help me. I am thankful to those in law enforcement who did listen to me.

There are times that I think of the victims who were killed during this terrible ordeal. I can't even begin to describe how deeply distressed I feel about the victims and their families. At other times, I have had experiences that have provided me with miraculous opportunities to heal.

During John's first trial, a coworker and I were on our way to a funeral when we stopped at Starbucks. While I was in the shop, a gentleman recognized me from my picture in the paper. He walked over to me and we began talking about the case. His name was Henry Smith and he said that at one time the police had suspected that he was the sniper since he had left the military dishonorably. He told me that he was a friend of Conrad Johnson, the bus driver who had been killed, and that they used to have breakfast together each morning. It was difficult to talk to him; I felt my emotions rising up. I tried to leave but when I moved, he moved. I didn't want to be rude since I sensed that he needed to talk to someone. So, I put my feelings in check and continued to listen.

I asked him if he was in contact with Conrad Johnson's wife. He said, "Yes."

"Please tell her that I'm sorry for her loss," I said.

As we parted, he said, "You are courageous and brave." Then he told me he was moving to Georgia on that same day. I was thankful that before he left, we had that "chance" meeting, which allowed both of us an opportunity for more healing and some closure.

Another time I decided to stop at Margellina, an Italian restaurant near my house. One of the people that was shot owns Margellina, which is less than a mile from where I live. The owner, Paul LaRuffa, was shot in the chest, neck, arm, and elbow. But by God's grace, he managed to survive his wounds. I went past Margellina almost daily, and for a long time after the shootings, I would stare at the restaurant and think about him.

One day, I felt moved to say something to him so I went into the restaurant to introduce myself, and to my surprise, he said he had always wanted to meet me.

"I read an article about you and my spirit brought me here," I said. "I wanted to know how you were doing."

He had always believed that John's ultimate goal was to get me. "I'm glad he didn't hurt you," he said.

We chatted for a short while and then he asked, "How do you live with everything that happened?"

"Day by day," I replied.

When I talk to my children about their dad, they want to know about him when he wasn't "The D.C. Sniper." They want to hear some of the good things about him. Fortunately, the prosecutors returned all of our video-tapes, pictures, and other items. For weeks, each day after they returned home from school, we watched a tape or looked at photos. They asked questions, I answered, and we laughed together about the good times.

Once Taalibah said, as if surprised, "Daddy does love us."

"Yes, ma'am, he does love you, Salena and John," I said.

People always ask me about how John was with the children. At the time, I believed that John was a good father. He spent time with his children and included them in his daily activities. In the evenings after work, he always took time with each one of them as individuals and together as a group. We went to the parks, museums, Lil' John's ball games and any school activities involving any of the children. Our children were well-behaved. They listened to us and followed our directions.

The only time we had problems regarding the children was when John tried to play board games with them. The children learned that John would change the rules or cheat or do anything he could to control the game to win. This made Lil' John so upset that he would walk away or come to get me to play with him. It happened whether they were playing board games or playing with action figures. After a while, the children stopped playing board games with their father. If we were playing and their father joined us, they stopped abruptly and did something else.

When I think about John and what happened with him, several different things come to mind: his feeling of being abandoned because his father disowned him and his mother died when he was young; his sense of being rejected by the military and not fitting in the way he hoped; his failure to really connect with the Nation of Islam (he wanted it to be more milita-ristic and less about spiritual development.); and his experience during the Gulf War.

I've said many times, and I'll say it again: The man that I married is still in Saudi; the man that returned is a complete stranger. I'm sure there are many military wives who experience this same feeling. We see the mental unhealthiness but don't know where to turn for help. Unfortunately, there isn't anyone for our husbands to talk to without jeopardizing their military careers. I hope and pray this has changed. I don't know if John was exposed to toxic chemicals, as some veterans groups claim, or if something else happened. The John that I lived with before the Gulf War had many problems, and he was far from perfect, as we all are, but he never scared me. The John who returned was different; he had changed completely. I didn't recognize anything except his physical appearance.

As time went on and my life regained some normal routines, I became more involved with Mosque activities. I found out there was a singles ministry online and decided to join the group. It was good to talk to others during this time in my life about spiritual development; I was beginning to trust again and my spirituality was growing. I felt good about that. Some nights we had online live chats. On one particular night the question asked of everyone was: *"What do you think is hindering you from finding your true mate?"*

Before it was my chance to answer, I began thinking about how I could put my circumstances out there and not be rejected. Others were stating their personal lives regarding this question and I'm sure they had the same anxieties I had. So, when it was my turn I was careful with the words I used and stated only the facts. At the end, I wrote, *I don't think there is a man whose shoulders are strong enough to handle this and treat me and my children like it is not our fault. I don't think there is a man who will love me as his wife or care for my children as a father should because of this.*

The response was not what I thought it would be. Instead of feeling rejected, I felt embraced by everyone. They told me I should not feel that God does not have someone for me. They told me that my children and I were in their prayers. *Hold your head high because you have nothing to feel ashamed of,* they wrote. They told me I was blessed and that they were proud to call me "sister."

Their responses moved me to tears. I had never felt that kind of love and acceptance from anyone during that time. I was overwhelmed. Then, I received a personal instant message from Reuben Muhammad. He wrote,

*You shouldn't feel that way.* We chatted privately for the duration of the session. He didn't ask any further questions. Before signing off he wrote, *I like your spirit.*

I had a major financial setback when it was announced that the Pennsylvania Coalition Against Domestic Violence, had to close its Washington, D.C. office due to budget cuts. I decided to pursue starting my own organization, which I had already begun outlining and had decided to call it "After The Trauma." The mission would be to assist survivors of domestic violence reestablish their lives. I had done some research and found that the survivors' needs were not being met. Being a survivor myself, I did not get the assistance I needed to move forward. I also found that my struggle was harder since I didn't have the physical scars to validate that I was a victim and am now a survivor.

The lack of help provided was always frustrating to me. I went to the victim compensation agency, only to be told that the agency only gives financial compensation to victims of crime who have physical scars. They offered other compensation but the red tape involved made help impossible in my case. For one, I'd have to file in the state of the crime, which meant Washington State. I called that state's office and found you have to submit an application within two years after the crime occurred. By this time, it was 2006 and I had missed my deadline. Besides, I didn't have a police report to validate the crime since John was never charged as an abuser, never charged with violating the restraining order, stalking, kidnapping, or threatening me.

My only resort was Social Services. I applied for assistance and was given food stamps and medical insurance for me and my children. I also applied for monthly cash assistance but the woman helping me told me that I had to inform John, and then they would also notify him and give him my address before they could give me cash assistance.

I looked in disbelief at the woman. "Whoa! Excuse me, ma'am. I can't let him know where I am," I said.

"Why?" she asked.

"My ex-husband is The D.C. Sniper. I can't let him know where I am."

"Well, I'm sorry this has happened to you, but you won't be able to get the cash," she said.

"Then I don't want it. I don't see why I have to put my life in danger for money."

She said, "I'm sorry, but those are the rules and there's no other way to do it."

As I left, I wondered how many disappointments I'd have to bear to find a safe place and environment for my children and me.

Other than God and my children, the other bright light in my life was communicating with Reuben, the man I had met through the Nation's online singles' ministry. We began talking regularly. We moved up from sending emails to talking on the phone and I found some solace in his baritone voice. He was a counselor working with teenaged and adult substance abusers for an agency in Compton, California. He was incredibly knowledgeable in the teachings and the scriptures of both the Holy Qur'an and the Bible. Since I am a praying woman and have relied on God throughout this entire ordeal, his words were a comfort to my spirit. He seemed to pick up, through my voice, how I was feeling for that day and knew what to say to make me feel better.

Once we got past the surface talk, we went deeper into who the other person was. He explained his past and where he was at that point. He was forty-one, divorced and raising five sons, ages ten to fourteen, on his own. I thought that was extremely courageous. I was nervous about going into the details of my past. Before revealing everything to him, I told him that if, after hearing my story, he did not want to be involved with me any further, I would understand; rejection had become a part of my life. He agreed. So, I told him and he listened. There were times when he was so quiet that I had to ask if he was still there.

After I finished, I asked him if he still wanted to move forward.

"I didn't hear anything that would cause me to move away from you," he said.

I was happy to hear that. "What's next?" I asked.

"Well, I'd like to court you, if that is okay with you," he said.

"That would be fine with me," I replied.

He asked for the information of the authorities at my Mosque and I gave it to him.

"I'll be in touch," he said.

He contacted my local Mosque to let them know of his intentions. He made arrangements to fly from Compton to Washington, D.C. for a weekend to meet me and the children and talk to the authorities at the Mosque. The Mosque officials met with us together to ask us about our feelings for each other and to find out if we wanted to move forward with a courtship that could possibly turn into marriage. After the meeting, we officially began courting.

He arrived on August 4, 2006, and we packed everything we could into a short time together. We spent hours talking, looking at each other, and studying our lessons. He met my children. They approved of him by giving me a thumbs-up when he wasn't looking. We all played football outside with some of the neighborhood children and they accepted him as well. My sister and brother-in-law spent time with him and told me they approved of him, too. Our spirits seemed to get closer as we spent quality time together. I tried to slow down my emotions and keep things in perspective.

The relationship felt like a perfect fit, as if we belonged together, but I didn't want to misinterpret this; it was, after all, our first time meeting. Yet we had so many mannerisms alike that it was uncanny. When we walked into the house, we removed our shoes the same way. As Muslims, we take our shoes off at the door. Reuben and I both did not untie our shoes; we lifted our left foot and slid our shoe off and then we slid off the right. We did this the first time; looking at each other and smiling over the significance of this similarity. These kinds of things happened throughout the weekend, but I had to focus on the present and not get carried away with my emotions. I decided to enjoy the moment and accept things the way they were, allowing Allah to take things where they should be. I had the best weekend I'd had in an extremely long time.

When it was time for Reuben to leave, my children and I took him to the airport to say good-bye. When it was time for his flight to depart, all of them—even John—hugged him. When Reuben came to me, I started crying. At six feet three inches, he towered over me and it felt good to have someone to lean on. I was trying to be a "big girl" and not cry at all; however, I couldn't hold in the tears. He hugged me and I cried more.

"I'll be back," he said.

"I don't want you to leave," I said.

I could tell he was holding back his emotions, so I tried to regain composure. As he waved, I could not stop crying. I believe our spirits connected and I was not ready for him to leave. My children came over to comfort me.

"Mom, I wasn't ready for him to leave either," Taalibah said.

I was so surprised to hear her say that. But John and Salena said the same thing. Then John decided to lighten the mood.

"Mom, when I go off to college, what are you going to do?" he asked.

"They are going to have to knock me out, because I won't be able to take that and I may not let you get on the plane," I said.

We all laughed.

"Knock you out, Mom?" Salena said.

"Yeah. You know that song, 'Mama said knock you out.'"

"You had to reach way back for that one, Mom," said Taalibah.

Once again, my children helped me to get through a difficult day and, although I didn't think it was possible, with the passing of time and their demonstrations of kindness and compassion, my love for them increased.

The Coalition's office closed that September 30th. Everyone received a compensation packet. We felt sad about the closing and, at the same time happy; arrangements had been made so projects could continue under other organizations.

I started working diligently on organizing After The Trauma. I took a class on starting a business at the Women's Business Center in D.C. Since I'd had a business, I figured I was ahead of the curve and focused more on the information about starting a nonprofit organization. Unfortunately, the school closed before I completed the course. Nevertheless, I was determined to make my organization a reality so I continued my research on my own.

I'd spoken to my children about speaking publicly about what we had gone through. They told me they were okay with it as long as I did not lie on their father. I explained that I wanted to speak about domestic violence; I felt it would help other women and I would never lie or sensationalize my story. The truth is the best way. They gave me their blessings.

In October, I visited Reuben in Compton. I was nervous about meeting his family, especially his sons. I found them to be very respectful. Reuben was the same at home as he had been visiting me—a no-nonsense, humble man with a warm and loving presence. He and I and one of his sons attended the Mosque on Sunday and I was pleasantly surprised to find that Reuben opened the meeting as the Assistant Minister. He hadn't told me that he held this position, but that explained why he was so knowledgeable about the scriptures and I could see how his easily approachable manner helped him in his ministry. When visitors were announced, I was recognized by the secretary, who stated I was visiting Brother Reuben and that we were courting. Then Reuben was asked to say a few words about our courtship.

As he began talking, I looked at his son and we smiled at each other. Reuben was explaining the courtship process to everyone; this was a wonderful gesture. However, then I heard him say, "I've done all the examining that I need to do and I've made a decision." I glanced at his son again and he seemed as puzzled as I was. So I turned back to the front and when I did, I heard Reuben say, "Sister Mildred, would you come to the front, please?"

I got nervous. I didn't know what he was doing or what he was going to say. I walked to the front. As I stood there, Reuben said, "Sister Mildred, will you marry me?"

I was thinking, *Wow, he has asked me this in front of all of these people.* Everyone was clapping and shouting. I was stunned. I couldn't say anything; I was focused on trying not to cry.

Reuben asked everyone to quiet down.

"I didn't hear an answer," he said.

I looked at him. "Yes," I said.

The clapping and chants started again.

And just like that, I was engaged. I certainly had not come to Compton expecting this to happen. After the service, when we got to the car, I asked him, "Why didn't you tell me you were going to do that?"

"It felt right to do it then, so I did," he said.

When we returned to the house, his son told his brothers what their father had done. They also asked him why he hadn't told them he was going to do that; they wanted to be there. He told them what he had told me—that it felt right to do it then and so he had.

Back in Maryland, I told my children what happened. They were happy and Taalibah began chanting, "I'm going to have a daddy. I'm going to have a daddy."

I was surprised, since I had never heard her say anything that indicated she wanted another dad in her life.


I received an email from a woman, Norma Harley, from the Office of the Sheriff, asking me to speak at a survivor's forum to be held at the Prince George's Community College. She wanted me to tell my story. I was delighted; it would be the first time I shared my story in an open forum. I accepted the invitation to speak; it was a chance for people to hear my side of The D.C. Sniper story, the side that people may not know about.

When the day came, I was terrified. I walked into an auditorium filled with many people. The children accompanied me and held the video camera, watching proudly. My mind returned to old thoughts. *These people are going to blame me like everyone else did*, the negative voice said. *No one is going to understand.*

I met two other survivors as well: Yvette Cade and Cheryl Kravitz. I'd heard Yvette's story before. She was doused with gasoline at her workplace and sixty-five percent of her body—including her face—had been burned. Cheryl had been physically abused by her ex-husband, a Rabbi. So three religions were being represented at this forum—Christianity, Islam, and Judaism. I looked at us and thought: *Domestic violence does not have a religion.* The three of us took pictures together and we would remain in contact with each other.

Someone called my name and I walked up to the stage, shaking. To this day I don't know exactly what I said during my speech. I told them the story of me and my children as best I could. When I finished, every person in the audience stood to applaud.

John, Taalibah, and Salena ran up, hugged me, and said, "We're proud of you!" Other people said it as well, but to hear my children say it brought tears to my eyes. We had made it across the emotional mine field together, with me leading, even though I didn't know where we were headed. Their compliments were gratitude and grace, a reminder that I did not give up and leave them behind. We had come through it all together, as family.

Salena was headed to high school. She said she wanted to be a singer and entertainer so I searched around for a performing arts school. She had to audition to be accepted to the school that I located. Her middle school music teacher helped her to prepare. Salena decided to sing "Yesterday."

On the day of the audition, we were both nervous. I accompanied Salena but had to wait outside the room. I stood close to the door, hoping to hear her, but I couldn't. When she finished, we waited in the hallway for someone to come out to tell us whether or not she had been accepted. I paced the floor as the clock ticked on. Finally, after about an hour, Mr. Boucher, the man who would become her music teacher, came out to tell us that Salena had passed her audition and would be attending the school.

We were so happy! We jumped up and down. All of her work had paid off. When school began, she was in the honors chorus. One of their first performances was at the Kennedy Center. I was so proud as I sat in the audience, amazed at how grown up she looked standing on stage with the other members of the chorus.

In late December, the children told me they wanted to recognize their dad's birthday. I wanted to support them, but it was going to be tough for me, emotionally. I asked them what they wanted to do and they asked if we could get a small cake and sing "Happy Birthday" to him. I put my feelings aside and bought the cake. Still, I questioned myself, asking, *Am I going too far by allowing this? Should I say something to the children about it?* In the end, I decided that I would go along with their wishes.

On December 31, I felt the stress as soon as I woke up. I prayed and read before the children got up. John used to say, "The whole world celebrates my birthday." And just as the children wanted, we lit a candle atop a small cake and they sang "Happy Birthday." I stood there smiling, waiting for the moment to be over. After they had cake, they hugged me and thanked me. I sighed with relief.

I gladly welcomed the new year of 2007, and the gift of friendships that had come into our lives. Lil' John worked out with Brother Leighton and Brother Mark, two members of the Mosque who have a physical training program that includes diet and weightlifting. They took John under their guidance to help him train for football. I noticed a real change in his behavior, the way he dressed, and his outlook on life. John needed positive male influence in his life; I was thankful they decided to help him. Because of their tender loving care, Lil' John started calling them Uncle Leighton and Uncle Mark. They continue to be a positive influence in his life today.

Thank God, after my unemployment checks ended, my speaking engagements began, which provided income. I also got a part-time job at the public library. Meanwhile, my thoughts were always on domestic violence victims and survivors. I wondered if other women struggled as much as I did. *Is it because I'm black that I'm treated differently?* I asked myself. *Would it be different if I was rich or had a different last name? Where are the resources that are supposed to help victims like me?* I asked these questions and yet I tried not to complain; it lowered my spirits. I was constantly in a tug-of-war with my emotions. "Oh, Allah, help me to be strong and of good courage," I prayed.

Soon it was time for my second daughter, Taalibah, to audition at the performing arts school. Taalibah had expressed an interest in becoming a model and she knew that a performing arts background would help her. She was still in middle school when she auditioned that February. She didn't even tell me what song she was going to sing. She wanted to prepare by herself and I respected her decision. Besides, I didn't want to make her nervous. She went into the audition and again, I tried to listen outside the door. Just as he did before, Mr. Boucher came out to tell me that Taalibah had also been accepted. I'll never forget he said, "Your girls should be together. They have been through so much. I'll take care of them."

While the girls were having their successes, I had one of my own. I incorporated my organization, After The Trauma. Now it was a legal entity but I needed to get board members and complete the paperwork to establish it as a nonprofit.

I had also been thinking about writing a journal that would assist victims and survivors in tapping into those emotions that we are afraid to talk about with others. I looked at other journals that asked questions to prompt thinking and writing and I found that those made me feel as if what had happened to me was my fault. Because of this, when I wrote, I used journals with blank pages. For me, journaling was truly a source of healing and help in understanding my own thoughts. I put my burdens on the page and they left my shoulders. I wanted other women to experience this. So I started working on a journal that would be an additional tool used in the recovery stages for victims of domestic violence. After hard work and research, I self-published "A Survivor's Journal."

I was asked to give the keynote speech at a conference on domestic violence at the University of Maryland, College Park. Stanley came from Houston as a surprise to me and my children. There were about 300 people in the audience, more than I had ever spoken to. CNN was there to film the event to be included in a piece on Lee Boyd Malvo. The reporter told me that at his prison in Virginia, John had a lower-level security status than Lee. This meant John was allowed outside for an hour each day and Lee was not. I found that to be so odd.

After my speech, a line of women were waiting to speak to me. Some wanted to hug me; others expressed how they were happy to hear me and know that I was still doing well. Others were victims who needed help. I was glad I had resource information to give out.

One woman said, "Ms. Muhammad, thank you for speaking up for us."

"Who is *us*?" I asked.

"Those of us who don't have physical scars. Continue to speak for us, please," she said. "Don't let them forget about us, Ms. Muhammad. Promise me you won't do that, please."

"I will do all that I can by God's permission to bring more light to *us*," I said.

She smiled, hugged me, and said, "Thank you."

Reuben and I decided we would get married on June 30th. I was giddy with excitement when I went to the courthouse to get the license. Taalibah went with me. Unfortunately, there was a terrible storm during the week of June 30th, so we had to postpone our wedding. It was a hard thing for both of us to do, but we set another date of August 4th. Actually, this date seemed appropriate since it was in August of the prior year that he had first come to visit me.

I was still trying to work and get funds to move the children and me into our own place. I wanted to take a step that felt like I was moving forward. I worked on After The Trauma, went to work, and cared for my children. But my passion was trying to make After The Trauma a separate entity so I could begin the work I viewed as my calling.

I attended a women's business conference and met a couple who helped move me a step closer to making After The Trauma a reality. All of us in attendance had to describe our companies. After hearing about my dream organization, a young woman named Kelly Rozwadowski introduced herself. She said that she and her husband would like to help me for a year and provide me with stationery, a website, and business cards. She said someone helped her when she was starting out and she wanted to pass on the kindness. She and her husband, Anthony, helped me design my logo and built my website, and I'm so grateful. To this day, they maintain my website.

On Saturday, August 4, 2007, Reuben and I were married in a simple and lovely ceremony at the Mosque. John escorted me down the aisle. Salena sang the Al-Fatiha (the Muslim prayer) and Taalibah was a bridesmaid. Reuben wore a brown, striped suit with gold tones to complement my dress, a long, soft-yellow Indian garment with a flowing head scarf. The reception was at my sister's home with a small group of my closest friends attending. We had some finger foods and a wedding cake.

It was a new beginning for all of us. Monday morning, he flew back to California, which is where we agreed he would live while we continued to work toward building our future and bringing our families together under one roof. I was feeling hopeful. In addition to a new husband, I had a new job working as an executive assistant at a construction company—and I was earning a supplemental income making speeches.

That October, which is Domestic Violence Awareness Month and also the month in which the random shootings took place, the CNN documentary aired. It showed how life was for Lee before and after he met John. The documentary really affected my children, especially John. He felt like Lee was all alone and that there was nothing he could do. I told all of the children that we would always pray for Lee and they liked that idea.

I was asked to be the keynote speaker at the 2007 Victim Justice Conference in Des Moines, Iowa in November. It was my first time speaking outside of the metropolitan D.C. area. I met some really good people and I got a comforting sense that I was connected to something larger. I believed I was reaching another level of awareness. I met two women in Iowa who offered to help me and my organization in whatever way I needed them. One decided to pay for the application fee for my 501c3, which meant I could apply to become a nonprofit. I was so thankful. I came home with a sense of purpose and a heightened spirit to move forward.

I saved every penny I could from my speaking engagements and my job at the construction company. Finally, in early December 2007, I secured the house that would be my first home in Maryland that I lived in alone with my children. It was a single-family home with four bedrooms in a quiet suburban Maryland neighborhood. Once I got the keys, I waited for my children to come home from school. Then I took them to Taco Bell for carryout. I didn't tell them where we were going. When I pulled into the driveway of the house, they said, "Who lives here?"

"We do!" I said, laughing.

They jumped out of the car and walked around outside the house. The girls were crying. John kept saying, "Yes!" over and over.

I opened the door and they walked from room to room, choosing which bedroom they wanted.

"Mom, we are free!" John said.

"Yes, we are, honey," I said.

It was a huge house for us. The four of us were used to spending most of our time in a basement. We took our food downstairs to the den, sat on the carpeted floor near the fireplace, and said grace. Then we ate, laughed, talked, cried, and prayed together. Before we left, we walked around and looked at every room again and then we did a group hug.

"Mommy, you did it. You got us our own place," the children said.

"By God's grace, we got it," I said.

"Mommy, we always had faith in you," they said. "And I had faith in God,' I said.

We didn't want to leave but we had no choice; the next day was a school and work day and we hadn't moved any of our clothes or belongings yet. We returned to my sister and brother-in-law's. But when we woke up that next day I announced, "We are moving today. When you get out of school, go to our new home."

My coworkers at the construction company helped me move while the children were at school. There wasn't a lot, compared to what most people probably have when they move into a house. We had beds, a television, computers, clothing, and some linens. I set up everything, nice and neat, and placed the children's personal items in their bedrooms.

That evening, they came home to *our* house. We woke up the next morning to find snow on the ground, the first snow we experienced in our new home. Now everything—outside and inside—looked shiny and new.

Two weeks after we moved into the house, the construction company shut down and I lost my job. I was thankful that the requests for speaking engagements continued to grow. To my surprise they came from universities and groups of attorneys, medical and mental health professionals, and law enforcement agencies as well as domestic violence groups. I discovered that I enjoyed speaking; each event helped me with my development and healing, as well as with fine-tuning my ability to affect change through others.

I have become a national spokesperson for domestic violence. I am an advocate and accompany victims and survivors to court. Women contact us for all kinds of assistance, from getting food to finding legal representation. When victims and survivors contact us for help, regardless of where they are, we find resources in their area so they can get the help they need. We keep in contact with them so they do not feel alone. Sometimes they simply want to talk.

Today, the focus of my work is through After The Trauma, which I operate from my office. I am living my purpose. I speak all over the country. I published and continue to sell and distribute a journal to help other women use the method I used to overcome my fears, calm my heart, and get strength. I assist women through emergency situations, accompanying them to the police station, the courtroom, and to social service agencies. I assist them through the legal process to get restraining orders, to file divorce papers, or to get custody of their children, and refer victims and survivors to other agencies as well.

Whenever I speak, women come up to me to tell me their painful stories of abuse. It takes everything I possess not to cry. They hug me and I hold onto them until they let go.

One woman told me, "You saved my life. I didn't know you didn't have to have physical scars to be abused."

Often, there is a woman standing silently to the side but she gives me a look that I recognize. It is a look that says, *Please don't tell anyone*. When I see a face wearing this expression, I hug the woman, give her my card, and whisper, "Call me, if you need me."

Usually, I get a follow-up email that says, *"Tell me what to do. I have nobody to talk to."*

Each night, before I go to bed, and again when I wake up each morning, I think of After The Trauma and the women who I help and those I can't. I am striving to enlighten more people to the fact that you don't have to have physical scars to be a victim or survivor of domestic violence. I publish and archive a monthly newsletter on the website, and send it to those on the mailing list.

I had a woman call my office one day to say, "Mrs. Muhammad, he violated the restraining order twenty-seven times. What can I do? I have followed everything they said for me to do."

I tell women, regardless of the ineptness of the law, or perhaps because of it, they must do everything legally to fight for their own lives and for those of their children. When I needed help, the lawyers I contacted wanted $2,500 as a retainer fee and I didn't have 25 cents, so I had to learn the law and file my own papers. At After The Trauma, we have two attorneys who provide legal assistance to clients; sometimes at a reduced rate and at times pro bono. The law failed me terribly. I didn't fall into a crack; I fell into a ditch and it took years to get out. I work hard and pray that through After The Trauma and other domestic violence organizations, this does not have to happen to other women. We all work together to assist as many as we can.

I have been on syndicated radio programs, and have appeared on CNN, BET, *Good Morning America*, and been interviewed on cable television and in various newspapers and magazines, including the *Washington Post* and *Newsweek*. TruTV also aired a documentary about me, which was produced by Barbara Kopple, titled "The D.C. Sniper's Wife."

I am honored to be a consultant with the federal government's Office for Victims of Crime and to be a board member on different domestic violence organizations. I recently received a Special Commendation Award from the Department of Justice, Office on Violence Against Women presented by Director Cindy Dyer for my work in domestic violence and was honored with the 2008 Shirley Chisholm Woman of Courage Award, presented by Executive Director Roslyn Bacon of Jonah Village, Inc. in Brooklyn, NY. I was also honored by No Jurisdictional Boundaries with the Leadership Courage Award, and Carolyn Washington, executive director of Sisters 4 Sisters, Inc., awarded the 2008 Circle of Grace Honors Award for my work in domestic violence.

My son, John, attends college now. His major is computer science engineering and his minor is civil engineering. He does not attend school in this area. I was glad he went away; I wanted him to be in a place where he would hardly, if at all, hear anything about his father. He is finding his own identity, developing just fine. When he calls home, he sounds so grown up and clear-headed.

Both of my daughters plan to attend a performance arts university. They are wonderful, talented girls.

Reuben and I have been enjoying our first two years of marriage with all of our children. We continue to build our lives together, keeping our focus on God, our children, and each other.

With John Muhammad behind bars, I certainly feel more secure. My brain still has difficulty coming to terms with the fact that John was going to kill me; that I am not supposed to be here. I was supposed to be a statistic. And at times, my imagination still presents to me a gruesome and graphic picture of a bloody, dead me.

I am not ashamed of the young woman I once was. That woman gave birth to a new Mildred, who rose out of the madness and trauma. The new Mildred walks proudly; she is stronger and wiser. She has, by God's grace and mercy, already led her children through an emotional minefield to safety. She holds a lamp high, to light the way for the women behind her, for those who are scarred and for those with perfect skin and invisible wounds.

My mother always used to say, "When your hand is in the lion's mouth, you can't just snatch it out. You have to ease it out slowly." I have been in the process of easing my hand out of the lion's mouth a little bit at a time.

One day my ex-husband and the father of my children will be executed. I am still processing this fact. Meanwhile, he has tried to escape three times. I'm told that the facility in Virginia, where John and Lee are being held, has five security levels. Level one being minimum, and level five being maximum. John is in a level four security while Lee is in level five. John is allowed outside for an hour, while Lee isn't. How can this be? We don't know how long the process of appeals will take because along with the death penalty, appeals are granted. And until those appeals are exhausted, then a date of execution cannot be set. Until that day, "execution" seems like just another word. I cannot begin to comprehend how I will feel when that day comes, but I will have to lead my children through their grief.

By God's permission, I am the support my children need to stand on, the tree on which they lean. I am humbled to be a new wife and also a servant to other women who have often forgotten their worth. I can remind them of who they are because, praise be to Allah, I am still here and the promises of God are true!

# ABOUT THE AUTHOR

Mildred D. Muhammad is a consultant with the Office for Victims of Crime and is a board member of various domestic violence organizations. She has become a "National Spokesperson" for domestic violence and has been honored as being a keynote speaker, telling her story for several conferences regarding domestic violence. She shares her expertise on what it's like being a victim and a survivor of domestic violence—without physical scars—to victims and survivors of domestic violence, advocates, law enforcement representatives, therapists, counselors, mental health providers, medical health providers, various universities and many others.

She has written a working journal, *A Survivor's Journal*, specifically for victims and survivors to help with those anxieties that others may not understand. The responses from those who have ordered the journal have been overwhelming.

She has three wonderful children, John, Salena and Taalibah, who remind her on a daily basis that the promises of God are true. She met and married Reuben Muhammad, who has five children.

## AWARDS

Carolyn Washington, Executive Director of Sisters 4 Sisters, Inc., awarded her with the 2008 Circle of Grace Honors Award for her work in domestic violence.

Cindy Dyer, Director of the Office on Violence Against Women, honored her with a Special Commendation for her extraordinary contribution to the prevention of domestic violence and in appreciation for her commitment to the mission of the Office on Violence Against Women, U.S. Department of Justice.

Roslyn Bacon, Executive Director of Jonah Village, Inc, in Brooklyn, N.Y., honored her with the 2008 Shirley Chisholm Woman of Courage Award.

Chuck Paris of No Jurisdictional Boundaries honored her and After The Trauma, Inc., with the Leadership Courage Award.

She has also received many Certificates of Recognition for her ongoing work assisting survivors of domestic violence.

Visit the author at www.MildredMuhammad.com. For information about the non-profit organization, After The Trauma, which assists victims and survivors of domestic violence, visit www.afterthetrauma.org.

A domestic violence resources guide and a personal safety plan have been provided at the end of this book. This information is also available at www.afterthetrauma.org.

# DISCUSSION GUIDE

❏ Who did you feel sympathy for in this story? Why?

❏ After reading this story, do you believe you have ever been in an emotionally abusive relationship? If so, what were the actions you now see as being abusive?

❏ How has the abuse affected your relationships with subsequent intimate partners?

❏ If you have not been in an emotionally abusive relationship, would you recognize the warning signs?

❏ Can you name five warning signs of an emotionally abusive relationship?

❏ How do you feel your family experiences have shaped the way you relate to past or present intimate partners?

❏ Do you believe you could find yourself in an emotionally abusive relationship? Why or why not?

❏ Do you feel emotional abuse is damaging? Why or why not?

❏ What does submission mean to you?

❏ Do you submit to your intimate partner? Why or why not?

# STATE COALITIONS
# AGAINST DOMESTIC VIOLENCE

**Alabama Coalition
Against Domestic Violence**
P. O. Box 4762
Montgomery, AL 36101
(334) 832-4842  Fax: (334) 832-4803
Hotline: (800) 650-6522
Website: www.acadv.org
Email: acadv@acadv.org

**Alaska Network on
Domestic and Sexual Violence**
130 Seward Street, Room 209
Juneau, AK 99801
(907) 586-3650  Fax: (907) 463-4493
Website: www.andvsa.org

**Arizona Coalition
Against Domestic Violence**
100 W. Camelback, #109
Phoenix, AZ 85013
(602) 279-2900  Fax: (602) 279-2980
Nationwide: (800) 782-6400
Website: www.azcadv.org
Email: acadv@azadv.org

**Arkansas Coalition
Against Domestic Violence**
1401 W. Capitol Avenue, Suite 170
Little Rock, AR 72201
(501) 907-5612  Fax: (501) 907-5618
Nationwide: (800) 269-4668
Website: www.domesticpeace.com
Email: kbangert@domesticpeace.com

**California Partnership
to End Domestic Violence**
P. O. Box 1798
Sacramento, CA 95812
(916) 444-7163  Fax: (916) 444-7165
Nationwide: (800) 524-4765
Website: www.cpedv.org
Email: info@cpedv.org

**Colorado Coalition
Against Domestic Violence**
P. O. Box 18902
Denver, CO 80218
(303) 831-9632  Fax: (303) 832-7067
(888) 788-7091
Website: www.ccadv.org

**Connecticut Coalition
Against Domestic Violence**
90 Pitkin Street
East Hartford, CT 06108
(860) 282-7899  Fax: (860) 282-7892
In State: (800) 281-1481
In State DV Hotline: (888) 774-2900
Website: www.ctcadv.org
Email: info@ctcadv.org

**Delaware Coalition
Against Domestic Violence**
100 W. 10th Street, #703
Wilmington, DE 19801
(302) 658-2958  Fax: (302) 658-5049
In State: (800) 701-0456
Website: www.dcadv.org
Email: dcadv@dcadv.org

**DC Coalition
Against Domestic Violence**
5 Thomas Circle NW
Washington, DC 20005
(202) 299-1181  Fax: (202) 299-1193
Website: www.dccadv.org
Email: help@dccadv.org

**Florida Coalition
Against Domestic Violence**
425 Office Plaza
Tallahassee, FL 32301
(850) 425-2749  Fax: (850) 425-3091
TDD: (850) 621-4202
In State: (800) 500-1119
Website: www.fcadv.org

**Georgia Coalition
Against Domestic Violence**
3420 Norman Berry Drive, #280
Atlanta, GA 30354
(404) 209-0280  Fax: (404) 766-3800
Website: www.gcadv.org

**Hawaii State Coalition
Against Domestic Violence**
716 Umi Street, Suite 210
Honolulu, HI 96819-2337
(808) 832-9316  Fax: (808) 841-6028
Website: www.hscadv.org

**Idaho Coalition Against
Sexual & Domestic Violence**
815 Park Boulevard, #140
Boise, ID 83712
(208) 384-0419  Fax: (208) 331-0687
Nationwide: (888) 293-6118
Website: www.idvsa.org
Email: domvio@mindspring.com

**Illinois Coalition
Against Domestic Violence**
801 S. 11th Street
Springfield, IL 62703
(217) 789-2830  Fax: (217) 789-1939
Website: www.ilcadv.org
Email: ilcadv@ilcadv.org

**Indiana Coalition
Against Domestic Violence**
1915 W. 18th Street
Indianapolis, IN 46202
(317) 917-3685  Fax: (317) 917-3695
In State: (800) 332-7385
Website: www.violenceresource.org
Email: icadv@violenceresource.org

**Iowa Coalition
Against Domestic Violence**
515 28th Street, #104
Des Moines, IA 50312
(515) 244-8028  Fax: (515) 244-7417
In State Hotline: (800) 942-0333
Website: www.icadv.org

**Kansas Coalition against Sexual
and Domestic Violence**
634 SW Harrison Street
Topeka, KS 66603
(785) 232-9784  Fax: (785) 266-1874
Website: www.kcsdv.org
Email: coalition@kcsdv.org

**Kentucky Domestic Violence
Association**
P.O. Box 356
Frankfort, KY 40602
(502) 695-2444  Fax: (502) 695-2488
Website: www.kdva.org

**Louisiana Coalition
Against Domestic Violence**
P.O. Box 77308
Baton Rouge, LA 70879
(225) 752-1296  Fax: (225) 751-8927
Website: www.lcadv.org

**Maine Coalition To End
Domestic Violence**
170 Park Street
Bangor, ME 04401
(207) 941-1194  Fax: (207) 941-2327
Website: www.mcedv.org
Email: info@mcedv.org

**Maryland Network
Against Domestic Violence**
6911 Laurel-Bowie Road, #309
Bowie, MD 20715
(301) 352-4574  Fax: (301) 809-0422
Nationwide: (800) 634-3577
Website: www.mnadv.org
Email: mnadv@aol.com

**Jane Doe, Inc./Massachusetts
Coalition Against Sexual Assault
and Domestic Violence**
14 Beacon Street, #507
Boston, MA 02108
(617) 248-0922  Fax: (617) 248-0902
TTY/TTD: (617) 263-2200
Website: www.janedoe.org
Email: info@janedoe.org

**Michigan Coalition against
Domestic & Sexual Violence**
3893 Okemos Road, #B-2
Okemos, MI 48864
(517) 347-7000  Fax: (517) 347-1377
TTY: (517) 381-8470
Website: www.mcadsv.org

**Minnesota Coalition
for Battered Women**
1821 University Avenue West, #S-112
St. Paul, MN 55104
(651) 646-6177  Fax: (651) 646-1527
Crisis Line: (651) 646-0994
Nationwide: (800) 289-6177
Website: www.mcbw.org
Email: mcbw@mcbw.org

**Mississippi Coalition
Against Domestic Violence**
P.O. Box 4703
Jackson, MS 39296
(601) 981-9196  Fax: (601) 981-2501
Website: www.mcadv.org

**Missouri Coalition Against
Domestic Violence**
718 East Capitol Avenue
Jefferson City, MO 65101
(573) 634-4161  Fax: (573) 636-3728
Website: www.mocadv.org
Email: mcadv@sockets.net

**Montana Coalition Against
Domestic & Sexual Violence**
P.O. Box 818
Helena, MT 59624
(406) 443-7794  Fax: (406) 443-7818
Nationwide: (888) 404-7794
Website: www.mcadsv.com
Email: mcadsv@mt.net

**Nebraska Domestic Violence
and Sexual Assault Coalition**
825 M Street, #404
Lincoln, NE 68508
(402) 476-6256  Fax: (402) 476-6806
In State: (800) 876-6238
Website: www.ndvsac.org
Email: info@ndvsac.org

**Nevada Network
Against Domestic Violence**
100 West Grove Street, #315
Reno, NV 89509
(775) 828-1115  Fax: (775) 828-9911
In State: (800) 500-1556
Website: www.nnadv.org

**New Hampshire Coalition Against
Domestic and Sexual Violence**
P.O. Box 353
Concord, NH 03302
(603) 224-8893  Fax: (603) 228-6096
In State: (866) 644-3574
Website: www.nhcadsv.org

**New Jersey Coalition
for Battered Women**
1670 Whitehorse
Hamilton Square
Trenton, NJ 08690
(609) 584-8107  Fax: (609) 584-9750
In State: (800) 572-7233
Website: www.njcbw.org
Email: info@njcbw.org

**New Mexico State Coalition
Against Domestic Violence**
200 Oak NE, #4
Albuquerque, NM 87106
(505) 246-9240  Fax: (505) 246-9434
In State: (800) 773-3645
Website: www.nmcadv.org

**New York State Coalition
Against Domestic Violence**
350 New Scotland Avenue
Albany, NY 12054
(518) 482-5464  Fax: (518) 482-3807
English In State: (800) 942-6906
Spanish In State: (800) 942-6908
Website: www.nyscadv.org
Email: nyscadv@nyscadv.org

**North Carolina Coalition
Against Domestic Violence**
115 Market Street, #400
Durham, NC 27701
(919) 956-9124  Fax: (919) 682-1449
Nationwide: (888) 232-9124
Website: www.nccadv.org

**North Dakota Council on
Abused Women's Services**
418 E. Rosser Avenue, #320
Bismark, ND 58501
(701) 255-6240  Fax: (701) 255-1904
Nationwide: (888) 255-6240
Website: www.ndcaws.org
Email: ndcaws@ndcaws.org

**Action Ohio Coalition
for Battered Women**
P.O. Box 15673
Columbus, OH 43215
(614) 221-1255  Fax: (614) 221-6357
In State: (888) 622-9315
Website: www.actionohio.org
Email: actionoh@ee.net

**Ohio Domestic Violence Network**
4807 Evanswood Drive, #201
Columbus, OH 43229
(614) 781-9651  Fax: (614) 781-9652
(800) 934-9840
Website: www.odvn.org
Email: info@odvn.org

**Oklahoma Coalition
Against Domestic Violence
and Sexual Assault**
3815 N. Sante Fe Ave., Suite 124
Oklahoma City, OK 73118
(405) 524-0700  Fax: (405) 524-0711
Website: www.ocadvsa.org

**Oregon Coalition Against Domestic and Sexual Violence**
380 SE Spokane Street, #100
Portland, OR 97202
(503) 230-1951  Fax: (503) 230-1973
Website: www.ocadsv.com

**Pennsylvania Coalition Against Domestic Violence**
6400 Flank Drive, #1300
Harrisburg, PA 17112
(717) 545-6400  Fax: (717) 545-9456
Nationwide: (800) 932-4632
Website: www.pcadv.org

**Rhode Island Coalition Against Domestic Violence**
422 Post Road, #202
Warwick, RI 02888
(401) 467-9940  Fax: (401) 467-9943
In State: (800) 494-8100
Website: www.ricadv.org
Email: ricadv@ricadv.org

**South Carolina Coalition Against Domestic Violence and Sexual Assault**
P.O. Box 7776
Columbia, SC 29202
(803) 256-2900  Fax: (803) 256-1030
Nationwide: (800) 260-9293
Website: www.sccadvasa.org

**South Dakota Coalition Against Domestic Violence & Sexual Assault**
P.O. Box 141
Pierre, SD 57501
(605) 945-0869  Fax: (605) 945-0870
Nationwide: (800) 572-9196
Website: www.southdakotacoalition.org
Email: sdcadvsa@rapidnet.com

**Tennessee Coalition Against Domestic and Sexual Violence**
P.O. Box 120972
Nashville, TN 37212
(615) 386-9406  Fax: (615) 383-2967
In State: (800) 289-9018
Website: www.tcadsv.org
Email: tcadsv@tcadsv.org

**Texas Council On Family Violence**
P.O. Box 161810
Austin, TX 78716
(512) 794-1133  Fax: (512) 794-1199
In State: (800) 525-1978
Website: www.tcfv.org

**Utah Domestic Violence Council**
320 W. 200 South, #270-B
Salt Lake City, UT 84101
(801) 521-5544  Fax: (801) 521-5548
Website: www.udvac.org

**Vermont Network Against Domestic Violence and Sexual Assault**
P.O. Box 405
Montpelier, VT 05601
(802) 223-1302  Fax: (802) 223-6943
Website: www.vtnetwork.org
Email: vtnetwork@vtnetwork.org

**Virginians Against Domestic Violence**
2850 Sandy Bay Road, #101
Williamsburg, VA 23185
(757) 221-0990  Fax: (757) 229-1553
Nationwide: (800) 838-8238
Website: www.vadv.org
Email: vadv@tni.net

**Washington State Coalition
Against Domestic Violence**
711 Capitol Way, #702
Olympia, WA 98501
(360) 586-1022  Fax: (360) 586-1024

3rd Avenue, #406
Seattle, WA 98101
(206) 389-2515  Fax. (206) 389-2520
In State (800) 886-2880
Website: www.wscadv.org
Email: wscadv@wscadv.org

**West Virginia Coalition Against
Domestic Violence**
4710 Chimney Drive, #A
Charleston, WV 25302
(304) 965-3552  Fax: (304) 965-3572
Website: www.wvcadv.org

**Wisconsin Coalition Against
Domestic Violence**
307 S. Paterson Street, #1
Madison, WI 53703
(608) 255-0539  Fax: (608) 255-3560
Website: www.wcadv.org
Email: wcadv@wcadv.org

**Wyoming Coalition Against
Domestic Violence and Sexual
Assault**
P.O. Box 236409
South Fourth Street
Laramie, WY 82073
(307) 755-5481  Fax: (307) 755-5482
(800) 990-3877 Nationwide
Website: www.wyomingdvsa.org
Email: Info@mail.wyomingdvsa.org

## US VIRGIN ISLANDS

**Women's Coalition of St. Croix**
Box 2734
Christiansted
St. Croix, VI 00822
(340) 773-9272  Fax: (340) 773-9062
Website: www.wcstx.com
Email: wcscstx@attglobal.net

## PUERTO RICO

**The Office of Women Advocates**
Box 11382
Fernandez Juancus Station
Santurce, PR 00910
(787) 721-7676  Fax: (787) 725-9248

# PLANNING FOR SAFETY

A safety plan is a "must have" in a domestic violence situation. Victims/ Survivors will need to plan a strategic safety route that will allow them to leave without incident.

Just remember, leaving is the most dangerous time, so be careful!

Please share this plan with ANYONE that needs information on what to do in a domestic violence situation for the safety of their lives and the lives of their children. After The Trauma, Inc., is here to assist in any way possible— email us: info@afterthetrauma.org.

## PERSONALIZED SAFETY PLAN

The following steps represent my plan for increasing my safety and preparing in advance for the possibility for further violence. Although I do not have control over my partner's violence, I do have a choice about *how* to respond to him/her and how to best get myself and my children to safety.

**STEP ONE:** SAFETY DURING A VIOLENT INCIDENT.

Women cannot always avoid violent incidents. In order to increase safety, battered women may use a variety of strategies.

*I can use some or all of the following strategies:*

A. If I decide to leave, I will _____ .
(Practice how to get out safely. What doors, windows, elevators, stairwells, or fire escapes would you use?)

B. I can keep my purse and car keys ready and put them _____
(place) in order to leave quickly.

C. I can tell _____ about the violence and request they call the police if they hear suspicious noises coming from my house.

D. I can teach my children how to use the telephone to contact the police and the fire department.

E. I will use _____ as my code word with my children and my friends so they can call for help.

F. If I have to leave my home, I will go _____ . (Decide this even if you don't think there will be a next time.) If I cannot go to the location above, then I can go to _____ or _____ .

G. I can also teach some of these strategies to some/all of my children.

H. When I expect we are going to have an argument, I will try to move to a space that is lowest risk, such as _____ . (Try to avoid arguments in the bathroom, garage, kitchens, near weapons or in rooms without access to an outside door.)

I. I will use my judgment and intuition. If the situation is very serious, I can give my partner what he/she wants to calm him/her down. I have to protect myself until I/we are out of danger.

## STEP TWO: SAFETY WHEN PREPARING TO LEAVE.
Battered women frequently leave the residence they share with the battering partner. Leaving must be done with a careful plan in order to increase safety. Batterers often strike back when they believe that a battered woman is leaving a relationship.

*I can use some or all of the following safety strategies:*

A. I will leave money and an extra set of keys with _____ so I can leave quickly.

B. I will keep copies of important documents or keys at _____ .

C. I will open a savings account by _____ to increase my independence.

D. Other things I can do to increase my independence include:

_____

_____

_____

E. The domestic violence program's hotline number is _____
My local coalition phone number is _____ .
I can seek shelter by calling both of these numbers.

F. I can keep change for phone calls on me at all times. I understand that if
I use my telephone credit card, the following month the telephone bill
will tell my batterer those numbers that I called after I left. To keep my
telephone communications confidential, I must either use coins or I might
get a friend to permit me to use their telephone credit card for a limited
time when I first leave.

G. I will check with _____ and _____
to see who would be able to let me stay with them or lend me money.

H. I can leave extra clothing with _____ .

I. I will sit down and review my safety plan every_____ in order to
plan the safest way to leave my residence. _____ (Domestic
violence advocate or friend) has agreed to help me review this plan.

J. I will rehearse my escape plan and, as appropriate, practice it with my
children.


## STEP THREE: SAFETY IN MY OWN RESIDENCE.

There are many things that a woman can do to increase her safety in her
own residence. It may be impossible to do everything at once, but safety
measures can be added step by step.

*Safety measures I can use/include:*

A. I can change the locks on my doors and windows as soon as possible.

B. I can replace wooden doors with steel/metal doors.

C. I can install security systems including additional locks, window bars, poles to wedge against doors, an electronic system, etc.

D. I can purchase rope ladders to be used for escape from second floor windows.

E. I can install smoke detectors and purchase fire extinguishers for each floor in my house/apartment.

F. I can install an outside lighting system that lights up when a person is coming close to my house.

G. I will teach my children how to use the telephone to make a collect call to me and to ——————————— (friend/minister/other) in the event that my partner takes the children.

H. I will tell people who take care of my children which people have permission to pick up my children and that my partner is not permitted to do so. The people I will inform about pick-up permission include: ——————————— (school), ——————————— (day care staff), ——————————— (babysitter), ——————————— ( teacher), ——————————— ( Sunday School teacher), and ——————————— and ——————————— (others).

I. I can inform ——————————— and ——————————— (neighbor, pastor, friend) that my partner no longer resides with me and they should call the police if he/she is observed near my residence.

## STEP FOUR: SAFETY WITH A PROTECTION ORDER.

Many batterers obey protection orders, but one can never be sure which violent partner will obey and which will violate protection orders. I recognize that I may need to ask the police and the courts to enforce my protection order.

*The following are some steps that I can take to help the enforcement of my protection order:*

A. I will keep my protection order ⸺⸺⸺⸺ (location). (Always keep it on or near your person. If you change purses, that's the first thing that should go in.)

B. I will give my protection order to police departments in the community where I work, in those communities where I usually visit family or friends, and in the community where I live.

C. There should be a county/parish registry of protection orders that all police departments can call to confirm a protection order. I can check to make sure that my order is in the registry. The telephone number for the county registry of protection orders is ⸺⸺⸺⸺⸺ .

D. For further safety, if I often visit other counties/parishes, I might file my protection order with the court in those counties/parishes. I will register my protection order in the following counties/parishes: ⸺⸺⸺ ⸺⸺⸺⸺ and ⸺⸺⸺⸺ .

E. I can call the local domestic violence program if I am not sure about B., C., or D. above or if I have some problem with my protection order.

F. I will inform my employer, minister, closest friend, and⸺⸺⸺⸺ and⸺⸺⸺⸺ that I have a protection order in effect.

G. If my partner destroys my protection order, I can get another copy from the courthouse located at ⸺⸺⸺⸺⸺ .

H. If my partner violates the protection order, I can call the police and report a violation, contact my attorney, call my advocate, and/or advise the court of the violation.

I. If the police do not help, I can contact my advocate or attorney and will file a complaint with the chief of the police department.

J. I can also file a private criminal complaint with the district justice in the jurisdiction where the violation occurred or with the district attorney. I can charge my battering partner with a violation of the protection of the protection order and all the crimes that he commits in violating the order. I can call the domestic violence advocate to help me with this.

**STEP FIVE:** SAFETY ON THE JOB AND IN PUBLIC.

Each battered woman must decide if and when she will tell others that her partner has battered her and that she may be at continued risk. Friends, family and co-workers can help to protect women. Each woman should consider carefully which people to invite to help secure her safety.

*I might do any or all of the following:*

A. I can inform my boss, the security supervisor and _____ at work of my situation.

B. I can ask _____ to help screen my telephone calls at work.

C. When leaving work, I can _____ .

D. When driving home, if problems occur, I can_____ .

E. If I use public transportation, I can _____ .

F. I can use different grocery stores and shopping malls for purchases. I can shop at hours that are different than those when residing with my battering partner.

G. I can use a different bank and take care of my banking at hours different from those I used when residing with my battering partner.

H. I can also _____ .


**STEP SIX:** SAFETY AND DRUG OR ALCOHOL USE.

Most people in this culture use alcohol. Many use mood-altering drugs. Much of this use is legal and some is not. The legal outcomes of using illegal drugs can be very hard on a battered woman, may hurt her relationship with her children and put her at a disadvantage in other legal action with her battering partner.

Therefore, women should carefully consider the potential cost of the use of illegal drugs. But beyond this, the use of any alcohol or other drugs can reduce a woman's awareness and ability to act quickly to protect herself from her battering partner. Furthermore, the use of alcohol or other drugs by the batterer may give him/her an excuse to use violence. Therefore, in the context of drug or alcohol use, a woman needs to make specific safety plans.

*If drug or alcohol use has occurred in my relationship with the battering partner, I can enhance my safety by some or all of the following:*

A. If I am going to use, I can do so in a safe place and with people who understand the risk of violence and are committed to my safety.

B. I can also _____ .

C. If my partner is using, I can _____ .

D. I might also _____ .

E. To safeguard my children, I might_____
   and _____ .


## STEP SEVEN: SAFETY AND MY EMOTIONAL HEALTH.

The experience of being battered and verbally degraded by partners is usually exhausting and emotionally draining. The process of building a new life for myself takes much courage and incredible energy.

*To conserve my emotional energy and resources AND to avoid hard emotional times, I can do some of the following:*

A. If I feel down and ready to return to a potentially abusive situation, I can_____ .

B. When I have to communicate with my partner in person or by telephone, I can _____ .

C. I can tell myself "_____"
whenever I feel others are trying to control or abuse me.

D. I can call _____ and _____ to help
me feel stronger.

E. Other things I can do to help me feel stronger are _____
and _____ .

F. I can attend workshops and support groups at the domestic violence
program or _____ , _____ ,
or _____ to gain support and strengthen
my relationships with other people.


## STEP EIGHT: ITEMS TO TAKE WHEN LEAVING.

When women leave partners, it is important to take certain items with
them. Beyond this, women sometimes give an extra copy of papers and an
extra set of clothing to a friend just in case they have to leave quickly.

Items with a check mark (✔) listed below are the most important to take
with you. If there is time, the other items might be taken, or stored outside
the home.

These items might best be placed in one location, so that if you have to
leave in a hurry, you can grab them quickly.

*When I leave, I should take:*

- ✔ Identification for myself
- ✔ Children's birth certificates
- ✔ My birth certificate
- ✔ Social security cards
- ✔ School and vaccination records
- ✔ Money
- ✔ Checkbook, ATM card
- ✔ Credit cards
- ✔ Keys – house/car/office

✔ Driver's license and registration
✔ Medications
  Welfare identification
  Work permits
  Green card
  Passport(s)
  Divorce papers
  Medical records—for all family members
  Lease/rental agreement, house deed, mortgage payment book
  Bank book
  Insurance papers
  Small saleable objects
  Address book
  Pictures
  Jewelry
  Children's favorite toys and/or blankets
  Items of special sentimental value

*Telephone numbers I need to know:*

Police department—home _____
Police department—school _____
Police department—work _____
Battered women's program _____
Battered men's program _____
County/Parish registry of protection orders _____
Work number _____
Supervisor's home number _____
Minister _____
Others _____
_____

*Safety Plan created by: Barbara Hart & Jane Stuehling, PCADV, 1992*

John and me on my birthday in December, 1986.

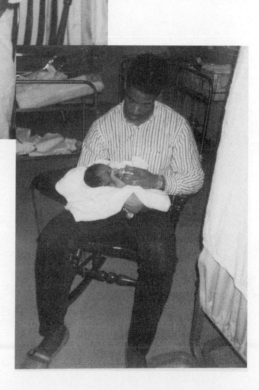

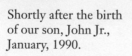

Shortly after the birth
of our son, John Jr.,
January, 1990.

John could be a loving father. ABOVE, he plays with Taalibah, 5; Salena, 6; and Lil' John, 8. BELOW, on a trip to the flight museum in Tacoma, Washington. Lil' John is 9, Taalibah, 6, and Salena, 7.

Taalibah, Lil' John, Salena and me at the Branch Avenue Metro station in Maryland on a reunion trip to visit museums in Washington, D.C., September, 2001.

Reuben and me on our wedding day, August 4, 2007.

ABOVE: Reuben, Taalibah, Salena, John and me on wedding day, August 4, 2007.
BELOW: Salena, John, Taalibah and me, 2008.

**SUPERIOR COURT OF WASHINGTON
FOR PIERCE COUNTY**

Mildred (Williams) Muhammad
Petitioner

John (Williams) Muhammad
Respondent

NO.

00 2 00701 4

**PETITION FOR ORDER
FOR PROTECTION
(PTORPRT) (Children)**

FILED
IN COUNTY CLERK'S OFFICE
A.M. MAR 03 2000 P.M.
PIERCE COUNTY, WASHINGTON
TED AUTL. COUNTY CLERK
DEP'TY

1. ☑ I am ☐ A member of my family or household is the victim of domestic violence committed by the respondent as described in the statement below.

2. ☑ I live in this county.
   ☐ I left my residence because of abuse and this is the county of my new or former residence.

3. My age is:
   ☐ Under 16  ☐ 16 or 17  ☑ 18 or over

   Respondent's age is:
   ☐ Under 16 ☐ 16 or 17  ☑ 18 or over

4. My relationship with the respondent is:
   ☐ Related by marriage (in-law)
   ☐ Related by blood
   ☐ Parent or child
   ☑ Spouse
   ☐ Former spouse
   ☐ Have child in common
   ☐ Presently reside together
   ☐ Resided together in past
   ☐ Presently dating
   ☐ Dated in past

5. Identification of Petitioner:

| | |
|---|---|
| Name | Mildred (Williams) Muhammad |
| Date of Birth | 12/20/59 |
| Driver's License or Identicard (# and State) | Muhammd411RD |

6. Identification of Respondent:

| | |
|---|---|
| Name | John (Williams) Muhammad |
| Date of Birth | 12/31/60 |
| Driver's License or Identicard (# and State) or, if unavailable, home address | ? 7419 S. Alaska, Tacoma, Wa 98408 |

7. Minors addressed in this petition:

| Name (First, Middle Initial, Last) | Birth Date | Age | Sex | How Related to Petitioner | Respondent | Resides with |
|---|---|---|---|---|---|---|
| John A. Muhammad Jr. | 1/17/90 | 10 | M | son | son | Mother |
| Salena D. Muhammad | 2/1/92 | 8 | F | daughter | daughter | " |
| Taalibah A. Muhammad | 5/1/93 | 6 | F | daughter | daughter | " |

8. Other court cases or any other protection order or no-contact order involving me and the respondent are:

| CASE NAME | | | |
|---|---|---|---|
| CASE NUMBER | | | |
| COURT/COUNTY | | | |

PETITION FOR ORDER FOR PROTECTION - 1 of 3
WPF DV-1.020 (11/98) - RCW 26.50.030

I did everything I knew how to follow the legal procedures necessary to protect myself and my children. ABOVE, and on the next three pages, is the first restraining order I filed in March, 2000. I truly feared for my life.

**REQUEST FOR TEMPORARY ORDER: AN EMERGENCY EXISTS** as described in the statement below: I need a temporary restraining order issued immediately without notice to the respondent until a hearing to avoid irreparable injury. I request a Temporary Order for Protection that will:

| | | **I REQUEST AN ORDER FOR PROTECTION** following a hearing THAT WILL: |
|---|---|---|
| X | X | RESTRAIN respondent from causing any physical harm, bodily injury, assault, including sexual assault, and from molesting, harassing, threatening, or stalking [X] me [ ] the minors named in paragraph 7 above [ ] these minors only: |
| X | X | RESTRAIN respondent from coming near and from having any contact whatsoever, in person or through others, by phone, mail, or any means, directly or indirectly, except for mailing of court documents, with [X] me [ ] the minors named in paragraph 7 above, subject to any court ordered visitation [ ] these minors only, subject to any court ordered visitation: |
| X | X | EXCLUDE respondent from [ ] our shared residence [X] any place I may reside. This address at present is [ ] confidential [ ] the following : 7302 S. Ainsworth Ave Tacoma, Wa 98408 |
| X | X | DIRECT respondent to vacate our shared residence and restore it to me. |
| X | X | RESTRAIN respondent from entering or being within _20 feet_ (distance) of my [X] residence [X] place of employment [ ] school [ ] daycare or school of [ ] the minors named in paragraph 7 above<br>[ ] these minors only:<br>[ ] other: |
| X | X | Subject to any court ordered visitation, GRANT me the care, custody and control of [X] the minors named in paragraph 7 above [ ] these minors only: |
| | | RESTRAIN respondent from interfering with my physical or legal custody of [ ] the minors named in paragraph 7 above [ ] these minors only: |
| | | RESTRAIN the respondent from removing from the state: [X] the minors named in paragraph 7 above<br>[ ] these minors only: |
| | | GRANT me possession of essential personal effects, including the following: |
| | | Grant me use of the following vehicle:<br>Year, Make & Model _____ License No._____ |
| | | OTHER: |
| | | DIRECT the respondent to participate in appropriate treatment or counseling services. |
| | X | REMAIN EFFECTIVE longer than one year because respondent is likely to resume acts of domestic violence against me if the order expires in a year. |

00 2 00701 4

**REQUEST FOR SPECIAL ASSISTANCE FROM LAW ENFORCEMENT AGENCIES:** FILED

I request the Court order the appropriate law enforcement agency to assist me in obtaining: IN COUNTY CLERK'S OFFICE

[ ] Possession of my residence [ ] Use of designated vehicle.

[ ] Possession of my essential personal effects at_____ A.M. MAR 03 2000 P.M.

[ ] Custody of [ ] the minors named in paragraph 7 above [ ] these minors only:___ PIERCE COUNTY, WASHINGTON TED RUST CO. CLERK

[ ] OTHER:_____

---

Domestic violence includes physical harm, bodily injury, assault, stalking, <u>OR</u> inflicting fear of imminent physical harm, bodily injury or assault, between family or household members.

---

**STATEMENT:** The respondent has committed acts of domestic violence as follows. (Describe <u>specific acts</u> of domestic violence and their <u>approximate dates</u>, beginning with the <u>most recent act</u>. You may want to include police responses.) The reason I did not meet the court appearance is because I was out of town and did not have an attorney to represent me.

Since the last restraining order, I've still be subjected to John threatening to destroy my life.

I have had my phone number changed three times within 5 days. I spoke with Bill Dorsett of U.S. West Communication. He said according to their records, John called today trying to find out my phone numbers. Because I have a special code on the record, he was unable to get the number. Bill Dorsett's phone # 206-504-0759. He said he would help me and change the number as much as possible and not charge me. I asked if he could get the number if he knew someone who worked there. He said it was possible.

➤ I am afraid of John. He was a demolition expert in the military. He is behaving very, very irrational. Whenever he does talk with me (Continue on separate page if necessary) he always says to that he's going to destroy my life and I hang up the phone.

I certify under penalty of perjury under the laws of the State of Washington that the foregoing is true and correct.

DATED_____3/3/2000_____ at _____Tacoma_____ Washington.

*Mildred D. Muhammad*
Signature of Petitioner

[ ] My residential address is confidential. Direct legal service by mail to:_____

PETITION FOR ORDER FOR PROTECTION - 3 of 3
WPF DV-1.020 (11/98) - RCW 26.50.030

**CHILD CUSTODY INFORMATION SHEET**     NO: <u>00 2 00701 4</u>

If you are seeking protection for your child(ren) from domestic violence or are requesting custody of your child(ren), please answer questions A - G below.

| | | | |
|---|---|---|---|
| **A.** | Do the child(ren) listed in Paragraph 7 of the petition currently live with you? | ☒ Yes | ☐ No |
| | (1) If your answer is yes, how long have the children lived with you? <br> *all their lives* | | |
| | (2) If your answer is no, explain_____ | | |

FILED <br> IN COUNTY CLERK'S OFFICE <br> A.M. ...? U 3 2000 P.M <br> PIERCE COUNTY WASHINGTON <br> COUNTY CLERK <br> BY ___ DEPUTY

| | | | |
|---|---|---|---|
| **B.** | Has the respondent, or any person other than yourself, had the majority of physical care and control of the minor children named herein during the last sixty days? | ☐ Yes | ☒ No |
| **C.** | Has there been any other court action concerning the custody of the minor children named herein in this state or in any other state within the past five years? | ☐ Yes | ☒ No |
| **D.** | Have you participated, as a party, witness, or in any other capacity in any other litigation concerning custody of the same child(ren) in this or any other state? | ☐ Yes | ☒ No |
| **E.** | Does the respondent, or any other person, have physical custody or claim to have physical custody or visitation rights to the minor children named herein? | ☐ Yes | ☒ No |

**F.** State the places the child(ren) has (have) lived in the past five years, and give the names and present resident addresses of the persons with whom the child(ren) lived during that period. <u>7302 S. Ainsworth Ave, Tacoma, Wa 98408</u>

**G.** If your answer to question B, C, D, or E is "yes", please explain: _____
*¢*

I certify under penalty of perjury under the laws of the State of Washington that the foregoing is true and correct.

Dated <u>3/3/2000</u>  at <u>Tacoma</u>, Washington

<u>Mildred D. Muhammad</u>
Petitioner

CHILD CUSTODY INFORMATION SHEET
WPF DV-1.030 (11/98) RCW 26.050.030